Trauma-Informed Treatment:

The Restorative Approach

by Patricia D. Wilcox

Trauma-Informed Treatment: The Restorative Approach

Copyright © 2012, Patricia D. Wilcox
2nd Printing 2014
3rd Printing 2017

All rights are reserved under international and Pan-American copyright conventions. No part of this publication may be reproduced, stored in a retrieval system, or transmitted in any form or by any means, electronic, mechanical, photocopying, recording, scanning, or otherwise, except as permitted under Section 107 or 108 of the 1976 United States Copyright Act, without either the prior express written permission of the author or publisher or authorization through payment of the appropriate per-copy fee, except for brief quotations in critical reviews.

Limit of Liability/Disclaimer of Warranty: While the publisher and author have used their best efforts in preparing this book, they make no representations or warranties with respect to the accuracy or completeness of the contents of this book and specifically disclaim any implied warranties of merchantability or fitness for a particular purpose. No warranty may be created or extended by sales representative or written sales materials. The advice and strategies contained herein may not be suitable for your situation. You should consult with a professional where appropriate. Neither the publisher nor author shall be liable for any loss of profit or any other commercial damages, including but not limited to special, incidental, consequential, or other damages.

Published by:
NEARI Press
70 North Summer Street
Holyoke, Massachusetts
01040 USA
413.540.0712

Distributed by:
NEARI Distribution
46 Development Road
Fitchburg, Massachusetts
01420 USA
978.829.2594
888.632.7412

ISBN# 978-1-929657-64-3

Dedication

To the children who are hurt through no fault of their own and who deserve the most excellent treatment possible in order to heal.

Acknowledgements

I would like to acknowledge both Presidents of Klingberg Family Centers, Rosemarie Burton and Steve Girelli. Both have generously supported the development, use and dissemination of these ideas, as well as supporting me personally throughout the writing of the book.

Leeora Netter was instrumental in the early development of this method.

Steve Brown has been a central part of further enhancing and refining these ideas and has helped me with both the thinking and the organization of the book.

Robert Davis also helped in the advancement of these ideas.

Megan Albanese has provided administrative help and emotional support.

Laurie Pearlman and Kay Saakvitne created the theory that lies beneath this book, constantly stimulated my thinking, and modeled how to write important books.

Euan Bear, Steve Bengis, and Joan Tabachnick at NEARI Press have been editors who immediately understood the philosophy of my work and helped me express it more clearly.

Dennis, Laura and Ryan France contributed the kindness and assistance that gave me space in which to write.

I would also like to thank my friends Bette Arey and Doris LaPlante for their encouragement throughout the book writing process.

My father, Thomas Wilcox, was an English teacher who delighted in words in all their aspects. He helped me find my voice and become a writer. In addition, he worked to implement ideas within his own profession that were philosophically similar to these. And his pride in me sustains me.

And most of all, credit goes to my extraordinary husband, Roger Nielson. He contributed ideas, did chores so I could write, was patient with the process, and always believed in me and in the importance of this message.

Contents

Introduction to Trauma-Informed Treatment

In this book I present the rationales and research for a trauma-informed treatment paradigm for our most difficult-to-treat children and adolescents: the Restorative Approach. I explore how it can and does work in congregate-care settings, how the dynamics among staff and between staff and clients can and will change as the approach is fully implemented, and how the outcomes for children change for the better.

The Creation of the Restorative Approach

The Restorative Approach is an integrated treatment method for child and adolescent-serving congregate-care settings, in which the clinical, medical, education, and support staff create a therapeutic milieu together from a common understanding of the healing power of positive relationships. It is more than a way to manage difficult youth behaviors. It is more than a replacement for points and levels, the traditional behavioral management systems in congregate care. The approach rests on the assumptions that children do well *if they can* and that symptoms are adaptations.

This newly developed trauma-informed approach to congregate care of children with serious emotional disorders was created at Klingberg Family Centers in New Britain, Connecticut (http://www.klingberg.org/). Many of the children treated at Klingberg came into care having suffered early neglect in which their basic needs were not met. They have also experienced trauma: physical and sexual abuse, witnessing domestic violence, parental exposure to drugs and alcohol, and multiple moves within their biological families. When they enter the child welfare system, they often suffer more abuse and experience many more moves and disruptions in caretaking. They present with serious problems of aggression, suicidality, self-harm, property destruction, and a continuing pattern of making unsafe choices.

The Klingberg Centers previously utilized a traditional points-and-levels approach in its congregate-care programs (residential, acute residential, extended-day after-school treatment, special-education therapeutic school). Rewards and punishments were thought to be the most powerful agents of change, and extensive periods of restriction were used to manage behavior. Youth who did not conform to rules for expected behavior would accumulate restrictions, and would become hopeless and feel they had nothing left to lose. Staff appeared to value compliance above all else. But this approach was not working, and also was not transferable to a home setting when it was time for a child to be discharged from the treatment facility. It is unreasonable to expect families to maintain elaborate point cards over time, and it is neither natural nor desirable for families to use inflexible reward systems.

The restorative method was influenced by the work of Daniel Hughes (1998, 2007, 2009), Jon G. Allen (2001), and Judith Herman (1997). The recent work of Bruce Perry (1999; Perry & Szalavitz, 2007) has also been incorporated. The Restorative Approach builds on the principles taught in the Risking Connection trauma-based training curriculum (Saakvitne, Pearlman, Gamble, & Lev, 2000). Risking Connection is a foundational trauma training curriculum which focuses on the effects of trauma, their influence on current behavior, how survivors heal through relationships, and the importance of paying attention to the person of the healer and the healer's experience of vicarious traumatization (pp. 20-21). Risking Connection was built on the theoretical foundation of constructivist self-development theory (McCann & Pearlman, 1990a; Pearlman, 2001).

Organization of this Book

The book begins with an introduction to current trauma theory and includes what we have learned about the brain from recent studies using modern technology such as Functional Magnetic Resonance Imaging. These instruments have allowed scientists to demonstrate the physical changes created in the brain by living with constant danger and neglect of basic needs. Chapter One introduces the trauma framework, a useful road map to understanding both the effects of trauma and how people can heal.

Although we have considerable new information about what helps people heal from trauma, many programs serving the children who have experienced the most traumas have not yet incorporated this information into their treatment or their programs' milieus.

In the following chapters I provide a specific treatment design using this new brain science as the blueprint for treatment programs for children. Chapter Two is an overview of the method, including its theoretical underpinnings, day-to-day operations, how it addresses shame, and answers to common questions and concerns.

Chapters Three, Four, and Five use case examples to convey the daily workings of the approach. Chapter Three focuses on demonstrating the daily workings of a trauma-informed treatment program. Chapter Four illustrates the power of how staff define and talk about the children and their behaviors. Chapter Five contains examples of the challenges of caring for traumatized children, and how the method works during difficult times.

Chapter Six examines one of the most difficult decisions in implementing trauma-informed care: how to respond when the children hurt others. This chapter asks providers to consider their theory of change, and to operate from a theory of what will actually help the child be less likely to repeat this behavior. It introduces the restorative task, a response that incorporates opportunities for healing and for making amends, and gives examples of such tasks. Suggestions for improving tasks and how to respond if the child refuses the task are included.

Chapter Seven focuses on the role of the clinician in trauma-informed care, the characteristics of a clinician who will succeed in this system, and necessary training. In the Restorative Approach, the clinician and the child-care team work closely together providing individual, group and family therapy as essential parts of the treatment program. Treatment planning reflects the therapist's theories of what steps help a child heal. As in all best-practice programs, the therapist will need support and supervision in order to lead the team in a clinical approach to behavior.

Chapter Eight covers the importance of providing trauma-informed care for the families. Most of the parents of children in treatment are themselves trauma survivors, which presents unique challenges in parenting. The program helps them by being attentive to their need to feel safe and to build trust. A key component is to recognize and honor their strengths, and to provide opportunities for the family to have fun and joy together. The families can be educated in the Restorative Approach and experiment with using it themselves when the client is at home.

Chapter Nine extends the Restorative Approach to foster care, describing how training in understanding trauma can help foster parents not to take behaviors personally and to keep the child despite behavioral problems. Formal training is important, and the support workers use of the theory to understand actual events will solidify the family's understanding.

Chapter Ten looks at characteristics of the agency as a whole that support trauma-informed care. The role of agency leadership is crucial in implementing this approach. The agency structure makes a big difference in the success of the Restorative Approach. Developing the necessary culture of connection takes time, but enables the approach to endure. The physical plant affects the experiences of both the clients and the staff.

Chapter Eleven, describes the processes that are essential to develop and maintain a good staff. Many agencies find that staff turnover decreases after the implementation of trauma-informed care. Hiring, training, supervision and promotion are all crucial tools. Certain skills that support a trauma-informed approach can be deliberately taught. Most crucial is attention to vicarious traumatization (Pearlman & Saakvitne, 1995; McCann & Pearlman, 1990b), the way the work affects staff and how they can take care of themselves and each other to stay alive and hopeful in the work.

Chapter Twelve covers the actual change process, and what steps an agency can take to facilitate the change. A transformation committee is a good mechanism to lead the change. Later steps include changing policies and procedures to solidify the changes. John Kotter's *Leading Change* (1996) forms a helpful guide to examine the process.

Chapter Thirteen concentrates on sustaining the change. Unfortunately there are many forces pushing the system back towards a punitive approach. Certain challenges can be predicted and addressed.

Chapter Fourteen emphasizes measuring and celebrating progress. The chapter presents various factors to measure and scales to utilize in measuring them. Results garnered from these data can be shared with funders, the Board of Directors, consumers and other stakeholders. Celebrating success will help sustain the transformation.

The Appendices contain useful tools for agencies to employ.

Although transforming an agency towards embracing trauma-informed care is a long and complicated process, it is well worth the effort. The following comments are quotes from two staff members who received Risking Connection trauma-treatment training and had implemented trauma-informed care for 3-6 months. In response to a question about what changes they had observed, they wrote:

> The everyday milieu is different – we avoid shaming the kids and remember that symptoms are adaptations. We are more hopeful and positive – we live in solutions. We teach about how to maintain and repair relationships, that it is okay to make a mistake, and you can fix it. The staff is talking more with the kids, finding out where their behavior is

> coming from. We engage the child more. Our focus on relationships and repair helps staff relationships. The direct-care workers and youth counselors are more involved in the treatment. There has been a decrease in AWOL and self-harm among our kids. The kids are involved in their own treatment plans. We are teaching the parents new ways to understand their kids' behaviors. We remember that a child is doing the best he can. We take better care of each other. We have more self -awareness. This place feels more like a real home. We are nicer to each other.
>
> We are more understanding of the parents. We understand that VT *[vicarious trauma]* is normal and we validate each other's feelings. We are saying, "yes" more to the kids. We have changed our hiring practices. We have more emphasis on strengths. We are more flexible. We are more hopeful.

The children and families we work with have experienced terrible things that were not their fault. Yet they remain engaged, strong, caring and hopeful. They deserve the absolute best treatment they can have, and this book offers a road map to create it.

Patricia Wilcox, LCSW
Vice President, Klingberg Family Centers
Executive Director, Traumatic Stress Institute
New Britain, CT
January, 2012

Chapter One

From Theory into Practice: The Importance of Trauma-Informed Care

This book is a manual about how to utilize what is now known about trauma's effects on people and what helps them heal in order to improve congregate care treatment programs for children and adolescents.

What is Trauma?

The first step in the process is to define trauma. One widely used definition formulates the central issue as follows: "Trauma is the unique individual experience of an event or enduring conditions in which the individual's ability to integrate his or her emotional experience is overwhelmed; and the individual experiences a threat to life, bodily integrity, or sanity" (Saakvitne, Gamble, Pearlman, & Lev, 2000, p.5). An important word in this definition is the word "individual," because similar events can affect different people in completely different ways. The description of an event (he was molested as a child) does not convey whether the experience was traumatic or in what ways. This impact can only be learned from the person.

Why is it Important to Pay Attention to Trauma?

Approximately 25 percent of children in the United States are believed to experience at least one potentially traumatic event in their lifetime, including natural disasters, life-threatening accidents, maltreatment, assaults, and family and community violence (Costello, Erkanli, Fairbank, & Angold, 2002). Among public mental health clients, 90 percent experienced multiple traumas (Mueser, et al., 1998). Teens in treatment for alcohol and/or drug problems are 6 to12 times more likely to have been physically abused and 18 to 21 times more likely to have been sexually abused than those without alcohol/drug problems (Clark, Lesnick, & Hegedus, 1997). Among youth in the Massachusetts inpatient and intensive residential-care programs, 82 percent have known histories of trauma (Lebel, et al., 2004). According to Briere and Scott (2006) 20 to 30 percent of women have experienced sexual abuse, and 10 to 20 percent of men have experienced childhood physical and sexual abuse. Up to 5 million children in the United States experience a traumatic event each year (Levine & Kline, 2007; Perry, 1999).

In *Trauma and Recovery* (1997), Judith Herman asserts, "The core experiences of psychological trauma are disempowerment and disconnection from others. Recovery, therefore, is based on the empowerment of the survivor and the creation of new connections. Recovery can take place only within the context of relationships; it cannot occur in isolation" (p. 133).

In 2005, Morrissey, et al., published the results of their nine-site quasi-experimental study of women with mental health and substance use disorders who had experienced physical or sexual abuse and who enrolled in either comprehensive, integrated, trauma-informed, and consumer/survivor/recovering person-involved services, or usual care. Mental health, post-traumatic stress symptoms, and substance use outcomes were assessed, controlling for program and personal characteristics. In sites where the intervention condition provided more integrated counseling than the comparison condition, they found increased positive effects on mental health and substance-use outcomes. Sites which provided significantly more integrated counseling, produced more favorable results in mental health symptoms and both alcohol and drug use problem severity. The same trend is observable for reductions in post-traumatic stress symptoms, although the difference does not attain statistical significance.

Also using a quasi-experimental design, Noether, et al., (2007), examined the effectiveness of a standardized intervention model designed to build resiliency in children of women with co-occurring mental health and substance use disorders and histories of interpersonal abuse. The children's intervention model consisted of three components: clinical assessment, service coordination and advocacy, and a psycho-educational skills-building group. Children in the comparison group received individual, group, and family services. Six-month and twelve-month outcomes were examined among 253 children using the Behavioral and Emotional Rating Scale, which assesses strengths across five subscales: Interpersonal Strengths, Family Involvement, Intrapersonal Strengths, School Functioning, Affective Strengths, and an overall strength quotient. In addition, to assess changes in the level of safety knowledge, mothers were asked to rate the child on the following statement using a 4-point Likert-type scale, where 1 represented *strongly disagree* and 4 represented *strongly agree*: "He/she knows what to do to keep himself/herself safe when he/she feels threatened by another person." Children in the intervention group improved significantly more than children in the comparison group (pp. 830-831).

As mental health practitioners begin to focus on and screen for traumatic events in their clients' histories, they discover that almost all of them, as well as their parents, have experienced neglect, trauma, and attachment disruptions.

How Much Does Trauma Matter?

The Adverse Childhood Experiences (ACE) Study is one of the largest investigations ever conducted to examine the connections between childhood abuse and neglect and adult health and life success. The study was the collaboration between the Centers for Disease Control and Prevention and Kaiser Permanente's Health Appraisal Clinic in San Diego.

In their report on the results of the study, Felitti et al., (1998) describe their methods:

> A questionnaire about adverse childhood experiences was mailed to 13,494 adults who had completed a standardized medical evaluation at a large HMO; 9,508 (70.5%) responded. Seven categories of adverse childhood experiences were studied: psychological, physical, or sexual abuse; violence against mother; or living with household members who were substance abusers, mentally ill or suicidal, or ever imprisoned. The number of categories of these adverse childhood experiences was then compared to measures of adult risk behavior, health status, and disease. Logistic regression was used to adjust for effects of demographic factors on the association between the cumulative number of categories of childhood exposures (range: 0–7) and risk factors for the leading causes of death in adult life.

Their results indicated that half of the respondents had experienced at least one category of ACE, and a quarter of the respondents reported exposure to two or more categories. Further:

> Persons who had experienced four or more categories of childhood exposure, compared to those who had experienced none, had 4 to 12-fold increased health risks for alcoholism, drug abuse, depression, and suicide attempt; a 2 to 4-fold increase in smoking, poor self-rated health, ≥50 sexual intercourse partners, and sexually transmitted disease; and a 1.4- to 1.6-fold increase in physical inactivity and severe obesity. The number of categories of adverse childhood exposures showed a graded relationship to the presence of adult diseases including ischemic heart disease, cancer,

> chronic lung disease, skeletal fractures, and liver disease. The seven categories of adverse childhood experiences were strongly interrelated and persons with multiple categories of childhood exposure were likely to have multiple health risk factors later in life.

In other words, childhood experiences of trauma matter: there are strong relationships "between the breadth of exposure to abuse or household dysfunction during childhood and multiple risk factors for several of the leading causes of death in adults" (Felitti et al., 1998, p. 245).

Diagnosing Trauma

Bessel van der Kolk, MD, and Robert S. Pynoos, MD, (2009) have been active in making the case for the need for a new diagnosis that accurately accounts for the experience and symptoms of children who grow up with neglect and trauma. They summarize that case as follows:

> The goal of introducing the diagnosis of Developmental Trauma Disorder is to capture the reality of the clinical presentations of children and adolescents exposed to chronic interpersonal trauma and thereby guide clinicians to develop and utilize effective interventions, and for researchers to study the neurobiology and transmission of chronic interpersonal violence. Whether or not they exhibit symptoms of PTSD, children who have developed in the context of ongoing danger, maltreatment, and inadequate care-giving systems are ill-served by the current diagnostic system, as it frequently leads to no diagnosis, multiple unrelated diagnoses, an emphasis on behavioral control without recognition of interpersonal trauma and lack of safety in the etiology of symptoms, and a lack of attention to ameliorating the developmental disruptions that underlie the symptoms (p. 3).

They note that the National Child Traumatic Stress Network was founded to address a growing "recognition of the profound difference between adult onset PTSD and the clinical effects of interpersonal violence on children, as well as the need to develop effective treatments for these children ...", and that "it has become evident that the current diagnostic classification system is inadequate for the tens of thousands of traumatized children receiving psychiatric care for trauma-related difficulties."

The proposed new diagnosis is:

Developmental Trauma Disorder

A. Exposure

- Multiple or chronic exposure to one or more forms of developmentally adverse interpersonal trauma (abandonment, betrayal, physical assaults, sexual assaults, threats to bodily integrity, coercive practices, emotional abuse, witnessing violence and death)
- Subjective Experience (rage, betrayal, fear, resignation, defeat, shame)

B. Triggered pattern of repeated dysregulation in response to trauma cues. Dysregulation (high or low) in presence of cues. Changes persist and do not return to baseline; not reduced in intensity by conscious awareness

- Affective
- Behavioral (e.g. re-enactment, cutting)
- Cognitive (thinking that it is happening again, confusion, dissociation, depersonalization)
- Relational (clinging, oppositional, distrustful, compliant)
- Self-attribution (self-hate and blame)

C. Persistently Altered Attributions and Expectancies

- Negative self-attribution
- Distrust protective caretaker

- Loss of expectancy of protection by others
- Loss of trust in social agencies to protect
- Lack of recourse to social justice/retribution
- Inevitability of future victimization

D. Functional Impairment

- Educational
- Familial
- Peer
- Legal
- Vocational

Dr. van der Kolk and his colleagues (2009) suggest that because "the study of complex trauma-related difficulties in children is still evolving," the proposed criteria, based on years of experience and study, as well as consensus among its formulators, may be subject to change based on continuing research. They conclude:

> In sum, Developmental Trauma Disorder represents consensus amongst leaders within the National Child Traumatic Stress Network and other leading researchers in the area of Developmental Psychopathology. We believe that this conceptualization has the potential to advance both science and the clinical utility of diagnosis within traumatized children (p.3).

What is a Trauma-Informed Program?

A trauma-informed program is more than a specific manualized treatment approach. It is a treatment environment in which all staff understands the prevalence and impact of trauma on the mental and behavioral health of youth in their care. It is a treatment environment in which all staff provides appropriate interventions that will decrease, rather than increase, the effects of trauma. Within the program, the agency provides clinical treatment which includes trauma assessment, and when indicated, evidence-based treatment for trauma-related problems.

In their article "Shelter from the Storm: Trauma-informed Care in Homelessness Settings" Hopper, Bassuk, and Olivet (2009) offer the following definition:

> Trauma-informed care is a strength-based framework that is grounded in an understanding of and responsiveness to the impact of trauma, that emphasizes physical, psychological and emotional safety for both providers and survivors, and that creates opportunities for survivors to rebuild a sense of control and empowerment (p. 133).

Roger Fallot (Harris & Fallot, 2001 pp. 7-12) has identified the following five critical dimensions of trauma-informed programs:

- Safety: Ensuring physical and emotional safety
- Trustworthiness: Maximizing trustworthiness, making tasks clear, and maintaining appropriate boundaries
- Choice: Prioritizing consumer choice and control
- Collaboration: Maximizing collaboration and sharing of power with consumers
- Empowerment: Prioritizing consumer empowerment and skill-building

Does Trauma-Informed Care Make a Difference?

Hopper, Bassuk, and Olivet (2009) summarize research on the efficacy of trauma-informed care (TIC), including studies of women with co-occurring disorders (substance abuse and mental health disorders) and interventions offering psycho-education to their children. They point out that trauma-informed, integrated services are cost effective because their use has improved outcomes but does not cost more than standard programming. Their qualitative results indicate that providers report positive outcomes in their organizations from implementing TIC. Providers report greater collaboration with consumers, enhanced skills, and a greater sense of self-efficacy among consumers, and more support from their agencies. Supervisors report more collaboration within and outside their agencies, improved staff morale, fewer negative events, and more effective services.

In the same article, Hopper, Bassuk, and Olivet further report on the importance of training and ongoing supervision in establishing trauma-informed care, citing a large multi-site study of trauma-informed models, and found that "training on trauma for *non-trauma [treatment] providers* was the first and most important step in making services more trauma-informed" (emphasis added).

The authors caution that ongoing supervision, consultation, and support are needed to reinforce trauma-based concepts. Ongoing supervision and support are important to ensure that the environment is trauma-informed and that staff members practice appropriate self-care. Many programs also used external trauma consultants and ongoing training to reinforce knowledge and commitment to building trauma-informed services (Hopper, Bassuk, & Olivet, 2009).

What Are the Effects of Trauma on Children?

The children who are served in hospitals, residential care, partial hospital or day treatment programs, juvenile detention centers, and specialized schools are not children who have had calm, happy lives and who then experienced one traumatic event. Instead, early in life these children have experienced neglect, during which their needs were not noticed or not responded to. They also experienced traumatic events, such as domestic violence, physical abuse, sexual abuse, and/or neighborhood violence. Both in their biological families and later in the child welfare system, these children experience attachment disruptions. They do not have a single committed caretaker throughout their childhood. Instead they have a series of caretakers: some better, some worse; some for longer periods of time, some for shorter periods. In addition, they may have many short episodes of treatment, such as a five-day hospitalization, a two-month course of outpatient therapy, or five weeks in an afterschool program. Within these treatment episodes come more attachment disruptions, and sometimes more traumatic events such as being sexually molested by another patient or a temporary caregiver.

All of these experiences combine to create a disrupted development. Both physically and psychologically, the child is changed.

Attachment

Prior to learning a language, the young child learns about relationships. His or her early experiences inform the child's ideas about what kind of world this is. Do people notice me? Do they respond to my cries? Do they bring comfort when they come, or do they bring pain? Are relationships worthwhile, or should they be avoided?

In a good-enough parenting situation, the child's cries bring a response in a fairly short time. The person comes close, and brings relief and pleasure. The child begins to associate other people with goodness, and this association deepens every day. The adult is focused on the child, and there are long periods of attuned interactions. Attuned interactions are those in which both parties are influencing each other: the baby smiles, the mother responds; the baby frowns, the mother coos, "Ooh, what's the matter?" and the interaction continues. These attuned interactions help the baby regulate his emotions, learn about herself, and create connections within his or her brain. When breaks in the connection occur, they are quickly mended.

In addition, as the child grows, he experiences many instances of distress.

He emits a distress cry, and the parent comes to soothe him. The parent may kiss the hurt and make it better, or apply first aid, or take practical steps, or just sympathize. But the child feels her distress go down. She associates the love of this parent with a relief from distress. Furthermore, with each of these many interactions, the child learns something. He learns that love heals, or that an adhesive bandage helps, or that you can leave the area if a large dog is growling. Gradually she begins to be able to apply some of these strategies herself to her smaller problems, while still asking for help in the larger ones. Over the years he or she learns a repertoire of methods to surmount life's difficulties.

In contrast, the children in treatment may be born to situations in which the parent, often also a trauma survivor, is unable to provide this kind of parenting. The parents may have turned to drugs or alcohol to relieve their own trauma symptoms, may be suffering from depression or another mental disorder, and/or may be enmeshed in a violent relationship. The child receives no response when he cries. The attuned connecting is minimal; he is left to himself a lot. Her needs may be perceived as burdensome or too much. Or, there may be periods of close connection that alternate with periods of physical or psychological absence and unavailability. What ideas is this child forming about the world and his or her place within it?

And when the child experiences distress, no one comes. Or the caretaker is angry: "Why are you bothering me with this little fall? Big boys don't cry, and I have enough on my mind already." This child, too, is learning. But he is not learning a repertoire of emotional skills. This child is learning that his or her needs don't matter and that people can't be trusted.

The child learns these ideas about relationships prior to having language, so the memories are stored deep within his body. She does not experience them as theories she has formed, even when she is older. She experiences them as the truth about how the world is. And by responding to the world from that assumption, she or he often draws more experiences that confirm those views.

So the child or youth comes to treatment with a deep distrust of people. In his life they have been associated with pain, or have left him. And he believes that all his relationship problems have been because he is an awful, unworthy person. Therefore he is sure that if he gets to know any new people, as soon as they know his inner evil core, they too will leave him.

The antidote to trauma is attachment. Jennifer, age 12, has grown up in a loving family, and as she walks home from middle school she is thinking about telling her mother about joining band. On her walk Jennifer meets Andrew, an older boy she has seen in the neighborhood. She responds politely when he talks with her, and is surprised when he suddenly grabs her arm, kisses her and touches her breast. As she struggles to get away he bruises her arm, and threatens to hurt her more if she tells anyone. As soon as she gets away she runs home crying. Her mother cares for her, calls the police, takes her to the doctor, and does everything she can to help. While this experience was horrible for Jennifer, her prognosis is actually good, because she had the antidote readily available: love.

But picture Jennifer's classmate Angela. The person who is touching and threatening her is her stepfather, Joe. She has hinted to her mother that something is wrong, but her mother is preoccupied and does not respond. Besides, Angela knows that Joe hits her mother, although her mother always tries to close the door and protect her. So Angela tells no one. Her grades start to slip in school because she can't concentrate, and then she starts skipping school so she won't be embarrassed by not knowing the answers. Angela does not have a good prognosis without trauma-informed treatment. In her case, the very people to whom she would turn for help are the people hurting her or not seeing her pain, so she experiences double problems.

Biological Changes

The development of new instruments to look at various parts of the brain and how they function has led to indisputable evidence of the biological changes that take place as a result of early trauma. Luckily, these same instruments have also produced evidence of brain plasticity: the ability of the brain to grow, heal and change at any age. So treaters now know that traumatized children are both physically different and less socially and emotionally capable than those who have not experienced trauma. And treaters now also know that their work can help heal this difference.

To understand the biological changes that occur in the body as a result of trauma, it is important to understand the human danger response. The body and brain are programmed to react quickly and automatically to any sign of danger, which often includes anything new or in motion. The amygdala is the part of the brain responsible for the danger response. When it senses danger it puts the body on high alert, getting ready to flee or fight. This preparation includes raising the blood pressure, stopping all non-essential functions (such as digestion), becoming extremely alert, and focusing only on danger and safety. The heart is beating fast; the muscles are tense, ready for action. In a healthy brain, the amygdala's instantaneous decision is combined with and moderated by information from other parts of the brain that add information regarding context, past experiences, reasoning, and observations from the sensory system. When there are fewer connections between the amygdala and the cortex (the thinking part of the brain), this integration of information will be harder to achieve, the process slower and less reliable. So the person will spend longer in the danger mode.

In order to feel what this process is like, treaters can remember a time when they felt seriously unsafe: a near car accident, an encounter with a threatening person, a weather-related event. Even a common example like trying to drive home from work after an ice storm can be illustrative. In fact, an even more appropriate example would be being a passenger in a car when someone you didn't know very well was driving through an ice storm. How does your body feel? What do you pay attention to? How do you feel later when you are safe? How do you calm down?

A third option available in danger is to freeze. When action is not possible, the body freezes, withdraws blood from limbs, and releases opioid painkillers to prepare for injury. This process is seen as dissociation, and like all coping mechanisms it can become a habitual response that is used when no longer necessary.

The danger response and the subsequent calming with safety are mediated through a complex combination of chemicals within the human body. However, when a young child experiences too much danger that is repeated, unpredictable, and beyond the child's ability to integrate, a chemical process happens which leaves the child essentially stuck in the danger response. It is as though the body said, "This world seems like a pretty dangerous place. I guess I have to stay on high alert all the time." High alert is a hard place to be stuck. It makes relaxation, sleep, learning, and play impossible. Not sleeping well can contribute to many other problems, such as general grouchiness and hopelessness. Play is the way children learn about the world. Learning is hard when you can't concentrate because you are constantly scanning for danger. So being stuck on high alert interferes with many of the normal activities of childhood.

To further elucidate the experience of danger, consider an experiment with baby mice (Panksepp, 1998). Some baby mice had been raised in cages. They had never seen or heard of a cat. Like all baby animals, they engaged in a lot of free play with each other. The experimenters put two cat hairs in the cage. Although the mice had no cat experience, the cat hairs were wired into their brains as signifying danger. Immediately, all free play stopped. And, also significant, when the cat hairs were removed, it took a few days for the mice play to gradually re-emerge, and it never returned to the level it had been before the cat hairs were introduced.

"Normal" people (short-hand for those who either have not experienced major, repeated childhood trauma or were provided with the resources to cope with it at the time) have arousal/relaxation cycles and know ways to calm down. Trauma survivors start at a higher alert level, have rapid spikes, and rely on the external environment to help them calm down. Since the brain of a child who has experienced repeated, unaddressed trauma produces constant danger signals, the child may become inured; he may no longer discern real danger and under-react (his body has "cried wolf" too often).

The child's brain is formed through the child's relationship with others; it is developed through attuned interactions. Therefore, children who have been neglected and/or abused have less well-developed brains with fewer connections between the parts. Children with trauma histories have fewer connections between their limbic system (emotions) and their pre-frontal cortex. The cortex is created by a caretaker doing cortex-functions (care-taking, safety, meeting basic needs, figuring out problems). If these functions are not done – and modeled – for the child, she will have a less well-developed cortex. The amygdala is involved with fear conditioning and aggressive behavior, and it triggers the fighting response. It gets bigger with increased use. The hippocampus is involved with the retrieval of verbal and emotional memory. It gets smaller with stress (Brenner, Randall, Scott, Bronen, Seibyl, Southwick, et al., 1995; Kim & Diamond, 2002; McEwen, 1999). Therefore, learning becomes more difficult.

Although attachment is necessary for safety, humans are also their own most dangerous predators. Therefore, humans are very sensitive to the moods, expressions, and gestures of others. Human stress responses are very closely tied to the systems that read and respond to social cues.

Thanks to the work of Bruce Perry (Perry, 1999; Perry & Szalavitz, 2007) and others, a great deal has been learned about the development of the brain.

- Brains develop and change sequentially. The lower part, which concerns the body, the danger response, and emotional reactions, develops before the higher part, which involves words and analytical thinking.
- Brains develop and change in a use-dependent way. If you use a part more, it gets stronger. If you don't use it, it withers away.
- What fires together wires together. Things that repeatedly happen together get associated in the brain, and the next time one happens it brings up the other.

- In early years of brain formation patterns are set in to the brain that will determine our assumptions and expectations of life. If a child is hurt by people in the early years, they expect people to hurt them from then on.
- If you want to change a part of the brain, you have to use it. So, if you are talking, you are not changing the lower part of the brain. You are only affecting the thinking part.
- Many repetitions are needed to change a previously learned association or pattern.

This new understanding of the brain and how it changes opens exciting new avenues of healing for all treatment. Especially in congregate-care programs, treaters have a captive audience and can use things like recreational time for planned brain building. At the same time, they can create new, more positive expectations of relationships. Clinicians can even adapt their therapeutic work to include more physical activity to open the deeper parts of the brain for influence.

The pre-frontal cortex controls emotional behavior through cognition. When there are persistent stressors in the early years of life, neurons do not grow and connect in the prefrontal cortex, therefore, less inhibition of the danger response is available. The prefrontal cortex is the site of executive functions, which are necessary to create a rewarding life. Adele Diamond in her work on interventions that develop executive functions in children (Diamond & Lee, 2011) describes "the core skills of executive functioning" as "cognitive flexibility, inhibition (self control, self regulation) and working memory. More complex executive functions are problem solving, reasoning and planning" (p. 959). Diamond and Lee suggest that the development of executive functions is inhibited by stress, loneliness, and lack of physical fitness. What help those functions grow are practice, movement, dancing, martial arts, art, mindfulness and sensory activities, narration, and enjoyable physical activity.

The message to all treaters is that the actual physical brains and bodies of the children they treat are inadequately developed, and that these brains can be developed further by the daily acts of attunement and caring within a treatment program.

Self-regulation Skills

As the child grows and experiences the world, he encounters difficulties. She observes others around her also encountering difficulties. Through this perception he learns skills that help a person survive and master problems. In the Risking Connection trauma-training curriculum (Saakvitne, Pearlman, Gamble, & Lev, 2000), the authors describe these survival skills as the "self-capacities." They are defined as: "The ability to stay connected to and grounded in one's sense of self even when one is experiencing strong feelings." These self-capacities (first described in Pearlman, 1998) are divided into three areas affected by trauma: inner connection, self-worth, and feelings-management skills.

Inner connection is "the ability to form connections with positive others AND to hold onto that connection when the other is not physically present" (p. 21). This skill allows us to think about someone who loves us and remember their wisdom and caring even when that person is not physically present. It helps us feel connected and cared for and to access sources of help even when we are alone. It is an absent or under-developed skill when a child has no reliable connections and people just disappear from his life, and his mind becomes full of hostile voices instead of comforting ones. Even small absences seem to last forever, leaving the child feeling horribly alone. She may resort to extreme actions or tolerate abuse just to keep someone with her.

Self-worth is the knowledge that you have a right to exist, you deserve the air you breathe. (p. 21) Even "normal" children are often convinced that everything bad that has happened to them is their own fault. Partly, this belief results from the tendency of children to think that the world revolves around them. When children have experienced multiple traumas, often the people in their lives have explicitly told them it is their fault. Plus, the child would rather blame herself than doubt the caretakers upon whom her life depends. So, the child develops a deep sense of shame and self-blame.

Shame is different from guilt. *Guilt* is a sense that you are a good person who has done something wrong: "I am a person who *has* a problem." *Shame* is the sense that you yourself are a horrible person, different and worse than anyone else: "I *am* the problem." Guilt drives us towards the other, to fix the problems. Shame drives us away from others, to keep them from seeing the awful self.

The antidote to shame is to be known and loved. It is very hard for a shame-based person to let anyone know and love them. But if they do, and that person is not horrified, they may begin to heal.

Feelings-management skills are taught by caretakers as they help a child through difficulties (p. 22). But if the child has been ignored or moved among several caretakers, they do not learn these skills. Children may not even be taught the words for feelings, or how to identify them within their bodies. Feelings-management skills include identifying, tolerating, modulating, and integrating feelings.

Without these skills, the person experiences feelings as coming upon them suddenly for no reason and as being scary and overwhelming. They are not able to accept the wisdom their emotions may contain.

The message is that all human self-regulation skills are learned. Babies are not born with them. If a child does not have reliable, attuned caretaking, he will not learn them. But treatment programs can teach these skills deliberately. Instead of demanding that children change their symptoms, treatment staff can teach them the skills that make the symptoms unnecessary (Saakvitne, Pearlman, Gamble, & Lev, 2000, pp. 20-21).

The Function of Symptoms

Mary is starting to do her math homework, a difficult subject for her. She notices that Jessica and Serena are talking and laughing. She immediately knows that they are saying bad things about her. They have always hated her. They have noticed how stupid she is in math … and in everything. That's why she is in this lousy place. She will never have any friends, and she will probably never see her family again. It's just what she deserves for being such a total loser.

And apparently out of nowhere Mary gets up and throws her math book at Jessica. It hits Jessica's arm, Jessica starts screaming, and she tries to attack Mary. Suddenly the room is in chaos and the bewildered staff is trying to calm people down.

What happened here?

> Mary came to school worried about her family, because she hasn't heard from them in a couple of weeks.
>
> Math is a stressor for Mary. She doesn't get it easily and she always feels stupid.
>
> Mary cannot ask the teacher for help. She is sure that the teacher would find this request annoying and would blame her for being stupid. She has received that response from plenty of teachers in her past. Plus, she wouldn't want the other kids to see that she needs help.
>
> Mary is constantly scanning the environment for danger, which is everywhere. She feels wired and didn't sleep that well last night.
>
> When Mary sees Jessica and Serena talking and laughing, it literally does not occur to her that they could be talking

about something else. She *knows* that they are saying bad things about her. And she has absolutely no way to ask them, or join in the conversation, because she *knows* that they hate her.

Mary herself doesn't realize how upset she is getting. But suddenly she can't stand one more second of these horrible thoughts and feelings. So she stands up and throws her book. And in the ensuing chaos, she does not have to do her math, people want to know what is going on with her, and Jessica has been taken out of the room so that she and Serena are no longer talking to each other.

What does Mary need?

She needs some relationships in which she can experience safety and kindness. Over time, she may learn to go to these people with questions and needs for comfort.

She needs gentle, safe, non-shaming help with math.

She needs help making friends.

She needs to learn to recognize the signs in her body that she is becoming upset.

She might be able to learn some skills to calm her body by music or physical activity.

She needs some experiences of her strength and success, maybe through a job reading to younger children, for example.

And she needs some hope for the next steps in her life.

Then, Mary will not need her symptoms as desperately. She will have less need to hurt others or herself, run away, or just withdraw. Her connections will provide a safe base for her to try new skills, explore her interests, and gradually develop a positive sense of herself.

Summary

Almost every youth who comes to congregate treatment has experienced neglect, trauma, and attachment disruptions. This experience has affected his development. The lack of attuned relationships in her early life leaves her with assumptions that people are dangerous and unreliable. His brain and body chemistry have been altered so that he is stuck in a hyper-alert danger-response, unable to relax or feel safe. Her brain has fewer connections between parts and less ability to perform executive functions. No one has taught him the basic skills of managing feelings and getting through difficulties. So, when a current stress occurs, he has no one he can turn to for help. His brain was already on overdrive, so this event pushes him even further. She does not know how to identify her feelings or what to do about them. So he is plunged into a deep hole of despair, hopelessness and fear. No one wants to feel that way, so she does something. He hits someone. She throws a chair. He runs away. This action helps in the moment, because she is not thinking those bad thoughts any more. But it hurts in the long run. He needs safety and caring relationships to build his brain. She needs skills to manage her feelings. He needs experiences of success. Through this remediation he can build new ideas about relationships and about himself and have a repertoire of other strategies that help in the moment and do not make things worse.

Chapter Two

The Restorative Approach: A Trauma-Informed Treatment System

As agencies learn about trauma and its effects on children, they begin to consider how to apply this knowledge in their programs (the training and transition process necessary to establish the new methods are discussed in later chapters). The Restorative Approach has been created as a bridge from theory to practice. It provides a blueprint for administrative, milieu and clinical interventions. It translates brain science into every day actions.

The Underlying Assumptions of the Restorative Approach

The basic tenet of this new approach is that positive relationships provide the strongest motivation for people to change. The Restorative Approach concentrates on how relationships affect behavior. Healing relationships provide the child with new models of interaction with people, demonstrating that others can be trusted and will help. The day-to-day interactions within the milieu and education settings provide the most powerful opportunities for change, and therefore it is essential to see *every* staff member as a potential healer. The concept that symptoms are adaptations, that the children are doing the best they can to meet their needs and to solve their problems, provides a road map for responding to them. All staff must ask, "How do we understand this behavior?" and use this knowledge to design individualized responses. It is difficult to know how to respond effectively until you understand what is causing the behavior. In order to do so, every staff member must receive foundational training in trauma, which should include how it hurts, its lasting effects, how people can heal through relationships, and how the treaters must take care of themselves and each other to continue to do this difficult work well.

Safety is a prerequisite to any treatment. When children feel they are in danger, they cannot form relationships, relax, sleep, or have fun. Within the Restorative Approach, programs look first to ways they can create a greater sense of safety for children and their families. Without safety, a child and his/her family cannot begin to trust a provider to help them examine the impact of trauma on their lives. In fact, a program that emphasizes the healing power of relationships becomes safer than one that operates through reliance on consequences, as there are fewer power struggles and less need for physical intervention.

The Restorative Approach emphasizes the importance of examining shame. Most of the children in congregate care have been seriously abused, which they feel is their own fault. It's hard for any child to understand why someone close to them (a parent, relative, or friend) would abuse them. Instead of viewing the abusive parental figure as a bad person, they come to believe – often because they are explicitly told – that they have done something wrong to cause the abuse. Therefore they feel great shame and are convinced that they are bad and worthless people. Any in-care behavioral setback (for example, they hit their teacher that day) reaffirms this basic belief. Consequences that include isolation and public humiliation further reinforce this internal certainty.

Therefore, the first step in the Restorative Approach is to understand that it is the job of treaters to form a relationship with every child and family they treat. When children trust a treatment provider to help them, they can begin to examine the causes underlying their shame. Then they can begin to allow providers to reach out to them to find the good in them, to learn about them.

Connecting Theory to Action

The Restorative Approach translates what modern science has learned about trauma's effects on the brain into specific strategies for daily interactions with the children. The following points summarize the connections between theory and daily actions. These techniques will be explained in greater detail in later chapters.

Understanding that the thinking parts of the traumatized child's brain are less developed helps staff realize that they must provide extra help for the children under their care in problem-solving, memory, self-soothing, and planning. A traumatized child's under-developed verbal skills and inadequate social understanding means the staff must use multiple modalities such as music and art to communicate. Since the child has not learned how to identify or manage emotions, the team must actively teach and model these skills. Because the child is stuck in the danger response, he or she will need support to play, relax, sleep, and to feel safe. When staff understands that the child's thinking is compromised, they will take the child's response to them less personally. In the trauma-informed response, when things go wrong, the children can experience the possibility of fixing problems in relationships, something that has never happened before in their lives. For all members of the team, knowledge of the damaging effects of trauma and how to heal them guides their daily interactions with the children.

The Restorative Approach recognizes that a traumatized child's brain is different, in that the prefrontal cortex is less developed. Because of that trauma-related difference, the child is easily overwhelmed by emotions. In treatment programs using the Restorative Approach, staff members understand that they will have to act as the child's prefrontal cortex for awhile, teaching problem-solving rather than punishing a child for apparently 'choosing' to act out emotionally when the child is doing the best he or she can. The staff members' brain-building tasks include helping the child with selective attention, working memory, self-observation, and response inhibition. Further, the staff responds to the child's emotional dysregulation with calming techniques rather than with thinking interventions.

A traumatized child typically has a strong, even over-developed, response to any situation perceived as dangerous. Using the Restorative Approach, staff members aim to soothe the child whose emotions are blowing up, to reassure him or her rather than get into a power struggle. The last thing a staff member trying to help an emotionally dysregulated child would do is back him or her into a corner. Instead, staff uses soothing techniques when the child is upset. They teach uses of emotions, and that emotions contain information, and teach self-soothing techniques. The staff provides and identifies safety, in part by talking before acting and providing predictability. The program uses crisis kits and crisis prevention plans. Staff is aware that the child will notice everything that they do, how they treat each other, their tone of voice, and their expressions.

Because of their focus on danger, the child may miss a large part of what goes on around them. Staff may need to coax child to have fun and to point out joys in life.

Traumatic events – especially those experienced prior to the acquisition of language – may return to the child as flashbacks, as though he were reliving, not remembering, the experience. At times the child may dissociate to manage the pain of her experience. Staff can teach grounding techniques that return the child to the present.

The physical underdevelopment of the child's brain results in more difficulty accessing verbal memory. Therefore, staff do not rely on verbal planning alone, and whenever possible they use multi-model interventions and communications, such as charts, pictures, art, dance and music.

The child whose life has been unpredictable has confused, few, or no regular bodily rhythms. Staff helps develop bodily rhythms by maintaining predictable structures and offering rhythmic activities such as yoga and dance. The child also has an under-developed ability to sort out social cues, so staff is clear in communication and uses simple language. They teach social interpretation through movies, books, and other social modeling opportunities.

Lack of early reliable care combined with trauma and attachment disruptions result in a child whose connection with his body has not been reliably established. Therefore, she may have difficulty regulating her body functions. Staff can help through offering repetitive, rhythmic, rewarding activities to rebuild the lower brain, the part that controls the body. The child may have difficulty sleeping, so staff will not respond to bed time problems with consequences, but instead look for ways to help the child relax, such as providing a night light, or allowing or encouraging reading or music. Staff in a trauma-informed program handle hygiene issues with sensitivity and understanding of their complexity (symptoms are adaptations), not with consequences, and find opportunities to teach healthy sexuality.

Because the traumatized child has had fewer attuned interactions, his brain is less integrated and he has more difficulty in generalizing experience and knowledge from one situation to another. Staff, therefore, makes connections explicit and specifically make comparisons between various aspects of life, distinguishing past from present. They give the child opportunities to practice her new skills in many arenas and settings.

Children who grow up with neglect and trauma have not been taught how to recognize or name emotions, so it is up to treaters to teach them the names of emotions – including the recognition of their bodily sensations – and to model healthy emotion. The child may experience her emotions as moving from extremely aroused to extremely shut down quickly with no apparent rationale. Staff can help the child develop awareness of his own emotions and their stages, and develop tactics for each stage.

The hallmark of trauma is the victim's lack of control. He could not influence what was happening to him, and he was used to fulfilling someone else's needs. She was not treated like a person. After repeated exposure this powerlessness generalizes to all situations. The child learns that no effective action is possible in her life. In order to effectively help these children heal, treatment systems must not replicate this experience of helplessness and lack of control; they must allow *many* opportunities for the child's active participation in decisions involving him or her. They can also respond to problems by guiding the youths to fix damage they have created and repair relationships they have hurt. Because of previous lack of control, the child may value control above all else. The program can give a child control whenever possible, collaborate with him, and focus on his learning to control himself as opposed to staff controlling his behavior. Because control is so important, and lack of control is associated with victimization, the child may cover up vulnerable feelings such as fear and sadness. Staff can create safety to allow the child to share vulnerable feelings, and model having vulnerable feelings in a healthy way.

The child believes that everything that has happened to her is her own fault. To heal she must develop a sense of safety in which she can share what she finds shameful and receive compassion. Staff can also point out her strengths and achievements.

The child's experiences have taught him not to trust adults. Programs can provide a different experience by being trustworthy, and by emphasizing trustworthy relationships. They can point out how relationships in the present are different from past relationships. The child expects the worst in relationships, and so may push people away. Staff understand the adaptive aspect of the child pushing the adult away, stay committed, and don't pull back. They verbalize and validate the child's fears.

The relationships in the child's life have often violated her boundaries, involving her in adult problems and activities, requiring her to perform tasks beyond her abilities, causing her to be the caretaker of adults. Therefore the child is uncertain about boundaries and tests them. Staff can maintain firm yet flexible, safe boundaries, be aware of the complexity of boundaries in the child's life, discuss boundary issues openly with each other and with the children, and also seek professional supervision around these issues to identify their own reactions so that they don't interfere with the work.

The child has not been taught how to handle problems in relationships. When he has had relationship difficulties, the other person has often just disappeared. He may have seen adults handle problems by drinking, using drugs, or violence. Staff has the opportunity to provide relationships that stick with the child. They can model relationship skills, speak from their hearts, and share their own modulated emotional reactions. They can always address the relationship aspects of events, provide paths to work through relationship difficulties, and actively teach social skills. Since he does not trust others, the child may have trouble asking directly for what he wants. Staff can encourage direct communication, and practice and model skills of making requests. They can say yes when possible.

Similarly, the child has not learned how to handle something going wrong without making it worse. Staff can teach distraction and calming techniques, help the child develop a list of tactics to improve a situation, offer the child alternatives, not consequences, when he is becoming agitated, and develop with the child a list of positive coping tactics for handling pain.

Because of both past and present situations, the child often feels hopeless. Staff can help through pointing out new skills and behavioral gains. Also, they can teach and support the child in self-advocacy.

Working with children who have survived trauma, neglect and attachment disruptions causes strong reactions in all treaters. The trauma-informed program is aware of the effects of vicarious traumatization, and imbeds in daily operations opportunities to discuss the effects of the work, provides training in techniques for care for one's self and other team members, and encourages practices that promote vicarious transformation.

Trauma-Informed Care in the Milieu

Trauma-informed care and the Restorative Approach is observable in many every day interactions on the unit, in the school, and in the therapist's office. Some indicators include:

- Staff displays an attitude of "the child is doing the best they can" **rather than** believing the child is acting out on purpose.
- Staff explores the problem (e.g., "What's going on? What's wrong?") **rather than** immediately talking to the child about consequences.
- Staff engages in active listening with children (i.e., listen carefully, restate the problem, empathize with feelings and needs).
- Staff avoids comments and responses that could intensify feelings of shame (e.g., insisting a child do tasks that stretch his/her ability too much; isolating the child; scolding the child in front of peers).
- Staff avoids power struggles with children (e.g., arguing with the child, proving the child is wrong).
- Staff refers to children in descriptive ways (such as, "He does not know how to ask directly for what he needs") **rather than** using negative labels (e.g., manipulative, borderline, troublemaker).
- Staff value flexibility in managing behavior **rather than** strictly following rules.
- When a child is upset, staff mainly works to help the child calm down **rather than** try to reason with the child or provide consequences.
- Staff tries to avoid restraint and seclusion of a child. They do **not** use restraint to get a child to follow the rules, stop property damage, and/or cut off a discussion with a child.

- Staff talks with their peers and supervisors about their strong positive and negative reactions to clients and doing this kind of work. Understanding their own emotions helps inform their work.
- Staff asks peers for help, or allow peers to help, when they get stuck trying to manage a child's behavior.
- Treatment team members work well as a team (e.g., they manage conflict, care for each other, avoid splits between each other).

Incorporating Brain Science into Everyday Life

The research of Bruce Perry (Perry, 1999; Perry & Szalavitz, 2007) has shown that when children are neglected and/or abused early in life – as most of the children in congregate care have been – the lower parts of their brain are underdeveloped. This is the part of the brain that manages bodily functions, such as eating, sleeping, toileting, alertness and relaxation, and other bodily systems. The higher functions of the brain, such as emotional regulation and critical thinking, are all based on the lower, which has connections with all other brain parts.

In order to reach the lower part of the brain to change it, treaters have to engage it. And how do they do that? They involve the child in physical activities with movement and rhythm, including music, dance, drumming, rocking, swinging on swings, planting a garden, shoveling snow. And, they pair these activities with positive interactions with other people. Treaters make sure the activities are fun and engaging and done in connection with adults.

There are revolutionary implications of this brain-changing approach to treatment. Trauma-informed thinking has always maintained that the daily life in the milieu and the relationships with the mental health workers are powerful forces for change. Now it is even more clear that having fun with the clients in physically engaged, active ways is the very thing treaters have to do in order to change their clients' brains and help them develop in healthy ways. And now they can apply this process more intentionally and with targeted goals.

Another implication is the need for true presence. As we know, traumatized youth are acutely perceptive about other people's moods and emotions, a skill that also reflects their earliest brain development. They had to develop this perceptivity to stay alive and anticipate the next dangerous event. So they know if the adult is actually engaged with them, actually having fun and feeling positive and affectionate. If the adult is distant, sarcastic, punishing, or distracted and texting on their phone, this activity or interaction will not change the child's brain. In fact, the lack of real engagement will confirm and further strengthen the patterns already established. So, in order to be successful in the change process, agencies need to take good care of their staff, so that they feel energetic, hopeful and available.

While activities in the milieu can go a long way toward restructuring the traumatized child's brain, therapy also plays a large part. Especially in the early stages of treatment, the therapist can be a primary source of reparative connection. He or she can incorporate these principles by having a rocking chair in the office, using art and music, walking together while talking, and making sure the appointments are positive and fun. As the child feels safer and calmer, he or she will be more available for cognitive approaches. The cognitive part of the brain inhibits immediate action on impulses, and it needs increased strength to successfully do so. Any discussion, reading, talking (about anything, like sports or the weather) builds this brain skill. When the child's brain has developed and his ability to control and calm his body is more secure, he will be able to participate in verbally- based therapies.

Two evidence-based therapy interventions are Trauma-Focused Cognitive Behavioral Therapy (Cohen, Mannarino, & Deblinger, 2006) and TARGET (Brom, Pat-Horenczyk, & Ford, 2009). Therapists can also incorporate these brain-changing principles into group and family work. They can assist the family and child in engaging in joyful games that may heal the brains of both. Groups that cook, read and discuss books, do crafts, or take walks together can build all parts of the brain.

Another area of the brain that is under-developed in a traumatized child is the ability to observe one's own behavior and create a narrative of one's own experience. The therapist can build this skill by any type of story creation about the child's life in the program, by talking about things they have done together, by making a life book – in short, by any form of story making. And with the team, the therapist has an essential role in leading staff to think beneath the behavior, consider how it is adaptive, and plan how we can help the child meet his or her needs in a less destructive way.

Use of Language within the Restorative Approach

An important part of the Restorative Model is the language that staff uses in talking with the children. Staff use primarily "I" statements. They emphasize how the child's actions affect them and how the behavior will likely affect the other children. They speak from their hearts. Examples of this method include:

> "It hurts my feelings and makes me sad when you call me a name."
>
> "Susie feels angry and less safe when you hit her."
>
> "When you run out the door that way, I get worried and can't trust you as much. So I have to keep a closer eye on you."
>
> "You just punched me. I am hurt and mad. I know we will be able to work this out, but right now I need some time to calm down. I'll talk to you in a while, and we can figure out what went wrong and how to restore our relationship. I still care about you."

"I am so delighted by the way you shared with Mark just now."

"I feel that I can trust you to go out and play, because you just shared what you were feeling with me."

Staff avoids using statements that begin with "You need." While it is permissible to talk about the consequences of the child's actions, consequences should not be the first or only topic. The natural outcomes of behaviors can be discussed, after staff communicates their reactions and feelings and the situation is processed.

Responding to Behaviors That Hurt Others

Within the Restorative Approach most minor misbehaviors are handled with re-direction, with no additional consequence necessary. If a child is doing something that staff consider disruptive or unsafe, they ask the child to stop it. If the child left a towel in the bathroom, staff tell them to go pick it up; no need for a loss of points. However, at times children's actions or words hurt others, present a danger to the community, or involve serious property destruction. If the program is not using points and levels, time-based restrictions, isolation, and loss of privileges when the child acts out, then what can be done?

In programs using the Restorative Approach, when a child does something that hurts others, the adult response is two-fold: the tasks given to the child as "consequences" teach skills that will help the child avoid similar problems in the future and provide an opportunity to make amends. How can a child who has had a fight with a peer learn skills to avoid future fights? He can be assigned practice in getting along, like playing a game positively with this peer for half an hour. She can role-play a relationship problem with a staff member that leads to a better outcome. He can interview three people and find out how they handle a situation when a friend lets them down. How does this kind of skills practice help the child heal? The theory is that the child was trying to solve a problem with his behavior (a negative behavior learned from past experience or that worked in meeting his needs in the past). She can only change that behavior when she has acquired better skills for solving problems and understands the reasons for her past behavior. If the team understands what problems he was trying to solve and what needs he was trying to meet, they can explore with him more effective ways to approach future problems. They can consider what skills she should have to be able to meet those needs with less negative consequences, and use the tasks as an opportunity to acquire those skills.

How can a child who has assaulted a staff member and damaged property make amends? There are many ways. He can do something for that person: write an apology, talk over what was going on, make the staff member a picture, write and sing him or her a song, or pick a bouquet of flowers. He can make popcorn for all the children on the unit as restitution for the disruption and turmoil he caused. She can help fix the damaged property.

How does making amends help a child heal?

These tasks can teach the children that when there are problems within a relationship, they can be resolved through effective action. Previously in the child's life, relationship problems have typically been handled through violence and abandonment. When something goes wrong, he feels hopeless. She sees the problems as one more sign that she is a worthless person, and she is sure that this new adult will leave her as all previous adults have done in the past. He often responds to these feelings by demanding to leave, asserting that he never cared about any of these people anyway. The steps of making amends allow him/her to resolve relationship problems and enhance connections with others. It also gradually chips away at their intense feelings of shame because they will feel better about themselves when they can work out issues with others. Instead of "doing time," a strategy frequently used in congregate-care settings, the child is learning new skills and reconnecting with people.

The Restorative Approach requires more flexibility and creativity on the part of the staff, and therefore it also demands a high degree of self-awareness as well as the ability of the team to talk honestly with each other. Each child does *not* have to receive the same response for the same action. Consistency (in the sense of sameness) is not the goal. Instead, staff can be consistent in their values and purposes. The response to each child and each instance of misbehavior will consistently be individualized, related to that child's goals and what he or she needs to learn.

In addition, it is important for staff to recognize and discuss with others their own thoughts and feelings about the child and his/her behavior. Through supervision and team discussion, staff can increase their awareness of when their own feelings get triggered and of the assumptions they bring to the work from their own childhoods. Examining these issues allows the staff to stay in control of their own emotions and prevents them from interacting with the child in a negative way.

Shame and the Restorative Approach

Why is it important to use restorative tasks when a child has hurt others? Why assign a task that offers the child the chance to learn, and the chance to reconnect with others, to make amends for the harm he/she has caused? An abused child is full of shame. He is sure that the abuse he suffered was his fault. After an explosive episode in a congregate-care setting, the child struggles with feelings of shame, an increase in the sense that she is a useless, worthless person. Traditional punishments, such as isolation in a room away from adults, increase this shame, and thus increase the likelihood of more aggressive behavior. People who are feeling deep shame feel they have nothing to lose. They distrust relationships, and believe, "If you really knew me you would hate me." They act to say: "Let's get this over with now. I'll show you how bad I am, and you will leave or hurt me like everyone else."

Restorative tasks that offer a way to reconnect and make amends teach a valuable skill that we all need: what do you do when you have messed up?

It is possible to do something wrong and set it right. It is possible to have a problem in a relationship and then to fix it. This is not something these children have previously experienced.

When a child makes a meal for the unit he has disrupted, when he does a chore for the staff member he has harmed, when she teaches a computer game to the child she has attacked, she is left feeling a little better, a little stronger. He is connected to others. She has given something valuable, from her own efforts and talents. He feels he may be worth something after all. She has a reason to try to act safely next time. He has a tiny ray of hope that gradually helps him feel better about himself and reduces his feelings of shame.

Frequently Asked Questions about the Restorative Approach

There are common areas of concern that arise when an agency first implements the Restorative Approach.

Does using the Restorative Approach mean we no longer have limits or rules? No. The adults are responsible to create a safe, orderly setting that maximizes the safety and success of the children. This approach means setting clear expectations, structuring daily routines, building organized schedules with plenty of activities, and intervening immediately when things start to go wrong. Unsafe behavior is stopped before it spirals out of control. In some settings, restraints may be necessary to maintain safety (although they are used infrequently and only in situations of imminent physical danger). Occasionally children need to be separated from others or from the group.

Does program staff have and use authority in the Restorative Approach? Yes. Staff uses their authority honestly, directly, and with respect. Authority is not exercised for personal emotional gain. Staff uses their teams as a sounding board to make sure of their direction. They are in charge of the children, and responsible for their wellbeing.

It seems like staff might be encouraged to ignore maladaptive behavior so as not to reinforce it. No. It is one more form of neglect of these children if staff just ignores their behaviors because it is easier for them, because they are scared, or because they don't know how to intervene. They must have the strength and support to be direct with the children about what they are doing and how it is affecting staff and the community. Staff does so in a context of their own self-awareness and emotional regulation. They engage with the children in a respectful, collaborative manner that is based in their complete conviction that behaviors are adaptations and have been learned for self-protection. They know that the child needs to learn new, more effective behaviors, and they help to demonstrate and teach these positive coping strategies.

Wouldn't the Restorative Approach suggest that our prime intervention is constantly asking the child how they are feeling? No. It is rarely helpful to ask the children how they are feeling, because they usually don't know unless it is obvious (e.g., furious). They react to the "therapy sounding" question with even more frustration and anger. Instead, staff can use the art of engagement, exploration, humor, distraction, looking for patterns, listening, repeating, until staff and child discover and begin to understand what is going on.

The Restorative Approach sounds great for when everything is calm and staff has plenty of time. If that were the case, it wouldn't be much use in congregate-care treatment. Whether staff is intervening in a crisis, whether they have to fill out a form for external requirements, whether they are in a hurry and only have ten minutes, they can still be respectful and collaborative with the children. Adults can be honest and share directly what their constraints are in working with the children. They can speak from their hearts. They can convey certainty that the child is doing the best he/she can, and that together they can learn ways to do better.

It does not take more time, or more staff, to do this method. However, it does take more skills and thoughtfulness on the part of the staff. Typical behavioral management methods lose their effectiveness over time. Since these systems are not addressing underlying issues of shame and other psychodynamics, the child often repeats negative behaviors, and the staff interventions become more extreme (e.g., restraints). Restraints take time. Restraints use a lot of staff. The Restorative method cuts down on restraints, seclusion (confining the child to an enclosed space), and holding doors shut to keep children in rooms. The Restorative method cuts down on power struggles and arguments over the loss of points that result in escalation and angry outbursts.

Restorative tasks do not necessarily take a long time. They do not have to take as long as the former restriction would have taken. In addition, quite a bit of time is freed by not having to fill out, tally, and record points in a points-and-levels system. That time can be used to have a straightforward conversation with the child. Restorative tasks can be done in groups, and at staff convenience. A relaxed, flexible atmosphere results in staff having more time, using their time in more meaningful ways and thereby forming true relationships with the children.

How can we have consistency with all this individualization? As indicated earlier, the Restorative Approach suggests that the staff response to each child's actions be individualized. One child bites a staff member, and he is required to do a chore with that staff before returning to fun, special treat activities. Another child hurts a different member of the staff.

She makes a poster showing a thermometer that represents her anger, and she draws pictures of the feelings in her body when her anger is at each level from mild to out of control. There are different possible responses for essentially the same behaviors, depending on what the child needs. People often wonder what happens to consistency. Isn't it essential that we respond the same way every time any child does a similar thing? Won't the children feel that these individualized responses are unfair?

First of all, even traditional behavioral systems, such as points and levels is not consistently administered by staff. Any child in care can tell you which staff is more lenient and which are stricter. Secondly, it is important to understand that doing the SAME thing is not doing the FAIR thing, because children differ in intellectual and emotional capability. In responding to a child who may complain about consistency, staff replies confidently, "Everything is individualized here. We do what is right for each child." In a typical family, this sense of what is right and fair differing for each child holds true as well. For example, older children may have a later bedtime than younger children because their needs are different.

Still, the adult must be able to explain to the adults on his team why he chose a given restorative task for a given symptomatic behavior. The choice should be based on the conceptualized plan, or formulation, of the child's treatment, identified treatment themes, the child's abilities and skills, and the severity and frequency of his/her actions. The Restorative Approach's team culture values staff members supportively challenging each other about being too strict or too lenient with a given child.

Consistency is found in individualization, our understanding of each child, and a compassionate approach to his/her symptoms. Consistency is not sameness, it is thoughtfulness, and it is giving each child a chance to learn and to make amends, to feel less shame, to be stronger and better connected after a difficult situation. Staff aims to be consistently caring and empathic.

Is the program preparing these kids for the real world? The idea behind this question is that if programs do not punish the children for their behaviors, they will never learn that these behaviors are not tolerated in the real world. In this view, treaters using Restorative Approach methods are coddling the acting-out children, spoiling them, and giving them an unrealistic view of life.

Consider the following analogy: An 8-year-old named Ryan is in Instructional Little League this year. In this league, the children get five strikes, some times more if the coaches decide that the ball-throwing machine isn't working right. The coaches and teammates always say encouraging things to the children: "Good swing Ryan" for a strike; "nice try" for a throw to a completely unpredicted part of the field. The coaches constantly teach the children skills: move your foot up a little, keep your eye on the ball, move your body to catch the ball, don't just stretch. Everything that the children do that is even remotely in the direction of what they are supposed to do is highly praised. They can only run two bases (otherwise everyone would get a home run every time, as no one ever catches the ball) and the innings are over when a team gets 5 runs. Obviously, the idea here is to begin teaching the children the necessary skills to play the game, and to limit the humiliation/ disappointment/ frustration they feel so they will want to play again. The game is set up to encourage success and limit failure. And no one ever says: "We aren't preparing these children for the real world if we give them special treatment like this."

Maybe treaters should consider treatment centers to be the instructional league for real life. In the real world, ideas and applications of Restorative Justice are gaining ground, and many more court systems are using them. Also, in the real world, it is widely acknowledged that punishment alone does not work, as evidenced by the high rates of recidivism.

One can also hope that the real world contains people willing to negotiate and demonstrate flexibility and understanding. One hopes that people will not be punished for everything they do wrong (luckily, most people are not). When they hurt someone, adults hope they will have a chance to make up for it and heal the relationship. We hope that their real worlds will not be characterized by unremitting harshness.

If punishment actually changed children, surely they would be different by now, as they have experienced a lot of punishment in their lives. Punishment when a child yells at a teacher will not show him how to appropriately handle anger in the classroom. What is required is to teach him how to recognize when he is becoming angry and how to express that feeling without getting himself in trouble. Just like the child who is learning to play baseball, she needs constant encouragement if she is to learn and develop the required social skills and the desire to remain engaged in life.

Aren't we just making excuses for the children? "I guess I can understand how his trauma history can be an excuse for his behavior yesterday," Sarah, a childcare worker, said. "But today, he was feeling fine and I don't see how his past is an excuse for today."

The fact is that a child's trauma history is never an excuse. It is always a reason. The child's daily life, emotions, and thoughts are *always* affected by their past. *This* child is biologically different from non-traumatized children: he/she has a hyper-responsive nervous system that does not change from day to day. Her distrust of others is always present. His fear of being weak or vulnerable directs his choices. Her lack of emotion management skills, his sense that he is not worthwhile, that he is to blame for everything bad that happens, and her inability to maintain a connection with others – all these factors and feelings control and influence every moment of every day.

This continuing influence from a differently developed brain does not mean that the child cannot change. He can begin to feel safe and to relax. She can slowly learn to trust a few people. Through experiences of success and approval from others, he can discover positive parts of himself. She can learn feelings-management skills.

When a child has diabetes, adults do not refer to his diabetes as an "excuse" for his reaction to sugary foods. They would not speak of his diabetes as an "excuse" to avoid eating certain foods. They would plan for the child to gradually increase competence in managing his/her diabetes using the skills and technology available from others so that he/she would lead a largely normal life. And, the diabetes would always be present as a reason for some actions and choices.

Even if a child had a temporary injury, such as a broken leg, treaters would not call the broken leg an "excuse" to avoid a hike. If caring adults were taking that child somewhere, they would make adaptations to promote the child's success on the trip. They might bring a wheelchair for long distances. They would plan frequent stops to rest. They would teach the child how to use crutches and bring them along. They would not blame the child for needing these adaptations. At the same time, they would expect the child to get better. They might enroll him in physical therapy and encourage him to work hard at the exercises. They would gradually do less and less for her as she healed. His leg cast would be reduced to a smaller cast and then to a support bandage. There would be a constant balance between understanding her pain and incapacity, and supporting her efforts to heal.

How treaters speak about children can strongly influence how they feel about these clients, and thus how they act towards them. Identifying the children's trauma histories as an "excuse," is to imply that children are not able to change, to simultaneously blame them for their incapacity, and to have low expectations. This formulation is the opposite of what will help. If, instead, treaters understand each child's trauma history and realize that he or she is a victim, they will know that praise – not blame – will create hope and lead to the child's healing and potential for greatness.

Most programs make the kids take responsibility for their behavior. That phrase is commonly heard in children's treatment programs. This concept usually means the children taking responsibility for their mistakes and *negative* behaviors, although the children also don't (and are not encouraged to) take much responsibility for the positive things they do.

Everyone is in favor of taking responsibility for one's actions. It is part of working through mistakes that one makes. For example, recently when an adult forgot about a meeting and thus caused others to scramble around to get the work done, he felt it was important to admit he had messed up and apologize personally to the people he inconvenienced.

However, as staff we often express indignation that children "won't even take responsibility for their own behavior!" This righteousness might be tempered by looking at ways we find it difficult to take responsibility for our own behavior.

Have you or someone you know ever attended Weight Watchers? It is a wonderful place to learn about adults who are trying to make difficult changes in their behaviors, similar to the tasks we are asking of the children under our care. These adults by and large have many more assets than our children do: supportive networks, emotional management skills, and intellectual abilities. Yet they still have difficulty taking responsibility for their behavior. If a person has not been following the eating plan, his/her first impulse is to skip the meeting all together, and to think of a good reason he/she cannot attend. If they go to the meeting, they may want to skip the weigh-in. If they have gained weight, they have many reasons and many extenuating circumstances (in the children, we would call this "making excuses," even though many of their reasons are completely legitimate). If a person has a bad day of over-eating, he/she often feels that all is lost, that he will never lose weight, and then he keeps on over-eating more and more. This pattern is similar to the way that the children are plunged into hopelessness and despair.

As adults, we can think of other situations in which we hide our failings, conceal our mistakes, and find reasons to excuse our less desirable actions. It just isn't that easy for any human being always to take responsibility for his or her behavior.

Then, why do adults imagine that children deny what they did, blame others, and claim extenuating circumstances? Is it actually because they do not know what they have done? Or is it because they are so ashamed, and feel so hopeless about their behavior that they cannot bear to face it? Maybe denial is the only coping mechanism they know. In the past, mistakes may have led to abuse. In many cases physical abuse came randomly, and it was difficult to figure out which, if any, mistake had caused it. But the children are sure that they must have done something wrong. In other cases, mistakes led to expulsion from a family. Certainly they have not learned that one can make a mistake and then work it out.

When programs punish children by isolation and restriction, does this action increase the likelihood that they will take responsibility for their actions in the future? The idea behind these traditional systems is that as the child consistently experiences punishments associated with certain behaviors and rewards with others, they will make the link and learn to admit and understand their mistakes. Yet this concept ignores the role of shame. When a child is banished, he feels hopeless and lost, and cannot bear to sit and think about what happened. So he becomes even more entrenched in blaming others to lessen his pain.

In the Restorative Approach, to make amends the child does a restorative task for the person or persons who felt the impact of his or her behavior. During this task the child will get an emotional understanding of how his/her behavior affected the other person, and can develop a deeper internal sense of responsibility. For example, Martin, a teenage boy who told three younger boys that he was going to blow up the school, is invited to meet with them with his therapist. He listens to their reactions to the event, apologizes, and assures them that he will not blow up the school. He explains to them that he was upset that day and is sorry he involved them. Then he returns twice a week to teach the boys the computer skills in which he excels. In spending that time with them, he can see that these little children were actually scared by what he said he was going to do and that his behavior mattered to them. And equally importantly, he learns that when he has messed up, there is something he can do about it. He can reassure them. He can work it through. The younger boys also learn that you can apologize when you do something wrong, and you can act to undo harm you cause. So, instead of feeling worse, more ashamed, and thus insisting more vehemently that it wasn't his fault, Martin feels better, knowing that it was his fault (and he is not worthless because of his mistake), and that he has done something to fix it.

Staff can help the children learn that what they do does affect others, both positively and negatively. Through creating strong relationships, they can help kids learn to care about how they affect others. And they can teach the children what we all practice every day: mistakes happen, the world doesn't end, your relationships don't have to end, and you can do something to make it better.

(See Appendix A for a training exercise designed to demonstrate some of the issues in taking responsibility.)

Summary

The Restorative Approach provides a blueprint to translate current scientific knowledge about trauma into a new caring and healing approach to treatment of children, youth and families. Through emphasizing the meaning of behavior and the healing power of relationships, it offers staff a way to make sense of the confusing and dangerous behaviors they experience every day. When all staff receives foundational training on trauma, in which they learn its profound effects, they will see behind the acting out, take it less personally, and ally with the children to help them meet their needs in more positive ways. As subsequent chapters demonstrate, the new treatment approach is supported by a strong team, clinical insight, agency structures, and an emphasis on taking care of each other.

Chapter Three

Stories from Everyday Life in Trauma-Informed Care

The Restorative Approach in Practice

The following true story is an example of a small interaction that captures the Restorative Approach in practice.

Cassidy, age 12, was yelling and swearing in the Main Hall. She had burst out of the dining room and was agitated and upset. A staff member approached her and said: "What's wrong?"

Cassidy yelled that she had not worn socks to school today, and now a boy was saying that she had stinky feet and that she smelled. Now no one was going to want to sit next to her and she would not have any friends ever again.

There were many educational and responsible things the staff member could have said, such as, "That's why you have to wear socks," or "You have to stop swearing or get a fine," or "You are out of bounds now," or "You can't let that boy upset you, and you have to go back to the dining room," or "I'm sure it's not that bad and you will still have friends."

Instead, she said: "I can see how you would feel that way." And then she stopped talking. No "but you have to … you must… you will get…."

Cassidy's voice volume went down ten decibels immediately. The next thing the staff member said was, "I don't think not wearing socks is really such a big deal. Look, I'm not wearing socks right now." After that they began talking in normal tones and discussed returning to the dining hall. Later they were eating together and talking about how Cassidy could react differently to what the boy had said.

Life in a treatment program is punctuated by regular outbursts by dysregulated children. Here's an example from an adolescent girls' unit.

The door from the Girls' Unit slammed open, and Sarita erupted out, screaming, "I am not going to the f***king mall! I can't go to the mall. Every night he wants us to go to the mall. But I have to get my eyebrows done tonight. Someone needs to take me. *Now*! I am not going to the mall!"

It was amazing how long and loud and with how many swears a girl could scream about not going to the mall. This episode was a perfect illustration of a choice point for the treatment philosophy. How should staff understand what is going on here?

One interpretation is that Sarita is a spoiled, demanding, and manipulative girl who just wants what she wants when she wants it (and she wants it NOW). She wants everyone to forget about everything else but her. She freaks out every time anyone says no to her. She thinks she's special.

And that attitude ordinarily leads to a response along the lines of, "Well, she is going to have to learn. People can't just drop what they are doing whenever she wants something. She will just have to wait her turn. Staff will have to teach her to stop yelling and disturbing people. That's not going to get her what she wants. Adults won't do one thing for her as long as she is making this kind of fuss."

Or ... there is another way to see it. Maybe, in fact, Sarita has very rarely gotten what she wants. In her life, few people have ever listened to her or cared about what she wants. She is not the center of anyone's universe. As she has grown up in chaos, and then equally as she has lived in congregate care, the only way she has been able to get anything has been to yell as loud

as she can.

Maybe when she wants something (to get her eyebrows done) and someone else does not seem to be listening to her and is just proceeding with their plans (to go to the mall), the words in her head might go like this:

He is not listening.

If I don't get my eyebrows done I will look ugly and no one will like me.

He does not hear me.

He does not care about me.

No one hears me or cares about me.

I have no one. I have nobody.

I am no one.

I am nobody.

Then Sarita becomes overwhelmed by unbearable emotions of despair and hopelessness, which she expresses (or tries to fend off) by shouting and slamming doors.

Where would that thinking lead staff?

> It does **not** mean that it is okay for Sarita to scream and swear whenever she wants something. Such a reaction would surely not give her a life worth living.
>
> It does **not** mean that staff immediately drop everything and take her to get her eyebrows done in order to quiet her down.

But what it does mean is that staff does not approach Sarita with lectures about being quiet. Instead, they start with "Sarita, what is the matter?"

And then, the staff part of the conversation includes statements like:

You definitely do not want to go to that mall.

You have had it with that mall.

It's very important to you to have your eyebrows done as soon as possible.

And where do you have to go to have that done?

So what you want to do is go to...

And you feel very strongly about this...

Because, in fact, Sarita will gradually stop screaming when she feels she is heard when she is talking.

And that is an experience staff using the Restorative Approach can give her.

Experiencing and Easing Difficult Transitions to the Restorative Approach

Sometimes things start to feel scary in the best of programs when the culture begins to change:

"Help!" the call comes in to the trauma-informed care trainer from a program that has recently received training and is trying to change their approach. "Ever since we moved away from points and levels, the children don't care what they do. They are getting worse and worse, rude, defiant, acting out. Since they don't lose points they have no deterrents to bad behavior. A two-minute apology letter means nothing to them. We need to put back some more consequences."

There are assumptions behind this plea for help: that the main reason that the children ever acted politely was because they would lose points if they didn't; and that the only response staff have to address problem behavior is consequences.

Do treaters really believe these assumptions? What about the relationships? It may be that what happens in some programs is that when the behavior management system changes, staff feel paralyzed. They can no longer use the old method of taking away points or dropping levels, and they are not yet comfortable with implementing the new approach. So they do nothing, and sit by helplessly, which makes the children and the staff feel hopeless and unsafe.

In fact, points, levels, and consequences are a small part of the treatment team's arsenal of tools to impact the children's behaviors. Here are some others:

- Talk about it. Say when you don't like it – and also when you *do* like their behaviors. Describe how the behavior affects you and the other community members. Express hopes that change will happen.
- Work hard and constantly to form caring relationships with the children so they care what staff thinks.
- Validate the feelings behind the behavior.
- Express an understanding that this is the best the child knows at the time, and the hope and confidence they will learn to do better.
- Develop in the child the basic feelings-regulation skills of maintaining an inner connection to others, feeling worthy of life, and feelings management.
- Teach specific feelings-regulation skills to help the child do things differently.

- While staff uses feelings-management skills themselves, label out loud that they are doing so.
- Have group meetings about what kind of place people want here.
- Have group meetings about bad things that happened and how everyone felt and how all can support each other to do better.
- As a team, discuss how the staff understands this behavior. What is their formulation about what is going on here? What problem is this behavior solving for this child? How can they teach her to solve that problem in a better, more effective way?
- With the child, develop a treatment theme: what is the basic thing this child is working on? Examples would be: feeling emotion without acting to make the situation worse; learning to trust; growing up. Then relate all behavior to that theme.
- As a team support each other in the long, difficult process of doing this work.
- Work on helping the child to develop self-worth.
- Address shame.
- Use (possibly as restorative tasks) exercises that help the child understand and manage his behavior, such as mood charts, emotion thermometers, collages of how they are feeling and/or things they can do differently, interviewing others about how they handle emotions, etc.
- In treatment, teams develop restorative ideas for each child that are significant, require thought, and are related to their treatment.
- Don't take the child on trips when they have just hurt staff – and explain why staff doesn't want to – the issues are trust and safety, not punishment.
- Make sure the structure and planning support success by providing a regular, predictable schedule with orderly transitions between carefully planned activities.

- And, TALK ABOUT IT – among staff, between staff and children. Address every problem. Take the children on. Tell them what kind of behaviors staff expect. Tell them how different actions make people feel.

And tell them, and show them, over and over again, all the good things adults see in them and how delighted staff is by everything positive (and even neutral) that happens.

Points and levels are so insignificant when compared with these more powerful tools. Changing to a trauma-focused approach does not have to mean paralysis in the face of destructive behavior. It does mean active, complete, and relationship-based engagement. And then both the staff and the children will be co-running a program that supports growth and change in all.

Despite changes in approach and even with thorough training, some mornings start out with learning about the previous night's problems.

For example, one night in one program it all started with Kathy, who was upset about boyfriend issues. She was irritable and started criticizing Mayla. Several others started shouting and threatening each other. Tenesha became so anxious that she pulled the fire alarm. Mayla threatened that she was going to kill Kathy, and began destroying furniture in the lounge. She could not calm down, was taken to the nearest hospital's emergency room for evaluation, and did not return until the following morning. The Program Director was called in to help the girls calm down.

In situations like this one, staff starts to wonder: are we accomplishing anything here? The program is teaching all these people about this new approach, and still there is a night like this. The program had just been enjoying a period of relative peace and calm with the girls. Why did this blow-up happen? It is part of the Restorative Approach to teach that staff cannot judge their work by whether the children act up; instead the way to evaluate the night is by how they, the staff, act, and whether they use the PACE attitude (Hughes, 1998). Daniel Hughes developed this acronym to describe the desired actions of helpers towards children. He suggests that healing is most effective when adults are playful, accepting, curious and empathetic (PACE). They cannot force the children to change, they can only change their own behavior. If adults maintain the attitude, the children will gradually change. However, at times it is hard to maintain our belief in this attitude. It is hard to believe that our efforts are actually making a difference when staff experience how things can go wrong.

Staff can notice changes from the old approaches in our programs. Staff can articulate the differences they experience during a crisis since they began the Restorative Approach. Staff is warmer and more compassionate with the girls. The emphasis is not on the rules, but on helping the girls calm down. If Katie wants to take a shower, although it is not 'shower time,' letting her do so is an excellent de-escalation technique. The team of therapists and staff works closely and calmly together. The team concentrates on reaching out to the girls and asking what is the matter. That approach allows Robin to switch away from anger at her boyfriend, and at Nicole who has talked to him, and at the staff that won't let her beat both of them up. She begins talking about what might be behind the immediate issue: her father, who said he was going to become re-involved in her life, and has instead disappeared. Now she is crying instead of yelling and threatening. Staff is next to her, sharing and validating her sadness. The next morning, the conversation centers on what is happening in the girls' lives and better ways to help them. Education staff comes to the unit to meet with the girls and gauge their mood, to make plans with them for entering school (where of course the boys are) and becoming students. The girls are calm and able to attend school. Life goes on.

Another example is a situation with Steve, who had not done his homework and was supposed to be in his room completing it. Instead he was sitting in the lounge refusing to move. In the program before the Restorative Approach, staff concentrated on the fact that there was a rule and a resident was not following it. They had to be consistent. The focus was on compliance. The therapist stood nearby, but she was not involved when the goal was to get the resident to do as he had been told. This situation would have rapidly escalated into putting the resident in a restraint. Now, with a new focus on relationships, staff asks Steve what's wrong. They noticed that he had been acting differently all afternoon, had been withdrawn and sad. They called in his therapist. They ignored the fact that he was still in the lounge. Soon Steve began talking about what was troubling him, went for a walk with his therapist, and then easily finished his homework.

These children come to treatment already severely damaged, or they would not be here. They have no ability to manage emotions, and every small setback escalates into despair and panic. A problem with a boyfriend evokes all of their many devastating losses, family disappointments evoke shame and loss and fear. Treaters cannot expect that there will be no crises, no emotionally overwrought nights. Instead, they can change how they act in those times. They can stay emotionally regulated themselves so the children have a chance of regaining emotional regulation. They stay calm and connected by having a plan and through strong team culture among the staff. They can shift their focus away from compliance to rules and toward compassion. They can concentrate on helping children calm down. And then they will experience crises that are shorter, less destructive, less frequent, and that provide opportunities for growth for the children.

And yet, even when everyone does everything they can and does it well, there are times when a program is not able to help a child. Then it is essential that staff talk about their feelings about this sad event.

Elements of Success in Using the Restorative Approach

Despite the difficulty of the work, often treatment is successful. The youth do get better, and do go on to have a life worth living.

Sam was discharged from residential treatment this week to a group home. At his discharge party Sam said, "I never thought I'd see this day. I was sure I would end up in jail."

The thing that helped Sam the most was probably just sticking with him, despite all the staff he assaulted, all the windows he broke, all the furniture he destroyed.

But what helped staff stick with him? It was the emphasis on relationships, the staff that could say from their hearts, "We love Sam. He is such a special guy," despite all the outbursts and difficulty. Staff was able to see the goodness in him because they understand trauma, and know that his agitation was a symptom, his dysregulated emotions were a result of Complex Developmental Trauma, that he was not defiant or bad and that he was doing the best he could. They saw that the center of his distress was relationships, his need for and fear of closeness, his struggles within his connection to his mother and her family.

It helped Sam when staff took seriously that he could not stand to be in his room alone for "Quiet Hour." He was not "being manipulative" or "just looking for attention" – he was actually experiencing flashbacks.

It helped Sam when the program converted their unit to a Dialectical Behavioral Therapy model (Linehan, 1993) and began to teach him specific skills of mindfulness, distress tolerance, emotional regulation, and interpersonal effectiveness. He began actively learning and practicing these skills.

It helped Sam when, as a result of converting to Dialectical Behavior Therapy (DBT), staff learned and began practicing their own distress tolerance skills, so they could get through a crisis, remain calm, stay mindful, and not make it worse.

And as his treaters watch this courageous young man hug the people he has come to trust, cry and say goodbye, and head out to create new connections and a new future, they know that it has all been more than worthwhile.

And sticking with the clients may be the most important thing a program can do.

A staff member in one day-school treatment program shared a letter he had recently received from a client, expressing her gratitude for the program's help and the changes she and her son had made. The letter started, as such letters often do, with the phrase: "Most of all, you didn't give up on me."

Perhaps that is the most important thing treaters do for clients: not to give up on them, sticking with them, staying around, something many of the children and families have not experienced before. These children have been in so many placements, so many families, and so many treatment facilities. In addition to undermining healing relationships, all these moves underscore the basic message that you are such a terrible person that no one is able to stay around you for any length of time.

In order for any of these trauma-focused techniques to work, programs have to keep the child with them. Many times programs have experienced situations in which they had completely given up on a child, and they were sure they could not help him. However, the child welfare system being what it is, the child did not leave. And time passed, and he got better.

The message there is that programs could pay more attention to exactly what makes it possible for them to keep a child. And when they are struggling with a particular child, maybe they could take a page from the Restorative Approach and have a staff meeting specifically focused on enhancing their ability to keep him or her.

What could a program do to increase their stamina with a given difficult client? Some ideas include:

- Increase staff stamina by dividing the responsibility for the child among several staff every night. If the program has a concept of a "primary" staff, then maybe a certain child needs two or three primaries. Maybe the team could plan that anyone who deals with this child for a long period gets a break off the unit.
- If there is a particular horrid task (such as cleaning the room of a child with hygiene issues), do it in teams, not one staff alone.

- Keep a shared notebook of any signs of hope staff see.
- The program must articulate clearly that even if they do not (yet) see any change, the fact that they're not kicking this child out is a victory in itself, and they can congratulate each other for that.
- The program can regularly review what happened to this child, and how they understand his/her symptoms. What problems are those behaviors solving for him? How are they adaptive and helpful to her in the short term, even if they have negative long-term consequences?
- The program can make sure they have a treatment theme (such as: Jeff is learning to trust adults) that everyone on the team including the child and family knows, and that they use this theme to frame all events and interventions.
- The program can plan some ideas for restorative tasks before the child is in crisis, during treatment team meetings. Each task can be an opportunity for the child to practice one small skill that he would need to develop to give up his current symptoms.
- The program staff can make sure to complement each other lavishly whenever anyone is particularly caring, giving or helpful to this child.
- Administration can attend meetings and praise the treatment team for their stamina.
- The staff can discuss if there is anything the program can do to help the child feel safer and more connected.
- The program staff can deliberately do something fun together, to acknowledge the effort they are making, such as a potluck lunch, little presents, and chocolate.
- The most important thing is for staff, therapist, and administrators to acknowledge to each other both how difficult and how valuable what they are doing is. If they can stick with the child, his or her entire life may be different, more rewarding, and more positive.

This is not to say that children should never leave programs, or that children never need a different form of care. That happens, but not as often as staff thinks. More often, staff is frustrated by the pain the child is feeling, and by her ways of making sure they feel the same pain. Treaters think, if only she were gone, the unit would go so well. But if a program does succeed in ejecting a child, another one always steps into the role.

Teams can talk actively about their feelings about the child, how hard working with him is, how much chaos he creates for staff, and how tempted the team is to get rid of him. They can talk about staff feelings of sadness, of inadequacy, anger and frustration. They can remember how he got this way, how the team understands him, and make sure there is a strong team plan.

And then the team can re-engage with the child and hang in there. Then after he gradually starts to get better, and finally achieves that positive discharge, and does fairly well, they will likely get one of those letters, like this one:

> Dear staff,
>
> I just wanted to let you know I am doing well at my new home. I really miss you guys! I want to thank you for not giving up on me.

Chapter Four

Changing the Definitions of Behaviors

Understanding symptoms as adaptations changes how treaters understand behaviors, and hence how they respond to them. The following stories illustrate how redefining the meaning of behaviors leads to more effective treatment.

In this example, a childcare staff member reacts to a teenager in the morning:

Scenario one:

> It's a school day and Dahlia is sluggish and half awake. She scatters cereal all over the counter and leaves the milk out when she goes over to the table to eat. Mary, a staff member says. "Dahlia! Clean up this mess you made! Put away the milk!"
>
> "No" replies Dahlia. "You do it."
>
> "Dahlia, I have given you a directive. Please get over here and put away this milk and clean up this mess!" Mary insists.
>
> "F*** you!" replies Dahlia as she storms out of the kitchen and leaves for school.

> Mary cleans up the mess and puts the milk in the refrigerator.

Mary is fuming. “These girls,” she says to a co-worker. “They are so lazy and they have no respect for me or for their home. They are hopeless. How will they ever be able to live on their own?”

Scenario two:

> It’s a school day and Dahlia is sluggish and half awake. She scatters cereal all over the counter and leaves the milk out when she goes over to the table to eat. Mary looks at the counter and says: “Hey, Dahlia, what a mess. How about I’ll put away the milk – will you get the counter after you are done eating?”
>
> “Okay I guess,” says Dahlia.
>
> Mary puts the milk in the refrigerator.
>
> After she is done with her cereal Dahlia cleans off the counter in a half-hearted way, leaving some cereal. Then she goes off to school.
>
> Mary finishes cleaning up the counter.
>
> “Ahhh, teenagers!” she thinks to herself as she goes on with her tasks.
>
> Notice that in the first scenario Mary issued an order, while in the second she made a request for mutual effort.

Even more important, notice that the meaning Mary attributes to the event determines the quality of her interactions with the child, both in the present moment and in the future. Is Dahlia an obstinate child defying a

Staff Directive, a sign of disrespect and a hopeless future? Is it clear evidence that Dahlia has no caring for Mary or for her home? Does it demonstrate beyond doubt that Dahlia will never manage her own life well? Or is it a sleepy teenager in the morning?

In the next example staff was able to see behavior not as defiance of rules, but as a child's difficulty with trust.

LaTasha came to the group home from a residential treatment facility where she had been for two years. Prior to that placement, she had been hospitalized seven times, was in a shelter for eleven months, had been in nine foster homes, and had suffered early abuse from her biological family. She pushed so hard to get out of the residential program and was so eager to be discharged to the group home that both she and her staff were surprised at how hard the transition was for her. When she first came to the group home, she showed all the signs of feeling unsafe. She tested the staff, insulting and mocking them. She asked questions about the locks and security measures of the home. If ever a staff was uncertain about what to do or if the staff changed a rule ("Yes, I guess you can go outside and hang out for a while before you do your homework.") LaTasha would say they were stupid, didn't know what they were doing and were too young to be staff anyway. A couple of times LaTasha's behavior had become so escalated she had been taken to the local ER for a psychiatric evaluation. When LaTasha first arrived, she completely refused to eat. She said she didn't like the food, it wasn't her type of food, staff didn't know how to cook. The treatment team wondered if she had an eating disorder, but there was no mention of it in her records. Then, she began taking food and smuggling it to her room, which of course was against the house rules and could bring bugs and other complications. She would sometimes eat snacks or make herself a late-night peanut butter sandwich, but she would never sit at the table with the group. Occasionally she tried to eat her sandwich in the living room in front of the TV, another behavior that was against the house rules.

Fortunately LaTasha's group home was using trauma-informed treatment and had an excellent treatment team. Led by the clinician, they looked at LaTasha's behavior and asked "why." What function was LaTasha's behavior serving for her? What was she expressing to the team? What emotion-management capacities did she lack and need help with?"

It was clear that LaTasha was scared and didn't trust them. Being in the house and in a strange community, very different from any she had previously known, made her feel unsafe. She was in danger mode. She didn't know the staff or the other children. Many other people, both professional and not, had let her down and rejected her. She had become used to a residential setting with its inflexible structure, many staff, and locked doors. This new place seemed very weird to her and she was not sure what to make of it. She was not going to connect with these people, act like they were her family, only to be hurt once again.

The treatment team decided that all their efforts should be focused on helping LaTasha feel safe. One key to that would be validation: letting her know that her reaction was completely understandable given her experiences, and in fact, anyone would feel uneasy in a new place. So, instead of insisting that she eat at the table with the group, staff began trying to support whatever arrangement felt comfortable for her, and expressing their hope that she would join them whenever she felt it was right for her.

They let her eat in the living room for a while – and started bringing her a tray of whatever they were eating, so she wouldn't be stuck with peanut butter sandwiches. After a while, she began eating in the kitchen near where the others were, but not at the table. Then she came to the table, but she was wearing headphones and listening to music. Instead of telling her this was not allowed, staff welcomed her and ignored the headphones. Later, she began to wear the headphones around her neck at the table ("I am in control, I can retreat if I need to"). LaTasha now eats regularly with the group, and her overall agitation has also decreased.

This is a perfect example of how staff can implement trauma-informed care in the daily details of life. The first step was for staff to move beyond "rules" and "misbehavior" and "defiance" to the meaning of what this girl was experiencing, and then to take it seriously, really let themselves feel what this move must be like for her. And then the whole team focused on helping her feel safe and welcome. They did not get caught up in worrying about what if she always wants to eat in the living room; what if all the girls start doing it; then no one will be following any rules. Instead they allowed themselves to honor the emotional reality of one particular girl, and had faith that as their needs are filled people can move on.

Here is another example of applying a "symptoms as adaptation" lens to an everyday problem.

Juan constantly lies, according to the staff of his group home. He lies to avoid consequences or to avoid admitting he has done something wrong. He also tells lies about things that are happening in his life, such as that he has a girlfriend in school. He doesn't have a girlfriend. He makes up whole stories that simply are not true. For example, staff gave him some new gloves the other night to replace the pair he lost. Now tonight he is saying that he doesn't have any gloves, no one will ever give him any, and none of the staff care if his hands are freezing off.

It is such a normal human response to argue with the truth of these assertions. Staff *knows* they gave him gloves Tuesday night. He has probably just lost them again or left them in school. Juan really has to learn to be more responsible! The program does not have enough money for an endless supply of gloves. And what is this story about a girl friend?! They know from talking with his teacher that Juan is a loner in school and has few friends. How is he going to manage life if he keeps lying? So it seems important to tell him that staff knows this is not the truth and will not be able to trust him if he keeps lying.

What is happening with Juan during these events?

His hands are cold and he cannot believe he can't find his gloves again. He feels like such an idiot and a loser. No one likes him, no one cares about him, and no one should, because who would want to be around such a jerk? He feels stupid and unloved, and plus his hands hurt. Saying no one has taken care of him enough to give him gloves expresses his emotional truth. Certainly he cannot admit to having lost the gloves again, if he did then everyone will be mad at him, as usual.

What if staff *ignored* the truth/falsehood dimension of the situation and just reacted to the emotional and physical reality? What if Mark, Juan's favorite staff member, said, "Hey Juan, I see you have no gloves, let's find some you can wear." And when Juan said, "No one ever gives me gloves," Mark could say, "You're feeling right now that no one cares enough about you to help you. So let me see what I can do to help you right this minute."

How hard would that be? Mark might feel that if he doesn't confront the lie, Juan will have put one over on him, or will never learn that it is not okay to lie, or will start telling more lies to get what he wants. He might feel that he needs to defend staff against Juan's charge of neglect, point out that staff has been responsive and would never let Juan go without gloves. But Juan will need to lie less when he develops a new view of the universe: that this world is a place where people will help you, where people care what you are feeling, where they do not shame and blame you. Only then would Juan be able to admit that he left his gloves at school.

And what about the girlfriend? Juan is desperately lonely at school and is sure he will never fit in there. He thinks none of the kids like him or ever could – especially not the girls. So when he comes home he creates a new reality, life as he wishes it could be.

What if Mark was to reply: "Wow, it would sure be nice to have a girlfriend at school. What do you like in a girl, anyway? What kind of girl would be the perfect girlfriend for you?" and start a discussion of girlfriends in general. At some point Mark could ask, "If you wanted to make friends with a girl, what would be the first thing to do?" and start teaching social skills.

Note that Mark just sidesteps the true/not true question, and again reaches for the emotional reality. He doesn't believe or challenge Juan's story. He just turns it into a discussion of an important subject to Juan: girls. He avoids shaming Juan further ("Juan, I talked to your teacher, and in fact you do not have a girlfriend.") That would just lead to Juan's needing to lie even more.

What would it take for staff to respond like this much of the time? When we are away from the situation it all sounds like a good idea, yet in the pressure of real life staff find themselves reverting back to arguing about the lie. Time off the floor is needed to think and plan, time to consider what needs the child is meeting, and to choose a more thoughtful and healing response.

In the following situation, the behaviors were more serious, and the staff more frightened by their meaning.

Marcus came into the psychiatric hospital after having been ejected from a previous residential program. He is adopted, and his current adoption is actually his second; he was removed from his first home because he was abused there. He is small for his age and a bit strange looking. In the month he has been at this center he has not made any friends; in fact the other kids seem to pick on him. Several times he has said inappropriate sexual things to female clients and to female staff, which does not increase his popularity. Generally he is the kid who is always doing what staff just told him not to do, then accusing staff of talking to him only when he does something wrong. Staff is finding it hard to engage with Marcus.

However, recently a more upsetting issue has emerged. Tony and Jarell, two of the other boys, and Amber, one of the girls, separately came to staff to complain that Marcus has been showing them some very disturbing pictures that he drew. A search of his room in fact produced many of these pictures, which are very graphic (and skillfully drawn) renditions of men torturing naked women, complete with blood and gore. Amber said to her staff member that she thinks Marcus is going to grow up to be a murderer;

the staff who have seen the pictures tend to be worried about the same thing.

At first when this stash of drawings was discovered, staff gave Marcus a sketch book and said he could draw the pictures in there, but not show them to anyone. However, yesterday his roommate Tim told staff that Marcus had been showing him his latest creation, one of the bloodiest yet. Lisa, Marcus's therapist, finds that the pictures make her very uneasy, and she does not know what to do to help Marcus. In fact, lately she has been avoiding meeting with him. In the staff meeting the most popular suggestion is that Marcus be forbidden any access to paper and writing or drawing materials in an attempt to prevent him from making these drawings.

Is this the best approach?

How does staff understand Marcus' behavior? In what way are these pictures adaptive for him? What positive results is he getting from drawing and sharing them?

What does Marcus need? What approach should his team take?

What should be done to support Lisa and the staff in helping Marcus to heal?

If staff keeps in the front of their minds the idea that symptoms are adaptations, they must consider what doing the drawings and sharing them with his peers is accomplishing for Marcus. They suggest several possible theories, such as giving him power, expressing his pain, giving him one area in which he is in control and can have an effect on others.

The drawings express a part of Marcus, however disturbing they are. If staff just tries to ban them, they are giving Marcus a message that they are turning away from his pain, and that they do not want to see, share, or accept all of who he is and what he has experienced.

Taking drawing supplies away from Marcus will not help at all. For one thing, staff won't win on this one. There are many more pencils and pieces of paper in the world than they can ever confiscate. But more importantly, that response tries to eliminate his behavior and not to understand it.

Treaters need to take seriously the effect the drawings have on the other kids, the staff, and especially the therapist. This reaction is something they have to discuss as a team and make deliberate plans to give themselves the stamina to take this on. For example, the therapist may wish to include a male staff member at first when she talks with Marcus about the drawings.

Then the therapist can explore the pictures with Marcus, and not in a judgmental way. What is happening? What are the characters thinking and feeling? What is likely to happen next? The therapist can express her thoughts: "Really? I think the woman might be scared and angry." But all discussion comes from a centered, calm place: "Tell me more. Explain how it feels. What does it remind you of?"

These discussions are entirely exploratory; they include *no mention of a need to change.*

Meanwhile, staff can talk with the other kids about how sometimes when people have had painful lives they draw painful drawings. Encourage the kids not to react, but just to bring staff into the conversation if Marcus shows them a picture. Of course, Marcus' showing them around would decrease if he got less reaction. Then staff would handle it more matter-of-factly: "You know, Marcus, better to save these for therapy. I'll give this one to your therapist and you can talk it over with her."

Another area of treatment could be to offer Marcus other opportunities to have power and control, using his drawing. Could he draw some posters for an upcoming agency event (subject to review, of course). Can he draw a picture for the unit illustrating some positive message, and can staff get it framed and hang it up?

Marcus has been hurt repeatedly over his lifetime. He has found a way to both express his pain and get strong reactions from others. His behavior will not change quickly. Staff must understand that the way that they feel in looking at these pictures is the way that he often feels in his life. And staff must support each other in doing the long hard work it will take for Marcus to develop a new, kinder view of life's possibilities.

Constant vigilance is needed to maintain a perspective that symptoms are adaptive, as the behaviors themselves are so persistent, annoying, and often scary.

The language staff use when they speak about a child can create or discourage hope, which can lead to more or less involvement with and effort towards the child.

In a treatment team meeting, the staff was talking about Jesse. They had gone over his childhood history, with his addicted mother and absent father. They had discussed the fact that his mother describes him as having problems since birth. They had reviewed his many attempts at treatment, his failed foster placement, and the other disruptions that had led him to their program's doors. Jesse is 13 years old and very intelligent. He is overweight, poor at sports, and has no friends. And he comes across as mean: he constantly says awful things to others, and because he is smart, often he finds the most upsetting thing to say to each person. He has trouble with boundaries, often touching others in ways they don't like, although not in overtly sexual ways. The staff has tried. They have explained to Jessie how bad he makes others feel. The therapist tries to draw out how bad Jesse has felt at times and link that to how he makes others feel. There has been no change. The staff is feeling hopeless.

Then the unit supervisor speaks: "There is nothing you can do about Jesse. We have tried everything. Jesse just **likes** making other people feels bad. He admits it. It makes him happy to hurt others."

It would be wonderful if when confronted with a child like Jesse, staff would automatically attribute his behavior to pain and hurt he is feeling. The amount treaters feel that this child *is* a pain is the amount that this child is *in* pain. Why does Jesse like hurting others? What has happened to him?

It would be great if staff saw Jesse as a child who has no sense of power, no sense of self-worth. The only way he can engage others is through making them feel bad – and he is very good at that. He sees others as likely to hate, hurt, and abandon him. Why not attack them first? He feels scared, shame-filled and hopeless inside, and can only escape from these feelings by making others (including the staff) feel as bad as he does.

Jesse will be able to decrease his meanness when he feels better. The task is not to explain to him how bad his actions are. The task, and it is a very difficult one, is to help him to see how good his actions can be: to help him see his strengths, use his powers for good, establish control in more positive ways, and connect with others through constructive leadership. If Jesse can experience (again and again) the many pleasures the world has to offer, he can find other things that can more reliably make him happy.

In other words, adults have to show Jesse that he can like other things besides hurting people: that friendship is possible, control can become leadership, intelligence can be admired and draw praise from the group.

How can programs possibly make this kind of thinking more routine in their settings? How can they begin to realize that change comes from helping a child to feel better, rather than making him feel worse?

At times treaters are called upon to look at a child's entire self-presentation rather than one or two behaviors, and try to figure out how it is adaptive for her. As this example illustrates, this kind of self-presentation can include some very scary behaviors.

When the child's behaviors are the most demanding, is when the treatment team must try hardest to understand their adaptive function and let that understanding guide their interventions.

Staff doesn't know what to do for Katrina! She keeps cutting herself, putting cords around her neck to hang herself, and recently she has begun using an eraser to create serious burns in her skin. She has given up running away and having sex with strangers, but she keeps up her unremitting self-harm. Staff can work with her for hours, and she seems better, but an hour after they leave, she cuts herself and they feel the whole effort was useless.

They are getting exhausted and feel depleted.

Discussions with Katrina, her mother, and her treatment team make clear how three facets of the effects of trauma interact to create dilemmas both for the child and the treatment team.

Katrina has a history, as so many of the children in treatment do, of repeated moves, changes of caretakers, and of serious abuse in each new home. Following her adoption at age seven, she had many treatment episodes: hospitalizations, emergency shelters, in-home interventions, and finally residential treatment.

This history had left Katrina with the following three characteristics (as well as others):

> 1. A deep sense of *shame* and *self-hatred*, resulting from blaming herself for all the abuse, the moves, the symptoms and failures she had experienced. Her self-hatred combines with a lack of a sense of self: who was she really? She has a tendency to take on the personality of whomever she is with. This lack of self and deep self-revulsion results in her conviction that no one could possibly just *like* her. It also produces the conviction that she does not deserve to receive anything good, or to have any fun, which results in self-sabotaging whenever something good does happen.
>
> 2. A *lack of inner connection to others*: for Katrina, when a person is not physically present it is as though they never existed. She cannot keep a representation of them in her mind to encourage her and help her, because she has not had the relationship stability in her life that would be necessary to develop that ability. So when a staff member moves away from helping her to complete tasks and talk with other children, it is as though that person disappears completely.

3. *No self-soothing skills*: Katrina has never previously been taught how to manage life's ups and downs. Her life-models had used drugs and violence to manage emotions. She has not been taught to recognize or name her own emotions, or what to do when she feels them. Through Dialectical Behavioral Therapy (Linehan, 1993) Katrina is learning some of those skills, and she can name and describe them when she is calm. However, due to her over-active nervous system, when something goes wrong she becomes so overwhelmed with emotions that her skills are no longer accessible to her.

Like everyone, Katrina needs connection, attention and support. However, both in her homes and in the many treatment programs she's been through, it has been hard to engage adults by doing well. Early on Katrina learned that the easiest way to draw adult connection was through her problems. Although her caretakers were usually absorbed in their own life pain, when Katrina was suicidal they had to pay attention to her. It is almost as thought she became addicted to having problems.

And this pattern becomes harder and harder to change.

Katrina starts with a conviction that no one would want to be with her just for herself. Then, something happens, and Katrina becomes upset. Her need for help is intense and unbearable. Life feels hopeless and frightening, and she blames herself. So she does something to hurt or erase herself, which has the added benefit of bringing in the resources she needs.

In an adult's calming presence, Katrina can sometimes gradually calm down. And when she does, what happens? The adult leaves. For Katrina, they disappear completely, never to return. And Katrina does not know how to re-engage them in a positive way. She does not even have any idea this is possible.

So, she tumbles into another problem.

The intervention strategy that will help to change this pattern is to give

Katrina a lot of attention whenever she is doing well, and to be less emotional, less intense and less involved when she is doing self-destructive things. But this approach turns out to be quite difficult. One reason is that Katrina is rarely doing well. Whenever she does start having fun or succeeding, she stops herself, because this is not her and she doesn't deserve happiness. However, staff can still catch the moments in which she is more relaxed or her behavior is more normal and engage with her then.

This counter-intuitive, vigilant intervention takes incredible stamina, planning and thoughtfulness from the staff, and demands much reinforcement and praise from those supporting the staff. Because if a child this needy is *not* calling your name, is doing well and enjoying life, who would want to approach her? Better to stay back and enjoy the momentary respite. And yet, this understandable reaction perpetuates the pattern that she only gets attention and caring by having problems. Staff will have to work hard for quite a while before this pattern changes, but what a gift they will give Katrina! The gift is the repeated experience (more powerful than any words) that she is a normal girl who can be competent and can receive attention, caring, and connection through achievement and everyday life activities. This new pattern is what she needs in order to move toward a life worth living.

Only a certainty that each child is doing destructive things for a reason will penetrate the shame the children in treatment feel, and create enough safety to help them share their deepest fears.

Understanding that Jonathan's defiance arose from fear helped his program's staff respond to him with compassion, which led to him eventually feeling safe enough to engage.

Jonathan is 14, small for his age, and has a history of severe trauma. He came into treatment snarling. He was vicious to staff and to other children, talked a lot about how tough he was, about his gang friends, and he made many threats to stab and otherwise harm everyone. He would not say hello or smile, much less talk about himself. He thought this whole treatment thing was so stupid. Yet, there were moments. Even the second day he was there he said: "You aren't helping me!" This was staff's first glimpse that he felt the need for help.

In the old treatment system Jonathan would never have emerged from consequences and punishments. Staff would have confronted his every behavior head-on. Instead, people kept their focus on the small, hurt, scared, confused boy who was desperately protecting himself with a wall made of hostile actions. Staff smiled, approached him, and said, "Life doesn't have to be this hard, Jon." He even said: "Why aren't you guys punishing me more?" That would have fit with his self-concept. Staff kept a log of "Hopeful Moments with Jonathan" to help them keep up their stamina.

Gradually Jon started to relax a little, connect a little. He began to say hi, and ask for things he wanted. One time when he was mean to a younger peer, he and that boy made brownies together for the unit, and Jon taught the boy how to play a computer game. He began to participate in family therapy, and shared with his therapist how angry he feels about how badly he was beaten. He even started to look at his relationship with the mother who is only intermittently in his life.

Jon's treatment was not easy. It included several short hospitalizations when he began to cry a lot, stayed in bed, and would not go to school. But these episodes were all part of the process, and he returned to continue his treatment. He did not change to earn privileges or to avoid punishments. He changed because compassionate people made him feel safe enough that he could finally share how scared he was, and finally begin to rely on help from caring adults.

At times teams fall into using simplified explanations like "She is doing it for attention." This tendency can blind the staff to a deeper understanding of the function of the symptom, and thus cause them to misapprehend which skills the youth needs to learn.

Alexandra, 14, has experienced trauma and multiple separations from her mother. She has a history of self-injury and suicidality. She has been in her current home for six months, and her foster mother has noticed that in the last month she's been opening up to them in a new way. Last week, it was announced that one of the other children who had been struggling in the home was going to be leaving to go to a group home because he needed more structure and support. This morning Alexandra's foster mother observed that she was wearing long sleeves even though it was 90 degrees out. When her mother asked why, she told her to "f*** off." She eventually revealed that she had been scratching herself bloody with a paperclip.

How might Alexandra's self-injury be adaptive for her? What problem(s) might it solve, how might it help in the moment, even though it leads to negative consequences in the longer term?

Practitioners often respond, "She is doing it for attention." So why does Alexandra need attention? She may be scared of opening up to the foster mom and then possibly losing her as the other child is going to. Why doesn't she ask directly for what she needs, or express her fear directly? Perhaps she doesn't know how, or she can't be that vulnerable, especially now when the relationship feels tenuous.

One staff member stated: "She just wants us to feel sorry for her."

The phrase "feel sorry for" (along with the dismissive "just") connotes an illegitimate need, something that she shouldn't want or need. It implies that she is trying to get some kind of unwarranted or excessive response.

Also, this phrase implies that adults should *resist* feeling sorry for her, and by extension resist coddling her, fussing over her, or being sympathetic. Yet some cuddling and caring may be exactly what Alexandra needs.

Of course, there is every reason to feel sorry for Alexandra, or rather to feel sorry about what has happened to her. She has had a very difficult life, and terrible things have occurred that were not her fault. Her basic needs have not been met. She has not been safe. These experiences have changed the biology of her brain. Her life has not included much relaxation and fun. She has not been taught that she is worthwhile, special, and that people love her. She has not been shown the feelings-management skills she needs for life.

Yet when adults say, "She just wants us to feel sorry for her," they are forgetting that Alexandra is doing the best she can, that her fears and needs are legitimate to her, and that she is using the only means she has to meet them. She will be able to change only when she feels safety within a committed relationship, and when she gradually learns new skills.

Although using the phrase "feeling sorry for her" seems like a small thing, it is important to stop and challenge that kind of adult thinking. This phrase can lead to an entire attitude that will infect treaters' responses to the child and interfere with her healing.

Another similar phrase is "playing the victim."

Overheard on a treatment unit: "Well, you know Jeff. He just likes to play the victim."

What is wrong with staff talking this way? How do we understand Jeff's behavior?

What can we do about it?

What is wrong with talking this way is the way it frames the behavior and blames the child – the statement that Jeff *likes* to play the victim, as though it is a deliberate choice he makes every day among the many delightful possibilities open to him. Although minor in itself, this language leads to an annoyance with the boy, a frustration that he doesn't see how much better his life would be if he would just stop this "preferred" behavior.

The language used shapes how we understand this behavior. When asked to describe Jeff further, the staff member said that he constantly uses his past abuse as an excuse for not trying or for failing. He also picks on other kids ("instigates," to use a favorite word in residential milieu) and then blames them for whatever fight begins. So why would a youth do that? It is most likely because he sees absolutely no possibility of success through competence. In other words, he has no confidence at all that he could succeed on the basis of his talents and natural skills. He has had no experience of being loved or appreciated for who he is. All the goodies of life and of relationships have come to him in the context of his problems, of reparations for his experiences of abuse, of sympathy for being picked on. That is the only way he knows to engage others.

So, what can treaters do about changing Jeff's behavior? The road to change is through helping Jeff experience other types of competence and success. And this task will be difficult, as he will be afraid to try things and will quickly revert to his old standby methods that have worked so well. But with patience staff can support him into positive experiences, achievements, maybe even triumphs. These experiences must include positive interactions with peers, fun, play, and everyday social back and forth. He doesn't know how these things work, so staff must teach and model the skills he'll need. It will take many repetitions for Jeff to believe that people will respond to him for other reasons than his problems.

When Jeff experiences the possibility of competence and fun, staff will notice that he "likes" to play the victim much less.

One element of difficulty in understanding that the children are doing the best they can is that their functioning is often varied from day to day. On Tuesday, a child handles a difficult situation with no acting out. However, on Friday a small disappointment results in a complete meltdown.

A frequent staff comment is, "She was able to handle this yesterday without acting out, so I know she can do it. So why is she so upset today? She must be doing it for attention." The implication behind such comments is that if a child can function without her symptoms on one day, she should be able to do so on all days. Therefore, her symptom today must be somehow contrived, phony, or unnecessary. Staff can become exasperated with children who are acting out when they have seen them do much better at other times.

What is going on when a child's functioning is uneven, when one day the tiniest little setback seems to completely destroy him, yet on another day he can get bad news from his family and react calmly and with understanding? As treaters consider what may be happening, it helps to look at adult experiences first.

To return to the previous analogy, when adults are dieting, some days it seems so easy and so obvious. The dieter just makes good choices. Why would anyone ever do anything else? On other days, however, every minute and every food decision seem like agony. Bread and butter feel essential to survival. A person can't even remember why he ever thought of dieting. Sometimes adults have some ideas why one day is harder: they are tired, or they are in a situation with a lot of special-occasion food. But sometimes it is inexplicable. People just wake up in an easier place, or a place of struggle. It is always this way with change, and with all improvements people try to make, such as quitting smoking, doing exercise, changing a behavior towards a person, or learning a new athletic skill.

So for the children, some days are just harder than others.

Staff can learn with them what may contribute to days of greater strength and resiliency. These contributions can include good self-care skills, such as getting enough sleep, eating right, and getting exercise. It can include changing the environment, such as spending time with positive people, finding interesting things to do, being in a safe and nurturing space. It can include setting up supports: friends, letters, pictures, sensory distractions, music, or art. Preparation for variability can also include predicting times of potential stress (such as phone calls from family, or special events at school that might involve social stress) and planning to have support and safe options available if distress occurs.

In the same way, dieting adults would do well to employ good-self care, not have the most tempting foods in their kitchens, seek out interesting activities to distract from food, cultivate supports such as other dieters, and plan for how to manage eating events.

And, adults have to understand that for themselves and for children, sometimes all this preparation just doesn't work, and there are inexplicable bad days. Each person must do what they can to limit the damage, get back on track as soon as possible, and realize that these bad days don't negate any progress they have made (although it feels like they do). The bad days are real, the difficulty is not "for attention." Change is not a linear process. Everyone needs relationships, compassion, understanding, and connection to just keep going.

The phrase "she has to learn to take responsibility for her behavior" can also block a more complex understanding of the role of shame and hopelessness in determining the youth's actions (as discussed in Chapter Two).

Martha, a therapist, asked: "I know we are not supposed to blame the kids for their behaviors. However, I am a firm believer in the kids needing to take responsibility for what they do. So what do you do when a kid just will not take responsibility for what she did and keeps blaming others?"

Martha explained that 15-year-old Malina was on a plan that she had to earn her weekend pass with her mother by maintaining good behavior in school. Last week, Malina had a major outburst in school, tipping over tables and completely disrupting the classroom. So, she lost her pass. When Martha attempted to talk with her about this incident, Malina would not admit that it was her own behavior that caused the pass to be withdrawn. She blamed her therapist, her teachers, everyone else.

What's wrong with this (very common) picture?

First, nowhere in this approach is it stated that, "treaters should not blame the kids for their behaviors." Practitioners believe and practice the idea that blame is not a useful concept here. Treaters can help the children understand their behaviors, and teach them the skills they need to act in new, more helpful ways.

Second, children do not have to "earn" their home passes. If the home situation and the child are safe, they go. The ties between the child and her family are essential for both recovery and the child's future. Staff will do everything possible to enhance them, and nothing to interfere. If the child is actually unsafe (such as suicidal) the family will be welcome at the agency and, when possible, transportation provided for them. Home passes are not part of a reward system.

The third point is that Malina was on this plan, and she blew it. What is her therapist asking of her when she asks her to "take responsibility for her behavior?" She is asking Malina to admit that she did the one thing she did not want to do, and in the process disappointed herself and her family once again. She is, in Malina's mind, asking her to admit she is a no-good, worthless person who will never change. How can Malina possibly do such a thing?

Finally, we must ask, "Why does the therapist think that 'taking responsibility' is so necessary?" It may be because she feels a person needs to admit something before they can change it, and as long as the client is blaming others they will not try to change themselves. There is some truth to this concept. Yet, there are many gentle, face-saving, non-shaming ways to discuss an incident and the factors that contributed to it.

Most importantly, we need to think about what will help Malina to stop turning tables over when she gets upset. It is not enough to provide mere increases in motivation. The "earn your home pass" plan is designed to make Malina *want* to behave better, and it did, she *wanted* to earn the pass. But the problem is, she does not know how. She is not able to be different yet; she has not been taught the skills she needs to deal with her emotions in a more socially acceptable way.

So what can the program do? Treaters can look carefully at the incident in school with Malina in any way she can participate: not in a blaming way – let's discuss this and get you to admit you were wrong – instead, to understand what happened. What upset Malina? Where did the incident start? What did she first feel? What were the warning signs that she was getting upset? What alternatives did she have then? What help could staff have given her at that point? This discussion is a search for better understanding, looking for patterns. It is a path to interventions that both staff and Malina can use next time to avert a meltdown. Was Malina frustrated by work she didn't understand? Did another girl make fun of her? Was she agitated because she hadn't heard from her mother in several days? These possibilities are not excuses for her behavior. They help staff and Malina understand the skills she needs to handle such events in the future without making things worse. What can the teacher do to make it easier for Malina to ask when she needs help? What skills and sense of self-worth does Malina need to withstand peer teasing, and how can staff help her build them? How can her therapist teach Malina techniques to get through anxious situations? These are things she has never learned in her disrupted upbringing, and staff is here to discover what skills are missing and to teach them to her.

This thinking will actually bring the team forward in their treatment. Making Malina earn her home pass undermines the only fragile support she has and increases her anxiety. Forcing Malina to admit that what she did was wrong will leave her feeling more shamed, more stupid, and in fact *more* likely to do the same thing again. Working with her to determine how she came to act this way, and to teach her other alternatives, will (after many repetitions) create real and lasting change.

Each of these examples illustrates the power of how treaters define behavior. When it is truly, deeply understood that both staff and clients are doing the best they can to meet their needs, each problem seems more a lack of skill than an act of defiance – and lack of skill can be improved with compassionate, gentle teaching.

Chapter Five

Dilemmas Encountered in Trauma-Informed Care

Even for programs employing the best staff with the best training and the best intentions, trauma-informed care is not easy. The clients have experienced multiple traumas and attachment disruptions in their young lives. They present with complicated problems. The whole endeavor of treating a group of disturbed children together, with staff of mixed cultures, backgrounds, experiences, professional training, and beliefs, is also very complicated. The following examples illustrate a few of the dilemmas that arise.

The children will act better when they feel better, when they feel safer, more connected, and more relaxed. Yet, although most treaters agree with this statement when it is made, it is difficult for treatment programs to emphasize making the clients *feel* better.

Adults learn through their own upbringing that punishments are the best way to change behavior. Yet any examination of human behavior will reveal that in general, people *act* better when they *feel* better. When a person feels safe, loved, effective, powerful and competent he or she is more likely to be kind to others. People who feel hopeless, scared, vulnerable and hurt are more likely to terrorize or hurt others. It would be a radical change if programs actually operated from this premise.

If treaters deeply believed and put this concept into practice, then their mission would become to help the children feel better. Of course, treaters do that already in many ways, but what if they deliberately made helping the children to feel better their top priority?

It would be essential to define "feeling better" in a complex and multifaceted way. Each area has many parts and they overlap. It would include:

Feeling better physically:

- Addressing any health problems
- Establishing good nutrition
- Helping with sleep
- Engaging the kids in exercise, helping them overcome their fears and shame around moving their bodies
- Providing nice, comfortable clothes
- Addressing sensory distress

Feeling safer:

- Eliminating bullying
- Addressing signs of danger
- Being caring, welcoming, sensitive to their needs

Feeling calmer:

- Teaching self-soothing skills
- Teaching yoga, meditation, neurofeedback
- Help with life problems

Feeling less shame:

- Exploring areas of self-blame
- Forming relationships
- Experiencing competency
- Feeling more competent
- Building on strengths

- Teaching new skills
- Encouraging self expression
- Providing opportunities to help others
- Providing praise and recognition of achievement

Feeling more effective:

- Providing many opportunities to control ones own life
- Teaching and practicing conflict resolution skills
- Providing opportunities to make a difference
- Developing leadership

Feeling more connected:

- Developing strong relationships with adults
- Providing assistance to help them maintain relationships with family and friends outside the agency
- Providing assistance to help maintain connections with communities such as religious organizations, their own school, sports teams, etc.
- Encouraging and facilitating appropriate relationships between the youth
- Encouraging exploration of their own culture and history

Obviously these are the things good programs do anyway, but does this perspective help staff understand or organize the work in a new way? When a child acted out, staff could wonder in what way that child is feeling bad, and how can they help him/her feel better. The treater's response will focus on helping them feel better, not on explaining what was wrong with what they did.

The question of what should be "earned" in a program is connected to helping the children feel better. One perspective asks, "If children are given privileges (trips, parties, special activities) just because they are alive, what will be their incentive to act better?" The Restorative Approach suggests they will act better because they are having these happy activities with caring adults.

In creating traditional behavior-management systems, treaters operated from the premise that earning rewards and privileges would be the principal motivator for the children in treatment to change. They expected the children to change their behaviors so that they could earn more points and go up in the levels of access to "privileges." In order to interest the children under their care in participating in this system, the program had to have as many aspects of daily living as possible to be contingent on good behavior. Staff was already limited in what parts of life they could make the children earn; they were not allowed to use food, for example. So, program planners looked through the day and considered what could be part of the level system. They even asked the children. And each system ended up with lots of things that the children could not have unless they were on a certain level. These earned privileges ranged from extra TV and Nintendo time, to later bedtimes, to posters on their bedroom walls, to trips and special events, to lining up first in lines, to contact and visits with their families. The theory was that the more important the privilege was to the child, the harder he or she would try to control their behaviors and earn the higher level.

However, this formulation ignores many aspects of what is known about trauma, how it affects people and how they heal. Points-and-levels approaches assume that the main problem for these children is *motivation*. Rewards and punishments increase motivation to do well. But these children are already motivated to do better, they just do not have the skills. When you do not have skills, increasing rewards and punishments actually makes behavior worse, as children feel pressure and resentment at being rewarded and punished for something they cannot control. Imagine if some part of an adult's paycheck was based on his flying from office to office (without mechanical help). He might make a few tries, but quickly he would give up and be angry and resentful. Another factor ignored by level systems is the role of shame. When a person has experienced significant trauma, he/she often becomes shame-based: they feel that they are no good, different and worse than others, and totally unlovable. Being on a low level reinforces this familiar shame, especially when the levels are posted on a public board in the program. Since success seems so impossible, the client thinks, why even try.

What if treaters actually believe that children act better when they feel better? If children are safe, happy, enjoying life, feel cared about, and are surrounded by trustworthy relationships, they will in time be able to be kinder, calmer and more trustworthy themselves. This assumption would lead programs to give the children everything they could as soon as they were admitted. Their rooms would be warm and welcoming and personalized. There would be many fun activities and warm relationships. They would experience support so they can experience success. The goal would be to make the units places where the child learns that life can be good, safe, warm, and happy.

More specifically: children's contact with their families *never* has to be earned in programs using trauma-informed care. The greatest predictor of success after residential treatment is how often the child connects with his family during treatment. There are already so many barriers, both practical and psychological, between the child and her family. The provider's job is to facilitate as much safe contact as possible. Trauma-informed treatment programs do not have visiting hours because the families are welcome at any time. Staff tries to provide whatever practical help they can in areas such as transportation and childcare. And they make sure the family feels welcomed and not shamed when they visit. If the child or family is unsafe, programs can provide visits at the facilities, supervised if necessary. But such a visit is a right, not an earned privilege.

Also, treaters must keep in mind that **children *need* fun, leisure activities and play** for many reasons. It is through play that children learn and grow, experience success, develop friendships, and experience joy. Many activities such as music, electronic games, dance, art, and crafts can also be ways to self-soothe, to get through difficult periods without making things worse, and to develop the lower brain. How are children going to learn to use coping skills if staff tell them that they can't have coping activities until they show through their behaviors that they have already mastered coping?

The only time it makes sense to have a privilege be earned is when a child needs skills to be able to use that privilege safely. For example, a child who is repeatedly running away should not be given the privilege of going on walks alone. More autonomy and less supervision are a result of responsible behavior. As children achieve their treatment goals, and as they show increasing ability to let adults know when something goes wrong or is bothering them, they can be supervised at increased distances. If a program wants a formal system for this kind of earning, it is best handled through a long-term phase system linked to treatment goals. Advancement through the phases is a team and child decision reached after discussion, and not based on point totals. Children do not go down (lower in status) in these phases.

It is certainly a good idea to suspend a given activity in response to a child's behavior. For example, perhaps a child has just hit a staff member then wants to go to the mall. The staff member replies: "Of course we are not taking you to the mall today. I do not trust that you will be responsive and not have a meltdown like just happened. However, let's work on your restorative tasks, let's figure out together what just happened, and I'm sure we will go to the mall together in the future." How long this suspension lasts is not based on a pre-set time period, it is determined by the child completing his restorative tasks and his attitude.

People worry that without many things to be earned the child will have no incentive to get through the day. Why would he finish his dinner, do his chores, go to bed if there are no points to be earned by doing so? Well, he will finish his dinner because it tastes good and he is hungry, or, it is fine that he does not finish his dinner. She will do her chores and go to bed because she is asked to and is part of the community, because she gets help and encouragement from those around her.

Many treaters report that when they were young, romantic relationships were a source of both joy and learning. But do treatment programs dare to acknowledge romantic ties between their clients?

How does staff in trauma-informed treatment programs respond to romantic relationships between the youth in a treatment program? Do they forbid them, in the interest of preventing distractions from treatment? Do they set limits, and if so, what are they: no sex? No holding hands? Does staff respond differently to a homosexual couple that lives on the same unit than they do to a heterosexual one living in separate housing? Does staff facilitate normative teenage activities such as dates to the movies?

Anyone who treats adolescents has had to struggle with these and many more questions. And the relationships are often fraught with drama, anger, broken hearts, agitation, and obsession. In addition, parents, social workers, and licensing and accreditation boards and agencies are watching and have strong and differing ideas about what a program should do.

Sally and Mark are in love. Or at least they were this morning, as they have been for the last couple of weeks. As they return from school this afternoon, they are angry and agitated. Rosita just told Sally that she saw Mark talking with Leticia in school. Three other girls have told her that Mark said he thinks Leticia is cute. But Kendra said that Mark told her that he only cares about Sally. The girls will not get ready for their planned softball game because they are gathered in clumps discussing this. Even worse, Sally and Leticia were good friends. Now Leticia is in her room with the door closed, and Sally and several of her other new friends are considering ways to kill her.

Meanwhile on the Boys' Unit, Mark is inconsolable. He is in bed with the covers over his head. He refuses to do his homework or attend an activity. He knows that Sally is going to break up with him and he cannot live without her. He doesn't even *like* Leticia! He sticks his head out and begs his roommate Devon to call the Girls' Unit and convince Sally that this is all a big mistake. When staff says that it is not phone time, Devon becomes belligerent and insists that this is an emergency.

What's a staff to do? All this relationship stuff is getting in the way of treatment. It is paralyzing the entire program. It is so over-dramatic and messy.

However, all the drama and mess *is* the treatment. First of all, of course, every part of this episode is normal teenage behavior. Programs cannot keep youth in treatment programs for several of their teenage years and not allow them to have teenage relationships. So much is learned in these relationships, so much practiced. If staff forbids them (as if they could, but then the relationships just go underground), the youth who have been in treatment will be behind their outside-community peers and incapacitated in one more way. Isn't it better to let them experiment in the relative safety of treatment programs?

Trauma-informed care asks, "What is going on here? What needs are being met? What can be learned?"

Can we assist Sally and Mark in direct communication? Instead of relying on the highly unreliable assistance of all their messengers, can they take the risk to talk to each other about whether Mark wants to break up with Sally and go out with Leticia?

What about the other teens? All of them are feeling important and excited by their roles in the drama. That's okay. The youth don't really need to go outside to play softball. Maybe staff can pull the girls together and have a group about relationships: a respectful and real group. How do you know if you can trust someone? How do girls keep on being friends when boys enter the picture? How do you decide whom to believe? What are you looking for in a boyfriend? And so on. These topics are central to all teenagers and they are great to discuss in groups, where many important issues come up. For example, in one group a therapist talked with girls about who they can trust and was saddened by how certain they were that there was no one, especially no boy that could ever be trusted. In another group, one girl had called another a slut. So the group leader wrote on a white board all the characteristics they considered slutty, and they had a great discussion of whether they wanted to be slutty and in what ways they were or were not presenting themselves that way. The trick is for the adults to be real, hold to their own values, but remain curious and respectful about the kids' thoughts and values.

Maybe one of the male staff could go in and talk to Mark about women: "you can't live with them, you can't live without them." He could talk man-to-man about how to show a woman she can trust you, or about whatever topics emerge. Neither the boys nor the girls have known very many good men, and they desperately need to know that it is possible to be strong and kind at the same time. Another staff member might talk to Devon about what a good friend he is and how he can best support Mark.

Programs have to have limits. One is: no sex with anyone in the program. But if staff can facilitate normal teenage activities, it will be so much more helpful to the clients than pretending those needs don't exist. For example: could staff take Sally and Mark to the movies (after they recover from this setback) and sit one or two rows behind them? We also have to make sure we are equally respectful to homosexual couples, despite the added complexity of sharing their living quarters.

Programs cannot forbid romantic relationships. They do not need to see them as a distraction from the real work. There is nothing more real or important to teenagers than their romantic relationships. And treaters have seen youth grow and change because of love, start to have more confidence because someone cares about them, learn how to share themselves more directly and experience the joys of being understood. Staff has also seen heartbreak, despair and regression. But adults see all these in their adult friends as well. This messy connection is what life is all about, and treaters can use every piece of the emotional upheaval as an opportunity for growth.

There are often heated debates in treatment programs about whether or not a child was "in control" when he did a certain action. Is this an important distinction to make?

Luke and Jason ran away last night. But they didn't go far: they broke into the school and destroyed the kitchen. They broke several appliances, wrote mean things on the walls, and dirtied the place.

As staff discussed this incident one question that came up was whether the boys were in control of their actions.

This issue of control (which connotes conscious choice of destructive behavior) often seems to be a key question for staff. It has many ramifications as to how they feel an incident should be handled. Although people do not usually articulate their assumptions, they seem to include these two ideas: the more a child is considered "in control" by staff, the more the staff feel they should respond with punishment; and the more the child is considered "not in control," by staff, the more the staff can be understanding and respond in a more "helping" or "treatment" way.

Treaters' sense of how "in control" the children are is typically based on factors like whether the children generally are psychotic, whether they appear emotionally dysregulated, whether the act is an impulse or required planning, etc.

This "in control/not in control" concept is a false dichotomy.

First of all, adults can all identify acts which require planning, but in which the person is not in control, such as compulsive sexual or other addictive behavior.

There is also a moral component here. The "in control" side includes elements of being deliberate, doing this on purpose to hurt others, and slides rapidly into labeling the child a bad child.

But most importantly, saying a child is "in control" does not answer any questions or even change the questions.

Let's postulate that those two boys had total control of their actions, planned this event for weeks, and were not apparently dysregulated at any time.

The question still remains: why?

With all that control, why did they choose this particular action? How was it adaptive to them? What needs was it meeting? What message was it expressing? What kept them from meeting those needs or expressing that message in a more positive way?

Treaters can still assume that the boys' attachment disruptions, lack of consistent positive parenting and early trauma is relevant to the needs they are meeting with their action and to their inability to meet those needs in other ways.

And the response does not change. What would make a child be less likely to consider trashing a kitchen? After all, most children don't. Why not? This behavior would be less likely if the child:

- Felt loved
- Cared about some people and did not want to disappoint them
- Knew that others expected the best from him
- Expected that adults would most often meet her needs
- Felt hopeful
- Cared about the people who would suffer from his actions
- Even knew that people would suffer
- Had a sense of a future, of goals and a trajectory towards them that seemed possible
- Had some skills to manage sad, disappointed, scared and hopeless feelings
- Felt that she was a good person who doesn't do things like this
- Had a sense of belonging to a community and being responsible to that community

How can a program increase these things? Mostly, such increases in connection happen in day-to-day life, before and after the behavior, through all their treatment strategies that honor and build relationships, help children internalize relationships, increase self worth, and teach feelings-regulation skills.

But in response to the behavior, will punishment increase or decrease these feelings and life assumptions?

Restorative tasks, making amends, working with people to fix the damage, and looking at what was going on will increase the above protective attitudes.

And the question of whether or not the boys were in control will fade into insignificance.

Another false dichotomy is that staff must choose between relationship and discipline. There is an implication that relationships form because people ignore harmful behaviors, and that discussing problems would destroy the relationship. This belief is no more true in treatment settings than it is in the rest of the world.

Relationships are central to the Restorative Approach. Staff often wonders if imposing discipline will harm these relationships. For example, a therapist asked: "I am often called onto the floor to intervene with a child who is acting up. I take on the role of the childcare workers. I end up giving him consequences. When that happens how can I preserve my relationship with him, and not seem to him like just one more person trying to manage his behavior?"

There are dangerous assumptions beneath that question, and these assumptions often underlie thinking and actions in treatment programs.

This question assumes that the therapist has a special healing relationship with the child, which would be threatened by the therapist addressing the boy's behavior in the normal way of the program. The childcare workers, on the other hand, are expected to address behavior routinely, and therefore whatever relationship they have with the child is considered expendable. They are "those people" who are just trying to manage behavior.

However, there do not need to be any people in a treatment program "just trying to manage behavior." In a trauma-informed care program, the first priority of every person who interacts with the child is to form, maintain, and strengthen their relationship with the child. Every relationship can be healing. Every relationship is important.

No staff member, whatever their role, is ever "just" managing behavior. Of course, in a crisis one has to direct traffic to restore safety. But with regard to any individual child, the constant focus should be to understand the meaning and adaptive function of every symptom, and teach the child more positive ways to meet those same needs. Treatment programs and all staff, in every way, promote a sense of safety and caring. Staff does not ignore behavior or remain paralyzed as the child becomes increasingly upset and out of control. They intervene actively and constantly from their base of relationship to help the child calm down, and, when he/she is calm, to figure out how to get what the child needs. Their goal is not to control the child's behavior. It is to help the child to feel calm and safe enough to try new ways of meeting his/her needs.

It is essential that everyone in the program be thinking this way, every childcare worker, every therapist, and every teacher. Everyone should be engaged with the child from a carefully formed relationship. Naturally, the child may be angry, unappreciative, nasty, upset, and uncooperative with any one (or all) of the many people on her team. In such a situation, any team member then acknowledges and validates her feelings, and (when she is calm enough to hear) shares their experience of whatever happened from their heart.

When programs acknowledge the central importance of all the relationships between the child and the team members; when they truly believe that the child is doing the best he can; when they see symptoms as adaptive; when they react by helping the child to learn better ways to meet his/her needs; then they can all do all parts of the job of treating and raising these children, and they can all enrich their relationships as they do them.

There are always times in treatment programs when things are not going well. Often dangerous and dramatic behaviors are taking place and people are getting hurt. It is difficult but essential to hold onto trauma-informed thinking in these times.

It may be triggered by a concerned call from the licensing agency. It may be from a review of the quality-improvement numbers. It might come from staff complaints, or a feeling of staff panic in a team meeting. But, somehow a program becomes aware that one of their programs, cottages or units is not doing well. Chaos has struck. There are an unusually high number of restraints, runaways, hospitalizations, staff and child injuries, police calls, negative discharges or other signs of dysregulation. What should the program do? Where should they start in their attempts to improve the treatment environment?

Usually these times are accompanied by a staff cry for increasing the severity of consequences. As staff feel more frightened and out of control, they reach for some sense of power. They turn towards more punitive responses as a way to feel in control and powerful. Similarly, the children are feeling frightened and out of control. They turn to violence, aggression and threats to give them a sense of power and control. A destructive cycle takes place.

Feelings of helplessness and futility lead staff to blame the chaos on one or several clients. If the unit could only get rid of Marci! Joshua needs to be discharged – he needs a place with more structure.

In such times it is hard to step back and think about what could be happening. Yet, it is exactly during these difficult periods that treaters most need to examine the patterns, think about how they understand the children's symptoms, and take measured, careful action. Also, amidst the crises, the very things that will help prevent crisis tend to disappear: regular activities are not done; routines break down; individual time for the children with their therapist or the staff is cancelled; and everyday positive interactions decrease. It is essential, but very difficult, to reinstate routines and activities during crisis times. Relationships, predictability, and positive activities are the most powerful interventions.

As staff considers what may be going wrong, staff and treatment team-related issues are the first things to think about. Often, these concerns decrease a feeling of safety for both clients and staff, and thus create a greater need for control and aggression. Here are some examples:

There is an influx of new staff without enough training, which leaves the team without enough knowledge and skill to maintain the balance of the trauma-informed perspective.

There are festering staff splits, and tensions between different groups such as therapists/childcare, staff/teachers, and first/second shifts. When staff is not getting along, blaming each other for the problems, and not talking about their differences directly, the children pick up on the tension and feel unsafe.

Therapists are staying in their offices rather than being active on the unit and helping to manage crises. As a result, they are not working closely with childcare staff to examine the meaning of behaviors, which leads to a decrease in clinical thinking and reflection.

Staff vicarious traumatization spikes with no way to talk about it or take care of ones self and others. When staff is unable to process the effect of painful events or are overworked, they have difficulty responding with compassion and become more controlling.

Frequently, agencies engaged in trauma-informed change experience a paralysis because they are caught between the old model and the new approach. They know what they are NOT supposed to do, but they are not sure what to do instead. So, they ignore behaviors and don't engage with the clients. Instead they stand by feeling helpless as a child's emotions and behavior escalate.

If the team comes to the conclusion that staff issues are at the center of their problem, what can they do?

The first and most important thing is to talk about it. Bring any issues into the open. Bring groups in conflict together to hash out differences. Of course, this is hard to do when a program is in the midst of problems, but it actually is the best way out. Part of the discussion might focus on staff members' emotional reactions to recent events and their experience of vicarious traumatization. Pain shared in the team is decreased and better tolerated. Loss of hope and cynicism are addressed directly. Consider additional training on the new method, on management and supervision, on policies and procedures. The program may need to address an individual staff in supervision, perhaps strategizing with him or her on a specific performance improvement plan. And, the agency may need to invest more resources in hiring.

Another area to look at is the schedule and structure of the program. It can be helpful to examine the program's serious incident reports to search for patterns. Are there specific times, days of the week, staffing patterns that correlate with the most incidents? One must be careful in interpreting these results, as many factors can contribute to them. Still, such analysis can provide a place to start.

One common pattern is not enough structure or activities, too much down time, TV or electronics time, or time when the clients are forced to stay in their rooms. For clients with racing, hopeless, and despairing thoughts, these times can feel awful. The clients then will do something to distract themselves from their thoughts, such as cause a commotion. One unit that analyzed its patterns of restraints discovered they were scheduling high-energy gym activities right before bedtime, and then having many problems while trying to get the clients to sleep. They reduced restraints by instituting quiet activities in the evening.

Another common occurrence is that children become anxious in situations with unclear expectations, unpredictability of schedule, and confusion among staff about what happens next. Planned schedules that are posted for all to see help the children feel safe. In addition, too much noise, activity, and chaos can be overwhelming to clients. If an analysis reveals patterns to the problems, staff can change the programming and see if it helps.

Of course, some of the sources of program distress are client-related, including:

- A large influx of new clients, or negative events that have affected clients and made them feel less safe, such as observing an out-of-control event that required police intervention, can lead to acting out.

- Client secrets, things that may be going on that staff do not know about, can be sources of disruptive behavior that need to be discovered and addressed. Sexual acting out and/or bullying and intimidation are prime candidates. Getting the truth out in the open can begin a change and a healing process that will result in greater safety for all.
- Clients are affected by individual or collective losses, such as staff leaving. If the departures have not been discussed or grieved, they can lead to problem behaviors.
- Of course, the children are constantly facing overwhelming individual life stresses. And, as all teams know, certain times of year such as school starting or holidays are difficult for the clients and thus lead to many behavioral expressions of trauma symptoms.

In these cases, staff needs to be active advocates for the clients. Again, talking collaboratively with the clients about what is going on, what is happening in the community, and what everyone wants to do about it can begin a powerful and mutual process of change. And staff may also need to institute extra precautions of supervision, observation and staffing to increase safety.

The bottom line here is that we assume that the escalation in behaviors is happening for a reason, and the reason is not that the children are obnoxious. The team remains certain that the program symptoms are adaptive in some way, for the clients and for the staff. They assume that everyone is feeling unsafe and is doing the best they can to protect themselves. They start from these assumptions to think about what could be going on, and then take directed action to enable everyone in their community to experience less pain and more joy.

An essential part of feeling better is hope. If a child has no hope of a positive future, why should he try to do the right thing, or form relationships, or achieve difficult goals?

Hope is essential to all our endeavors. Do programs make enough deliberate efforts to strengthen hope in organizations, staff, and our clients? How can they do this? Here are a few ideas:

Organizations:

- Hold regular celebrations.
- Communicate successes.
- Share stories of clients who return to visit and are doing well.
- Reward all sorts of staff efforts.
- Share any honors, recognitions, or praise widely.
- Regularly and publicly reflect on where the agency has been and where it is now and where it is going.
- Articulate a vision of what kind of organization it wants to be. Specify values and refer to them often.
- Organize many child activities such as plays, field days, art shows, and science fairs. As many staff as possible attend and applaud.
- When something goes wrong, pull together and identify the parts that were done well. Praise the staff for those. Be specific about what has been learned from the event.
- Articulate pride in the agency and specifically what there is to be proud of.
- Have fun, make jokes, do silly things.
- Celebrate staff milestones (new babies, weddings, etc.)

Staff:

- Praise, praise, praise – little and big things.
- Comment on any instance of staff doing their work well.
- Assist staff in meeting their personal goals through providing training and education reimbursement.
- Provide supervision.
- Share client success stories.
- Promote from within when possible.
- Deliberately groom people for their next job.
- Remark on extra effort.
- Make room for creativity and individual interests, like the childcare worker that hooks the kids up with a horseback riding stable through their personal interests.
- Do something different.
- Encourage staff to say yes, and say yes to staff.
- Be flexible whenever possible.
- Maintain a clean and beautiful environment, and fix damage quickly.
- Create fun events together such as potluck lunches or volleyball teams.

Personal:

- Reframe experiences to focus on what has been learned.
- Maintain balance with work and non-work connections.
- Take breaks and vacations.
- Decorate personal space when possible.
- Notice changes in clients even when small.
- Notice changes in self such as increasing skill, and point them out in others.
- Notice ways the work has grown you as a person.

- Set goals for areas you would like to learn more about or new things you would like to do.
- Connect with others in the profession.
- Talk about your experiences. Use supervision and therapy.
- Laugh.

Clients:

- Point out small changes.
- Set small goals with them, notice when they are met.
- Express sincere delight.
- Celebrate their achievements, attend their plays, and admire their art.
- Arrange for them to take extra classes in an area of skill.
- Fantasize the future when they are a famous football player and are returning to your place to speak with the kids who are there then – what will they say?
- Show that they matter by speaking from the heart.
- Allow them to take some risks and try something new.
- Offer new responsibilities.
- Arrange ways they can help others.
- Encourage the older to teach the younger, and the more skilled of any age to teach the less skilled.
- Put them in charge of things.
- Have a Youth Council that has real power.
- Tell stories of other successful kids.
- Have fun together.

The core of creating hope is through forming relationships. Yet treaters often feel confusion about what kind of relationships are healing, and whether relying on relationships means there is no discipline or rules. We have already seen that discipline and rules both play a part in trauma-informed care, just in more flexible roles that reflect compassion, understanding, and teaching new skills to children with different brain development due to trauma.

And yet, at times the team is left with sad situations, clients they cannot help, circumstances that are beyond their control. At these times it is especially important to support each other and talk about the pain.

The difficulties in treating Mario exemplify some of the key dilemmas of trauma-informed care.

Mario is twelve years old. He experienced severe early abuse, and has lost his entire family. He has been ejected from three foster homes. His IQ is low average, and his mother may have used substances during her pregnancy with him. He has been in the group home for a year and three months.

During the first few months of Mario's placement, he destroyed a lot of expensive property at the agency. He trashed the gym, broke windows, destroyed a part of the school, and more. After each event he was deeply ashamed and further confirmed in his sense of himself as a horrible, bad boy. He hid under the furniture and refused to talk with anyone. When he was not upset, he could describe some strategies he could use when something went wrong. But when something did go wrong, and it was often something very minor, his emotions would well up and completely take over his mind.

For example, a staff member says that he has to wait ten minutes before going to dinner. Mario becomes overwhelmed with a sense of total hopelessness. He knows he will never eat again. His mind becomes muddled and he is unable to think. He is plunged back into his basic reality in which his needs are never met, no one can be trusted, and he has to fight for anything he gets. So he reacts: he throws something, breaks something, or threatens someone. Anyone around him would be bewildered. What happened? Waiting ten minutes is no big deal. They try to explain this to Mario but he literally does not hear them. Mario's pain gets worse and he tries to express and escape it by increasingly aggressive actions. Finally, he is contained and the storm passes. Afterwards, he feels worse than ever.

Elliot is Mario's teammate (a child care worker with a special relationship with and responsibility for Mario). Elliot is a caring young man, and he sees Mario's shame and pain. He works hard to form a relationship with Mario and not to give up on him no matter what he does. When Mario is calm, he and Elliot have some great times together. Elliot is proud that he is able to connect with this difficult child, and thinks that their relationship may be part of the reason that Mario has gone a month with no major episodes. Yet, not long ago Mario got into a minor argument with a peer that rapidly escalated into violence. When Elliot tried to intervene and get Mario to take a walk with him, Mario looked at him blankly and said: "I don't know you. You don't know me." Elliot felt hurt.

Overall Mario's behavior had improved, his property destruction had decreased, and his episodes had become further apart. The treatment team members were proud of what they had accomplished, and Mario himself was feeling more hopeful. So he was referred to a therapeutic foster home and began to visit a family. Almost immediately his aggression returned. After several episodes the family withdrew from consideration.

Now, Mario appears to be regressing. He has become aggressive towards people instead of just property. He has had several major, dangerous high-end events. He was hospitalized, and did well in the hospital. Staff felt hopeful and lifted all his restrictions when he came back. As one person described it: "We gave him a blank slate and he smashed that slate into pieces." Shortly after coming back Mario went on an agency trip to a baseball game. On the way back he got into such a major unstoppable fight that several policemen and supervisors needed to intervene. At this point, the team is investigating transferring Mario to a long-term hospital program.

It is always painful when programs are not successful in treatment of a child. When staff have been working on forming and strengthening relationships, with their hearts open, it can feel personally distressing. Treaters doubt themselves and wonder if there is more they could do. They feel hopeless for this child, and perhaps less hopeful about their work in general. In short, they feel much the way the child feels.

So how do treaters react to their pain? And how do they understand what is happening with Mario? It is easy to begin seeing Mario's behavior as intentional: "He waits until staff are vulnerable and attacks." It is natural to think punishment would help: "He needs to go somewhere where he will get serious consequences for his behaviors. This program is being too nice to him. He needs to understand that in the real world he cannot get away with these sorts of actions." It feels like Mario is uncaring: "We don't have a relationship. When he is upset he does not even know me. He never seems to consider the needs and feelings of anyone else." A common reaction is to retreat, to treat Mario with distant politeness, and stay emotionally closed. It is natural to feel angry, betrayed, sad and hopeless.

Mario may need to be in the hospital. In a hospital adults can physically keep him and others safe, using tools a residential care program does not have (such as high staff-patient ratios, locked units, etc.). He probably did well in the hospital because right now he needs the feeling of safety that a hospital provides.

Yet it is important to reconsider what is going on here, no matter what the outcome.

Here are some points for thought:

Remember that Mario is *not* deliberately planning his aggressive outbursts. When he says he is going to try some strategies, he means it at the time (just as adults mean it when they say they are starting a new diet on Monday). When he is connecting with adults, he is not planning to trick them. When the chemicals in his muddled brain are calm, he can enjoy other people and plan a different future.

Mario is *not* looking for times when staff are vulnerable because there are fewer people scheduled or all females on the shift. It is possible that at these times he feels less containment and safety, and thus more anxious and more likely to over-react when something goes wrong.

Punishment will not help Mario change this behavior. Of course punishment will make him feel worse and more ashamed. Yet will it be a deterrent? Mario does not have cognitive access to an awareness of consequences when he is agitated. If he did remember them, he would not care or might feel that they would be just what he deserved. When his brain chemicals are raging he cannot think to himself: "If I do this, I will be in trouble so I shouldn't do it." Unfortunately he cannot even remember: "If I do this, Elliot will be disappointed." Instead he already feels that he is totally in trouble and already feels that Elliot is disappointed, or couldn't possibly be trusted to like him. So what is there to lose?

Staff sometimes overlooks the role of stimulation, even from positive events. Staff was being caring and compassionate when they decided to bring Mario on the trip. However, it is possible that the excitement of the trip, although a pleasant experience, was too much for Mario. Keeping his world's boundaries tighter and his routines more predictable might work out better.

What does Mario need? He needs to be kept safe so that he can experience positive relationships over a long period of time. He needs to learn and practice concrete steps he can take when he first starts to feel upset, and the first step is to realize when he is getting upset. He needs experiences of success and positive action. And he needs some hope, some pathway toward growing up outside an institution, some adults who will love him and stay with him.

These things are all very hard for the child welfare system to provide. And the pain of this situation leads Elliot to wonder: "Is there any hope for Mario? Are there some kids who never change, and who are destined to spend their lives in and out of jail?"

Can a 12-year-old be hopeless? Or does he need a situation our system does not have? That is a crucial question for all.

Chapter Six

When Children Hurt Others

The Challenge of Responding to Hurtful Behaviors: Why Punishment Doesn't Work

When children do something that hurts others, the goal of the program response is to decrease the likelihood that they will do so again. What response has the most powerful effect on decreasing repetition of symptomatic behavior? The child will be less likely to continue to hurt others when he/she has skills to meet his/her needs without doing so. The child will also be less likely to hurt others when he or she feels better, stronger, safer and more hopeful.

Traditionally programs have assumed that level systems using both rewards and punishments are the most powerful weapons they have to reduce the youth's problem behaviors. The idea of level systems is that a person will learn that when they do a certain behavior bad things happen, things they don't want. So they stop doing that behavior to avoid those bad things. In their excellent review of the use of points and levels systems, Mohr, Olson, Martin, Pumariega, & Branca (2009) point out: "By virtue of not taking into account their individual differences and symptoms it may undermine their progress, and at times can precipitate dangerous clinical situations" (p. 8).

They later add: "Level systems have no relationship to the environment to which the child will return, raising the issue of generalization or transfer of training, otherwise known as ecological validity. If compliance is achieved or behaviors changed, these tend to be temporary" (p. 12).

Another resource regarding both reinforcement and punishment is Karen Pryor's *Don't Shoot the Dog!* (2002), recommended in DBT (Linehan, 1993) intensive training. Pryor maintains that punishment is not as powerful as reinforcement, and must be used precisely: for example, it must happen immediately after the undesirable behavior. In congregate-care settings it is almost impossible to achieve such precision.

And surely the children in congregate-care settings have already had a lot of experience learning that their bad behavior brings negative consequences. In fact, they tend to blame nearly all the awful things that have happened to them on their own bad behavior. Because of what a terrible child he/she is, his mother left them, her father beat them, they were molested, they ended up in care with strangers. Because this feeling of unworthiness is so painful, children try to ward it off by blaming others.

If experiencing negative consequences could change these children, it almost certainly would have happened by now.

Staff members' own family backgrounds reinforce the idea that punishment is the solution to undesirable behavior. Many staff have said, "I was raised with strict punishments, and that is what saved me, what made me the person I am today." Others mentioned that they did not like it when their parents grounded them for sneaking out or other rule-breaking behavior. This comparison, while understandable, ignores the differences between the experiences of most staff and those of the children under their care. When staff talks about punishment in their own homes, they are usually referring to punishment in the context of a persistent, loving relationship. At least one parent raised them throughout their lives, loved them, and punished them. This experience is very different from that of the children in treatment, who have been moved around among many caretakers.

It is different from the relationship the children have with staff. Closer reflection often reveals that in most staff members' homes, it was much more difficult than being grounded when parents sat the child down for a talk that began: "Young lady, your mother and I are deeply disappointed in you." In other words, it is the injury to the relationship that had the deepest impact. The parents conveyed to the child they loved them, and that the child had let them down. That is what children really want to avoid.

The considerable societal context for the use of punishment as a response to problem behaviors is evident in both the religious and criminal justice systems.

But rewards and punishments primarily affect *motivation*. They make someone *want* to do something more to get the reward, or want to *stop* doing it to avoid the punishment. But if you do not know *how* to do anything different, it does not matter how much you want to. You need to learn the skills.

It may be helpful for staff to think of a time they have tried to do something they really wanted to do, but they were not able to. The examples can include playing tennis, rollerblading, knitting, learning a language. People readily see that if a person is having difficulty learning to play tennis, punishment for not playing tennis well wouldn't help. In fact it might make the situation worse, and/or contribute to the learner giving up. If someone wants to learn to play tennis, they need lessons from a kind and patient teacher, who will teach them the many small skills that go into the game.

In some ways punishments render children *less* likely to achieve better behavior. Punishments often contribute to shame and hopelessness, thus increasing the intolerable negative emotions that already overwhelm the child's ability to think. They accentuate passivity, encouraging the child's feeling that "I have messed up and there is nothing I can do about it." They undermine self-worth.

When a child physically hurts another person or damages something significant to another person, that child is overwhelmed with emotion, hyper-reactive, and often in the pit of despair. The child feels lost, alone, and terrified. He or she doesn't notice what they are feeling until they are in the midst of a hurricane. They see danger everywhere. They don't trust others and can't ask for or accept help. They feel worthless and have no hope and nothing to lose. They don't believe anyone cares, including themselves.

But if not punishments, then what? Adults often turn to punishment when they themselves are feeling overwhelmed and helpless.

Treaters may be concerned that if they take away punishment as an option, how will the children learn? How will they know that these behaviors are not allowed within society and that if the children keep doing them they will go to jail? In fact, the children already know this consequence. If asked when they were calm, they could readily explain all the negative things that will result from their continuing harmful behaviors: they have already experienced many of them.

What they need to learn is quite different. They need to learn that they are safe. That people can be trustworthy, that they are worthwhile and can have a meaningful future, and how to identify and manage emotions, ways to soothe and take care of themselves, and that when things go wrong between people, the rift can be mended. And most of all, that there is someone who likes them, sees good in them, and will stick with them as they struggle to heal.

They will learn these things through relationships, not through punishments.

Learning from Mistakes

Daniel Hughes points out in *Attachment Focused Parenting* (2009) that trauma makes it hard to learn from one's mistakes.

> These children also try to avoid any event that might be associated with prior events involving fearful and shaming experiences. They develop a strong avoidance of memories of those prior events as well as any current situations that

> might elicit those memories. These children, in a fundamental way, may never feel safe since they fear parts of their own mind. Not only are they hyper-vigilant about external events, they are equally hyper-vigilant about allowing parts of their inner life to enter awareness. They often react with intense rage or terror when seemingly routine events – associated with past traumas – elicit an intense emotional response.
>
> Their emotional experience and expressions tend toward the extreme, lacking a "thermostat" that will create flexible regulation. Their ability to reflect on the events of their lives tends to be weak, as they react to situations, often in a repetitive and rigid manner driven by fears regarding safety (p. 177).

The idea of the traumatized child being afraid of what is inside himself has profound implications for dealing with emotionally dysregulated children in congregate care.

Hughes (2009, p. 185) goes on to identify the importance of attachment and structure:

> Without attachment security, a child is less likely to turn to his parents for guidance as to how to be successful. He [*sic*] is also less likely to acknowledge his mistakes and try to correct them. He is less likely to communicate his difficulties and ask for help. As a result, he is less likely to learn from his mistakes and so correct them. Rather, he is more likely to make the same mistake again and again. This most likely will create a pervasive sense of failure. Rather than ask for help, he is likely to rely on himself more, become even more hyper-vigilant and controlling. With structure, supervision and limited choices, his environment makes success more likely and failure more difficult. Until he can

learn from his mistakes, they have to be kept to a minimum by his environment.

There are many different reasons why children who resist attachment have trouble learning from their mistakes. First, their pervasive sense of shame causes them to deny mistakes, have excuses for them, or blame others. Second, they often have developmental disabilities that place them in situations that they are not prepared for. They tend to be raised or taught according to their chronological age rather than their developmental age. Basic skills of self-direction, impulse control, frustration tolerance, and delay of gratification tend to be weak, leaving them at a high risk for failure in many situations.

The Restorative Response

If programs do not rely on punishment as a main source of change, what is an effective response when the child does something that hurts others? What response will truly increase his or her ability to meet emotional needs without hurting others? Responding to destructive, hurtful behavior with restorative tasks achieves this objective.

The restorative response includes an opportunity to learn or practice skills that would be necessary in order to act differently. Ideas for this task can be generated by answers to these questions: "What was the child trying to accomplish with this behavior?" and "What would this child have to know or be able to do in order to accomplish that goal without hurting others?"

The second half of the response may include an opportunity to make amends to people that the child hurt and to restore his relationships with them. Ideas for this task can be generated by answers to these questions: "Whom did the child's behavior hurt?" and "How can he or she make that person's life better?" (See Appendix B for a Restorative Task Planning Guide, and Appendix C for a Task Planning Worksheet.)

Healing Tasks

To create healing tasks, staff can consider what they want the child to learn from his or her mistakes. The team might want the child to look for patterns that will reveal what leads up to an episode of dysregulation, times when he is most vulnerable, pre-disposing factors. Recognizing these cues could suggest changes that might leave the child less vulnerable in the future. The DBT Diary card (Linehan, 1993) is one mechanism for looking for patterns. Other examples would be developing and using a feelings thermometer, keeping a mood chart, and creating a collage of what the child was feeling right before the event. If the child is working on developing empathy for others, a task would be to write the story (or draw a 'comic' or storyboard) of what happened from the other person's point of view. (See Appendix D for a Guide to Creating Healing Tasks, and Appendix E for examples of generating healing tasks from the case formulation generated by the treatment team.)

Some healing tasks teach a small part of emotion-management skills, such as "describing what I was feeling," or "what else I could do," or listing "ten good things I have accomplished," or drawing "pictures of people who care about me." Again, the task is based on asking what are *this* child's current emotion skills strengths and deficits; what are the next steps in his treatment, what is the team currently trying to teach her. The task is to give him/her some chance to practice the skills as part of his/her restoration.

The key to healing tasks is that they are individualized. They emerge from the team's formulation of how they understand the child's behavior, and the healing themes they are currently working on. They are also individualized in accordance with the child's skills and abilities. It would not make sense to assign an essay to a child who cannot write. An emotionally delayed child with few communication skills might be able to do only a short discussion in the moment about what happened. The staff is available to assist the child with the task, which provides another opportunity to teach the child that relationships help.

When considering a healing task, it may be helpful for the team to use the following questions:

- What led up to the problem behavior?
- What was the child feeling?
- What would the team like the child to do in that situation?
- What would the child need to know, feel, believe, and be able to do in order to utilize that alternative action?
- How can the child move forward in what he or she needs?

Here's an example of a hurtful behavior and how it was addressed through assessing the child's needs:

- Roberto hit Sam while they were playing basketball.
- **What led up to this behavior?** Sam was taunting Roberto about not making his baskets.
- **What was Roberto feeling?** Stupid, like a loser, ashamed of his lack of skill, sure he would never get better.
- **What would we like Roberto to do in this situation?** Ask Sam to stop, ask an adult for help, and use the emotion to improve his basketball skills.
- **What would Roberto need to know, feel, believe, and be able to do in order to utilize that alternative action?** That he was an okay boy, that he could trust adults to help, and that basketball skills can get better with practice.
- **What might help Roberto move forward?** Time spent with a caring adult working on basketball skills would help him to develop trust for the adult and, if his skills improved, could add to his pride and help him feel more inner strength.

Tasks for Making Amends

The first step in making amends is for the child to figure out who was affected by his behavior. Who was hurt, inconvenienced, upset, or insulted? Then, with staff help, the child can consider what he/she can do to work it out with that person and make their life better. This process may include listening to the other person's account of how they felt during the situation, and telling them steps she/he will take to avoid it happening again. Often the task will not be as large as the offense. Some examples include: making cookies (with staff help as needed) for all the units that were woken up by the pulled fire alarm; doing chores for children who could not attend an activity, or for staff who were assaulted; creating a bulletin board for the unit that was disrupted by destructive behavior; or reading a bedtime story to younger children scared by the child's threats. (See Appendix F for more examples of making-amends tasks in response to various behaviors.)

Making-amends tasks are also individualized based on the *abilities* of the child and the *receptivity* of the people hurt, plus other circumstances. Once the program has been operating this way for a while, the children tend to become quite adept at creating their own significant ways of making amends.

How Does This Approach Help?

When a child hurts others, he feels hopeless. Once again she has messed up. He is certain that all is lost, he will never improve and that he has ruined these relationships as he has ruined so many others. She suspects the team is getting ready to reject her as others have. Furthermore, he has a history in which he was not able to do anything to influence bad events. She has learned that there is nothing she can do to change things.

Traditional punishments increase his shame and self-hatred. They encourage passivity, because the child must only "do his time" and the punishment will be over. Often the punishment includes doing nothing in a small room. If the punishment is written on a white board (as is often the case) the public element is also shameful. And, the punishment does not teach anything about what the child should do; it only underscores what he should not do.

Restorative tasks give the child a chance to learn and practice new skills. They convey the assumption that the child is doing the best he can, and that he can learn to do better. They teach the child that when there are problems within a relationship, there are things she can do to make it better, and they teach her what those things are. By doing the restorative task the child reconnects with the people who matter to him. Restorative tasks require that the child take effective action to master the problem. At the end, she feels a little better about herself instead of worse and more hopeless.

How Much Restoration is Enough?

How does staff know how much restoration is enough? When a child does something that hurts another person or threatens the community, how do they decide how many or how large the tasks assigned for restoration should be? And how do they decide whether the child has completed these tasks with enough sincerity, effort or seriousness?

Some of the impetus for this question comes from thinking of restorative tasks as "punishments in disguise," and from believing that their effectiveness comes from being aversive. In other words, the tasks (like punishment) should not be fun to do, and then the child will change his/her behavior in order to avoid having to do them. In this framework, the tasks should be "as big as" the offense, and take a lot of effort and time, especially if the behavior was very serious or hurtful. This approach identifies the healing or relationship nature of the tasks as secondary. Some staff may be feeling like the child "got away with" his behavior because what he had to do was not hard enough. The person who was hurt by the child does not feel sufficiently paid back or restored, and thus feels resentful and disrespected.

In order to think further about this, staff may turn to their own lives.

Everyone has had experiences of forgiving people who have hurt them, and continuing the relationship. Imagine that a friend has done something that hurt. What would that be? Told a secret, let you down, forgotten to meet you for a planned appointment, said something thoughtless or mean to you, cancelled a plan with you at the last minute in order to do something else, borrowed money and not paid it back, or any of many other disappointments.

In order to restore this friendship and for you to truly feel better about this friend, what would you want from him or her? First, an apology and an acknowledgement of what went wrong and his/her part in it would help. You might want your friend to listen to you speak of how this behavior affected you and to seem to actually care and take in what you said. Then, you would want your friend to act differently from now on, or try to, or at least start to.

So these are the skills and behaviors treaters want the children in their care to learn.

The first thing that gets in the way of restoration or making amends is shame. In order for a person to deal directly with something they have done wrong, they have to be able to tolerate the bad feelings involved. In order to admit you have hurt someone and to face them, you have to have some inner core of believing you are okay, and okay people do sometimes make mistakes and hurt other people. You have to believe that forgiveness is a possibility.

The restorative tasks aim towards helping *this* particular child, with his/her particular abilities, needs, and treatment formulation, to become slightly better at:

- Acknowledging what went wrong and his/her part in it.
- Listening to the hurt others speak of how this behavior affected them, caring and taking in what that person says.
- Acting differently from now on.

In order to do any of these tasks, the child has to develop some sense of being a worthwhile person, someone who deserves the air he/she breathes, someone others could care about and could forgive. Much of treatment is designed to build this belief in many different ways.

A person gets better at these skills – acknowledging mistakes, and listening to the other person describe the effect on them – by practice, and by discovering that the world doesn't end and he/she can often repair the relationship. So, for one child the whole making-amends task could be a short conversation with the person hurt, because that could be a huge step. Another child perhaps can't do even that; the shame is too intense. But maybe he can draw a picture of the steps leading up to the event, and how he was feeling, and give it to the person he hurt. Maybe the recipient could respond by drawing a similar picture of the events from her point of view and how she was feeling, and the child could further respond with some communication that shows he paid attention to what she said. The goal here would be to think about what are *this* child's current abilities to face his/her mistakes, and what action would be one small step further than he/she usually can go. In the past in this child's life, making mistakes has usually led to abuse, and often resulted in the person hurt disappearing altogether. The goal is to make this time different, a restorative relationship experience, and to create a new template that includes the possibility of healing.

So back to the question of how much is enough? It is enough when the staff feels the child has made any little step on any of these dimensions. He has talked about what happened sincerely. She has actually listened to the person she hurt. He has explored the feelings that led up to his actions. It doesn't have to be the whole solution, just one tiny step, one new interpersonal experience, one moment of feeling "I am worth caring about," one building block in creating a new reality for the child.

When staff feels that the child has seriously grappled with what happened and tried their best to learn from it and make amends, the restoration is over. The child then returns to all normal programming. No amount of time is set in advance to do this. The child is not restricted for a certain number of hours or days. As soon as the child has completed these tasks seriously, it is over.

Dealing with Youth Resistance to the Tasks

Staff often wonders, "What if the child refuses to do the restorative task?" No staff member in a program using the Restorative Approach can *make* a child do a poster, bake cookies for someone, talk over a problem, or do a peer's chores. Staff may have less control than in the past systems in which they could make a child stay in a room and take away privileges.

Structural supports can be put in place to encourage the child to do the tasks. Some programs institute Restorative Task time blocks, e.g., from 3:00 to 4:00. If a child has an outstanding task, he is either doing it during this time, or staying inside not doing it. If she has no outstanding tasks, she is playing or doing something fun. Also, if a child has an outstanding task, he may have to go to bed early to get more energy for the task. She cannot go on extra off-grounds trips because she has not reconnected with the community yet.

It is essential not to engage in power struggles around tasks. The staff attitude is, "It's fine if you are not ready. Sometimes it takes time to become ready to work through a problem. We have confidence that you will get there, and we will be here ready to work it through with you when you are ready. In the meantime, we need to keep a closer eye on you and keep you near us, because we have not rebuilt trust between us."

Lastly, it is important to remember the reason for the task. The task is not punishment by another name. It is not designed to be difficult, to be a deterrent, to be arduous or unpleasant. The task is genuinely designed to be a vehicle of reconciliation and reconnection. People who have done something wrong or made a mistake want to make things right. Often in children who have experienced repeated trauma and attachment disruption, this impulse is blocked by a feeling that it is impossible to correct mistakes. The treater's job is to gently challenge that assumption, provide a step-by-step method for fixing mistakes, and to patiently and eagerly await the child's readiness to engage in the process with them.

Especially at the beginning of a program's use of tasks, it is important for staff to constantly review the restorative tasks they are using and restrictions or scheduling changes that they are making to support them. Administration can be alert to the fit between tasks and a child's abilities. Are the tasks ones that this child can do? Also, the administration can pay attention to whether the tasks are being misused as a roundabout way of administering a punishment. Open team discussion will help all members improve their use of tasks.

Concerns About Restorative Tasks

A program begins to use restorative responses. A child trashed the playroom because he could not watch the show he wanted to see on TV. Staff decided that if he worked to set it right, he would then be allowed to go on the planned trip to the movies once he was done, if he seemed calm and safe. He would not have a restriction that lasts beyond his having fixed the problem.

Some childcare workers thought this was crazy. "You mean he should be able to go to the movies just because he fixed the room up? But then the kids will think they can do anything they want, and all they have to do is clean it up, and everything will be fine. They will be going crazy destroying this place. The child care workers will have no control at all."

The therapist was skeptical too. "Won't we be setting them up?" she asks. "What about when they get to public school, where there are consequences for behaviors. We will have given them unrealistic expectations."

These are the crucial questions a team must answer if they are going to actually change the way children are managed within their treatment program. Let's look at the assumptions behind these questions:

- That children are eager to misbehave and will choose to do so whenever they can "get away with it."
- That only the fear of consequences prevents them from acting up constantly.

- That a childcare worker's most significant source of influence on a child is the wielding of punishments and rewards.
- That reward and punishment systems will teach the children to stop doing disruptive behaviors and that learning will transfer to their next setting.

What if we act from the basic belief that children do well if they can? Children do not *want* to fail, to anger the adults around them, to be kicked out of programs, to be placed in intensive care programs. They do not *want* to trash the playroom, and they are not looking for opportunities to do so when they can "get away with it."

What prevents adults from acting up constantly? What prevents staff from destroying their agency's staff lounge? Some of it may be fear of punishments, such as losing their job. But there is a lot more to it. For example, staff has people and goals that they care about. They have hope. They have a sense that there are people who love them and would be disappointed if they got fired or arrested. They have a positive idea of what kind of person they are. And when they are extremely frustrated (and child care staff can be *very* frustrated at the job), they have skills to manage these emotions. They talk to someone, they take a break, and they go for a walk. They have options other than room trashing.

Childcare workers have a chance to have a powerful and long-lasting impact on a child's life. They can help rebuild a child's brain – but not mainly through their use of rewards and consequences. They change children through connected, caring relationships in which children build new ideas of how adults can be, how trust is possible, and how people can care about their needs. Through many, many repetitions of attuned caretaking, a childcare worker creates a new view of the world for a child. And, childcare workers actively teach the child skills through that relationship. They teach the child that others care about him even when they are not physically present – and even when he has done something hurtful or disappointing; that he is worthwhile and special; and how to recognize and manage her emotions.

This brings up the question of what will help the child when she gets to public school. It isn't that the child has to learn that there are negative consequences when she trashes a room. She already knows that. She has experienced a lot of negative consequences in her young life. The problem is: when she experiences a setback, she is not able to get help from others or draw on an image of anyone who cares about her. She is already convinced she is a lousy no-good person. Her biology is over-activated and over-reactive. And she has no idea how to recognize her emotions and soothe herself. So she plummets into despair, fear and hopelessness. And her brain stops working. She is in danger mode; feeling like her very life is under attack. She has to do something to get away from all this pain, so she trashes a room.

In order to help her be successful in public school, the team needs to teach her that she matters, people care, and she can get help. They need to help her calm down and feel safe. And they need to teach each child specific emotion-management skills.

This is where the staff members' power is. This teaching, connecting, and caring are what will make a difference. This crisis is where they have the ability to influence (rather than control) a child's life.

So, they help her clean up the room. They have a brief discussion of what she was feeling that led up to this event. They validate her feelings as much as possible. They talk a little about what else she can do when she feels this way. And then they take the child to the movies, if that's the next fun activity.

How Can Staff Respond to Hurtful Behavior and Promote Healing?

When programs first begin to use the Restorative Approach, staff often thinks of restorative tasks as a new type of punishment. This leads them to attempt to create tasks that take as long as their traditional punishments did. Staff are still thinking that the power of the tasks lies in their deterrent value; in other words, that the child will stop doing the behavior because the tasks will be so hard and they will not want to have to do them. In other words, that the tasks are **punishment**. This leads to the piling up of tasks, and continuing hopelessness on the part of both the child and the staff.

Instead, let's go back to the theory of what is wrong, and what do we actually think will promote change.

Why are the children hitting people and throwing chairs and running away and cutting themselves? Is it because they lack motivation to change, that the previous punishments they have received for their destructive and harmful behaviors have been inadequate?

In trauma-informed care, we remember that the children continue these behaviors because they are doing the best they can to solve current intolerable problems. They do not have safe, strong, trustworthy attachments in which they can relax and learn new skills, and they never have. They do not know how to resolve problems that arise within relationships. Trauma has changed their biology, sensitized their nervous systems, and left them hyper-reactive. They have not been taught the basic human-feelings skills: how to hold onto the belief that someone loves you; believing that you are worth the air you breathe; and what we do when we experience strong emotions.

Because of this lack, they over-react to current setbacks, do not believe that anyone can or will help them, and have no way to manage their emotions. So they act out. Punishment will not help build skills and change behavior. The children have already been repeatedly punished; if that would solve these problems the children would be over them by now.

The Restorative Approach is designed to provide what will help:

Attachment-safe, regulated relationships in which people speak from their heart and are honest about the relationship effects of behaviors, and are RICH: Respectful, Informative, Connected and Hopeful (Saakvitne, Pearlman, Gamble, & Lev, 2000).

Containment of hyper-reactivity: an environment structured for success with available regulated adults helping children become regulated.

Modeling and teaching feelings-management skills: noticing, naming, self-soothing, distracting, and utilizing feelings.

Opportunities to develop relationships and active effort towards creating inner representations of those relationships.

Many different methods and opportunities to experience competence, help others, examine shame, surface what is shameful, and to see delight in another's eyes when they look at you.

Teaching relationship-repair skills: when something goes wrong between me and another, there is something I can do about it.

The power of change happens in these areas. The restorative tasks are designed to take a small step in any one of these areas. Often, the healing piece is in the area of feelings management: what was I feeling; what happened? Or, it could be feeling worthy of life: make a list of my skills and good points. The amends piece works in the areas of attachment, relationship skills, and also contributes to self-worth.

So the idea of making amends is not to make up a task for everything the child does wrong. The idea is to figure out what treaters think is going on in a given event, what skills the child is lacking, and assign a task that will help develop these skills. It does not have to be aversive. It has to be something that will work by helping the child to learn a little something new, and be a little more connected with the people around him.

It is not fear of punishment that will change the child. It is developing the capacity for relationships and learning the skills that will allow him/her to weather current setbacks without having to resort to such desperate behavior.

Improving Restorative Tasks

Here are three ideas to make restorative tasks more meaningful to both youth and staff:

1. Mapping the Effects of Behaviors: After each incident, meet with the child and create a map of who was affected by the child's recent actions. Include any one who was affected positively! Then the child has a chance to think about how to make it up to those who were hurt or frightened. Some children would be unable to do this cognitive task because their shame would produce overwhelming and intolerable emotions. But for those who can, taking this step formally would be a way to underscore the meaning of the restorative tasks.

2. Practicing Positive Ways to Meet Needs: A key tenet of trauma-informed care is the belief that symptoms are adaptive, that every behavior results from a person's trying to meet their needs the best way they know how at that moment. The behavior (hurting yourself, running away, throwing a chair) may be an escape from intolerable feelings of despair and hopelessness. It may be a way to draw humans closer and avoid deep aloneness. It may be a mask for desperate fear or unacceptable confusion. But the behavior serves a function, and it helps in the moment. It actually makes things better for a time, even if it also brings long-term negative results.

Led by the clinician, the Treatment Team tries to understand the needs that this child's behavior is meeting. They can do this by talking with the child, by noticing patterns, by knowing the child and his history, even by guessing. And then their job is to teach the child how to meet these needs with less negative consequences.

Use the healing part of restorative tasks as ways to discover and practice these new ways of meeting needs. An example: Yolanda is angry and destructive many nights before bed, and the team speculates that nighttime is hard for her, and she has trouble falling asleep due to racing, unhappy thoughts. What if her restorative task is to read a story to a younger girl on the unit every night? Or (with staff help) to put together a CD of soothing sounds and make copies for some other girls whose nights she disrupted? Or to make a stuffed animal filled with lavender for someone – and make one for herself too? Yolanda learns some ideas of how to fall asleep, while making amends to others.

If the team postulates that Andre becomes aggressive and assaults staff whenever he feels afraid, what would the adults prefer him to do when he becomes afraid? Probably, they'd want him to tell someone. So how could he practice that? He could talk with three of the male staff about times they felt afraid, and what they did about it (experience modeling of the desired behavior). Could he read or write a story about a boy who was afraid and handled it well?

In Treatment Team meetings, think about the needs a behavior is meeting and the desired way of meeting those needs. Then think of some possible ways the child could experience or practice that more positive alternative.

3. Peace offerings: When a person hurts a friend, she may bring her friend a peace offering when she apologizes (such as cookies, or wildflowers, or some small item she has made). The concept of a peace offering conveys what can be accomplished in the making amends part of the restorative task. The tasks to make amends can never be as big as the things the children have done wrong (at least, not if programs want to stay licensed). So using the phrase "peace offering" might help convey the spirit of the action – a sincere gesture of apology.

We Need to Find More Tasks!

"It's the tasks," a program manager says. "We just cannot seem to think of enough tasks to assign to the kids in my unit. And those we can think of they don't take seriously, they are done quickly, and I just don't think they are significant enough to deter the behavior."

This quandary is a sign that more training in trauma-informed care is needed. The focus of the manager's statement shows that staff is still considering the tasks as punishments, and thinking that their power for change is found in their deterrent function. That is, the kids won't want to do the tasks so they will avoid that behavior. When you're thinking that way, you start to wonder whether the tasks are hard enough, significant enough for the bad behaviors. You become concerned when the kids seem to enjoy the tasks. You hear statements from other staff members (or even the children) like, "They did [X] ... and *that* is all they have to do?"

Let's step back a few steps. Remember the basic premise that symptoms are adaptations, that the children are doing the best they can, and they are doing these behaviors because they do not know any other way to handle their intolerable feelings. Therefore, in the Restorative Approach we respond to behavioral problems with tasks that are designed to help the child to learn new skills and to repair damaged relationships. An example:

Kayla has a difficult phone call with her mother. (A setback happens in the present.) Kayla does not trust relationships and cannot ask for help. She is already over-activated and is now completely lost in her stress response. She has no sense that anyone loves her and will care how this turns out. She feels pretty worthless anyway, and she knows this latest event is just one more sign of what a lousy person she is – and that's why her mother gave her up. She does not know how to notice, identify, or soothe her feelings. She cannot (yet!) hold onto the image or idea that several staff members care about her. So, Kayla is plunged into the depths of fear and hopelessness. Who wants to feel that way? So she does something, anything, to escape these feelings. She cuts herself. She throws a chair. She runs away. She hits a member of the staff.

So what Kayla needs to be able to handle a setback in a better way is:

- Relationships she can trust.
- A way to calm herself physically.
- A sense that people care about her, and the ability to remember them when they are not present.
- The knowledge that she is worth the air she breathes.
- Skills to identify and soothe her feelings.

When the team knows Kayla, they know the neglect, sexual abuse, and multiple placements she has experienced. They know her strengths in drama and her ability to teach younger children, and they know that mornings are hardest for her. They have a formulation, a theory about what is going on with her, and their primary theme in working with her is learning to trust others and ask for help.

So this is where the tasks come in. The tasks are a chance to *practice* some part of what she needs, to put one building block in her foundation of creating a competent self.

Kayla will act better when she feels better. After her blow-up she is feeling worse, more shame, more self-hatred. And that can send her into another acting out episode.

This perspective suggests possible tasks:

- Making amends helps strengthen relationships and teaches how to fix problems in relationships.
- Doing a task with a staff member is practicing trust and accepting help.
- Practicing effective action: when something goes wrong, Kayla can do something about it. She does not have to freeze.
- Practicing what to do when upset (a feelings chart, a poster to illustrate what Kayla was feeling or "Six Steps I Can Take" when she is angry, interviewing others, making a plan for her next contact with her mother, etc.) helps to develop feelings-management skills, and includes methods to create a calmer body.
- Doing something to make things better (chores, create a bulletin board, make brownies, helping a younger child with her homework) increase self worth.

The idea is to use the opportunity an episode provides to help give Kayla what she needs to handle life better. Kayla doesn't have to hate the tasks. She has to take them seriously and do them well. Then it's over, and she goes on, hopefully just that little bit closer to what she needs.

This understanding is the best response to feeling a need for "more tasks."

A Restorative Approach for Aggression?

In an in-depth email discussion about in-care challenges to the use of the Restorative Approach, Robert Davis, Psy.D., Director of the Brain Analysis and Neurodevelopment Center in Amherst, MA, the Perkins Neurotherapy Center, and Director of Clinical Services at Devereux shared the following case example (personal email correspondence Sept. 7, 2007 – Oct. 13, 2007), and has allowed its use here.

Everyone is talking about it – staff and children. Yesterday at school Aaron punched Charles, a staff member, and Charles has a black eye. The children are agitated, worried, and making fun of Charles. Aaron is bragging: "Yeah, I really showed him." The staff is furious. Charles is feeling helpless and humiliated.

It was during math class, and Aaron was being his usual loud, obstructive, insulting self. The teacher tried many times to redirect him. Finally, she called the crisis staff and asked that Aaron be removed from her classroom. Charles came and talked with Aaron, and he seemed to calm down a bit. He walked out with Charles, which did not require any physical intervention. But ten minutes later in the intervention room Aaron became agitated again, and hit Charles in the eye.

The worst part is, the staff is saying, that Aaron did the same thing two weeks ago. He hit another staff member, a friend of Charles.

Some of the staff talk includes rather pointed questions.

If Aaron had been more severely punished the first time, would that have resulted in his not hitting Charles this time? It is possible that if Aaron had a threat of jail, or parole, or had been somehow given more severe consequences, he would have been able to keep that in his mind during this incident and use it to help himself control his impulses. It is also possible that severe punishment would have left him more angry, more shameful, less connected, more hopeless and less able to feel any reason not to hit.

What about the fact that he seemed to calm down for ten minutes or so after his agitated behavior and prior to this hitting incident? Does that mean this was not a trauma-related emotional reaction? Should the fact that he appeared calm lead to his being held responsible for this incident in some different way? If the incident was emotion and trauma-based does it mean he should not be held accountable?

What about Charles? He is feeling pretty lousy now. Is he right to blame the administration for not punishing Aaron more the first time? How should he handle the children's teasing? How can he use what he is going through to understand Aaron better?

What about Aaron? If we had control of what happens next, what should it be? Should he leave the program? What interventions would contribute to his being less likely to hit again?

While a program may have to struggle with these questions, the most important thing is to have these discussions out loud, in team meetings, with openness to everyone's point of view. If the discussions are held in secret and outside the normal channels, resentment will build.

The episodes that tend to increase punitive responses from staff and produce more resistance to a trauma-informed response tend to be those in which:

- The client is physically large and imposing.
- The client has no documented trauma history.
- The client appears to have had a "good day" and was quite calm leading up to the moment of aggression.
- Staff members appeared to have avoided any actions that could have been misconstrued as a posture of intimidation towards the client (e.g., surrounding the client).
- The client boasts after the incident (often viewed by staff as a 'lack of remorse' and seemingly inviting 'power-over' responses from staff).
- The client was heard making threats earlier in the day/week (suggesting a planned attack rather than the client becoming overwhelmed in the moment by intolerable feelings).

- The client is gang-involved.
- The client assaulted an equal-sized or physically smaller female staff member.

It is difficult for providers to hold to a trauma-informed model of care when these types of emotion-heightening factors are present. How can providers inoculate treaters against the contagion of staff fear, anger, and/or silent wishes for retribution? What efficient mechanisms can teams use to regularly remind their staff of the role of shame in driving many incidents of disruptive behavior? How do providers avoid becoming complicit in over-relying on physically large, male crisis staff whom typically become, over time, the primary responders to aggressive incidents?

Children like Aaron do not change quickly, and it is not punishment that changes them. It is the long, slow process of experiencing trustworthy relationships. After Aaron had been at the program for six months, he began to form a bond with Michael, a staff member in his cottage. He and Michael shared a love of NASCAR racing. As they watched the races on TV together, Michael would comment on how the drivers reacted to adverse experiences, to what happened when they were aggressive, to the control and cooperation that was necessary for success. Michael and Aaron noticed the way the driver relied on the pit crew, and how important it was that the driver let his pit crew know when he began experiencing problems with his car. They developed a habit of calling Michael and the other staff "Aaron's pit crew." Michael supported Aaron in completing his restorative tasks for Charles, which included cleaning and organizing the Intervention Room. They knew they were making progress when Aaron burst into the unit one day after school and said, "I need your help, you guys. I am about ready to kill my teacher."

During this period it was important that Charles' feelings were acknowledged and validated. At first, he did not work directly with Aaron for a while. Then Michael deliberately reached out to include Charles in some of his events with Aaron. Charles even accompanied Michael to a basketball game

Aaron was playing in at another school. As Charles and Aaron began to know each other better a tentative relationship formed between them. At school, Aaron showed Charles a math test he had done well on, and thanked him for helping him to learn the math.

Treatment of severely traumatized children is not easy. All staff brings their own histories and values to the task. There are no easy or simple answers. Our best hope is to consider these questions as a team, and to openly discuss what actions we think are most likely to result in the child reducing their use of aggression.

An Example of the Use of Restorative Tasks: Trevor and His Restorative Experience

What staff heard on the grapevine Monday morning: a kid trashed Susan's office! He even broke her computer! Can you believe it?

Trevor worries about everything. He loves his mother, and his worrying may have started very early in life when he observed her being beaten by his biological father. His anxiety continued to mount as his mom's mental health problems caused her to have extreme, fluctuating moods, at times feel suicidal and need hospitalization, and often need a lot of help from others. Trevor blames himself whenever his mom is unhappy or having trouble. His stepfather tries to take care of Trevor, but his rigid standards result in him using "discipline" such as tying Trevor to the bed and stuffing socks in his mouth. Trevor worried when one of his brothers died from a congenital illness, and worried when another was placed out of the home. Trevor knows all these events happened to his family because he is a bad kid.

Trevor wants to be good. He tries to please everyone. Yet he gets so anxious so fast, and at age 14 he becomes completely overwhelmed by sudden changes, uncertainty, unpredictability, and things going wrong. The pressure in his mind is so intense that he resorts to behaviors such as head-banging, self-cutting, screaming, and physical agitation.

When another boy, Marvin, broke off the antenna of Trevor's new remote control car, the one his mother gave him on her most recent visit, it was more than Trevor could bear. Aside from being angry that the car wouldn't work and sure that it could never be fixed, Trevor believed that his mother would blame him for not taking better care of this expensive present. She spent her hard-earned money and already it was broken! It was just one more example of how he could never do anything right.

Trevor could not stand how horrible he felt, so he started screaming, and the staff was just making it worse by talking to him. Trevor ran off the unit and outside. As he was storming around the yard he noticed an office window that was open right over a porch roof. A refuge! He easily climbed up and got in the window, closed and locked it, and found himself in the secretary's office – but staff saw him! They couldn't get through the now-closed window, but they were knocking on the door and trying to unlock it.

Trevor knew that if they got in all sorts of horrible things would happen: people would yell at him, he'd be kicked out of the program, he'd have to go to jail, and he'd never see his family again … so he decided he had to barricade the door. He began moving furniture frantically towards the door. As he pushed the desk, the computer monitor fell off and broke. A whole lot of plants toppled over. The fax machine fell and shattered. When he moved the bookcase, lots of papers scattered around. But he kept pushing furniture towards the door – he had to make himself safe.

The staff became worried. They could not get the door open. The banging continued. And the sounds Trevor was making made them wonder if he was hurting himself, so they called the police for help. The staff was able to disable the lock, and with the police present, they opened the door, as Trevor moved some of the furniture so they could get in. The staff and police decided Trevor needed to go to the emergency room for evaluation since he was still making suicidal statements. The policeman told staff that he would call later about whether or not the treatment staff wanted to press charges.

A boy did major – in fact *very* major – property damage, and destroyed the office of someone staff all love. What should they do?

Susan was surprised when her boss met her at the door on Monday when she came in. He wanted to warn her before she opened her office door. And when she did, she was horrified. Who could have done this to her? And why? She was always nice to the clients and in fact she had had some pleasant conversations with *this* boy. Why would he target her? And all the work she was going to have to do to clean this up and restore order!

Susan was a little apprehensive when the team suggested that Trevor would need to work with her when he returned from the hospital. Would she even be safe with someone who could do all this? What on earth could she have him do? What should she say to him? Should she talk about what happened and her reactions or not? And besides, she was quite angry that he had caused all this devastation – and she wasn't at all sure she wanted to be around him.

Susan talked all these concerns over with the team. They validated her feelings and encouraged her to talk to Trevor about her reactions and listen to his experience of what had happened. She agreed to participate in the restorative process.

Meanwhile, the team also discussed whether it would be helpful to have Trevor arrested for the property damages he caused. For some boys, being arrested could provide a deterrent next time. Yet when the team talked it over, this did not seem to be the case for Trevor. His main problem was that he worries too much and gets overwhelmed by anxiety about all the ways he has disappointed everyone and all the bad things he knows will happen. Being on probation would probably make that anxiety worse, cause him more panic, and make it more necessary for him to do something to escape his horrible feelings. So the team decided not to press charges.

While Trevor was in the hospital he did not really want to come back to the program. He was so ashamed of what he had done he did not want to see any of the people who knew about it. He assumed they all hated him now; in fact he was surprised he was even allowed to come back. He was especially worried about seeing Susan, and said, "I thought she would yell at me."

Trevor was scared when he started working for Susan. She had him carry some heavy boxes of files to the downstairs storage area. He was proud of how much he could carry! He was afraid he would do it wrong but soon saw that he was actually helping her. The next day they started to re-pot all her plants. During this process they talked a little about what had happened. Susan told Trevor how upset she had been walking into that mess. He apologized and said he had just been so scared.

Susan now says that the experience of working with Trevor made a difference in how she thinks about this event. "I realized he was not attacking *me*. I could see he was just so scared. And it meant a lot to see how genuinely sorry he was. He even brought me back pictures from a trip he went on. I am not left with anger or fear. I don't feel like I am working with a bunch of dangerous kids. I feel sad about how scared Trevor is, and I hope we can help him feel better."

Trevor says that he liked working for Susan. In fact, he kept doing things for her and making her things long after the restorative tasks were over. When asked if he thought the fact that he liked doing the tasks would encourage him do something wrong again in order to be assigned new pleasurable tasks, he looked puzzled and couldn't get that concept. "Maybe it would work that way for some kids," he said, "but not for me. Not for me." When he imagined just being grounded instead of doing the restorative work, Trevor said, "Then I would still be worried and nervous around the staff, and especially Susan, and I'd still be feeling so bad about what I did. Now, I am friends with Susan."

Trevor is leaving the program soon and going to a therapeutic foster home. When asked if he thinks he has changed Trevor says, "Oh yes, now I can use some coping skills." What are those? "Art – I really like art. And music. I have a guitar now. And drama – did you see me in the last school play? And I am going to be Jack in the next one." What helped him most was "the staff – not the kids so much, although some kids helped me." He thinks that the kind of staff that help kids are the kind that "listen and don't get an attitude," although he does feel they should be "strict." And Trevor says that it has helped him that staff has been his friends – especially Susan.

Chapter Seven

The Role of the Clinician in Trauma-Informed Care

The Experience of the Clients

As they have traveled through the child welfare system, the children currently in congregate-care have often experienced many episodes of therapy. Often these therapeutic interventions have been short-lived, limited by funding sources, program design, the child's move, or the therapist leaving. The child may have been moved out of a specific therapeutic environment because the severity of the problems that brought him/her to treatment placed too large a demand on any mission and skill-related limitations imposed on the program and its therapists. In many cases the therapy is provided by interns or new therapists, and is not informed by knowledge of trauma. Children are placed on sticker charts, and caretakers award and take away points. The children may form strong relationships with some of these providers but the relationships do not endure.

By the time they are placed in congregate-care treatment (hospitals, residential facilities, day programs, special ed schools) the children can no longer best be helped through an outpatient therapy model. A delivery method in which the child has an appointment once a week at a set time will often not provide enough continuity for the child to truly heal. The goal of trauma-informed treatment is to help children create new templates of relationships, develop a calmer biological response, and learn emotion-management skills. A therapeutic milieu in which the therapist, childcare workers and other team members work closely together to assure that all aspects of interaction with the child contribute to healing will have the most power for change. The therapist must be embedded in the daily fabric of the program, often available to both the child and staff whenever he or she is needed. Within such a program, the therapist has a unique role as the leader of the child and family's treatment.

Characteristics of a Trauma-Informed Therapist

The most essential characteristic of a therapist who will succeed in a trauma-informed congregate-care treatment program is that *he or she likes the children and their families.* This quality probably cannot be taught. These children can be difficult, demanding, and try anyone's patience. If the therapist does not find them delightful, cannot see their goodness, does not look forward to being with them, he or she will have nothing to help get through the bad parts. The children generally feel hopeless. They do not see their own worth and cannot imagine a positive future for themselves. If the therapist cannot do that, who will? And at times the therapist holds the hope for the whole team. One role of the therapist is to see a picture of how this particular child would be at his or her best, even while remaining aware of the child's current reality. The therapist who genuinely cares about and appreciates the children and their families can do this.

A therapist in a congregate-care setting must be *flexible.* The day never turns out as one expects. Things rarely go as planned. It is time for an important family meeting – and the child is at the park. An individual session is scheduled but another child is threatening suicide. The therapist is going to do paperwork – and the licensing inspector drops in on her for an unscheduled visit. Roles shift between people. A child not scheduled to be seen for two more days needs to talk with him now. A person who needs a predictable day would not be happy in this setting.

Working with a therapeutic team is a unique experience. For some, it feels wonderful to have so much help and support. For others, it is difficult to have to share everything, discuss everything and make decisions within a group. The therapist who *enjoys teamwork* will be the most successful in congregate-care. Often the teamwork is frustrating. There are factions, problems, and disagreements. The therapist tells 26 people about something and the 27th complains that he wasn't told. Decisions are made and then not carried out. Interpersonal issues between team members can be intense. And yet the treatment team can be the most powerful intervention possible in helping a child to change. As the therapist struggles with the pain and difficulty of the work, it can be sustaining to have a team to share with. The team can laugh together, cry together, and care together about the clients. The therapist who flourishes working in this complex environment will have the ability to form relationships with other staff, will assume good intentions in fellow workers, will give and accept feedback, will handle disputes openly, and will notice and praise the positive efforts of others.

At this level of care, a therapist must be able to *tolerate chaos and intensity*. The symptoms that the children display are frightening and are often life-threatening. There is usually more than one child in crisis at once. The families too can be angry, demanding, sad, and scary. The systems around the child are often inadequate and frustrating. The therapist must know how to stay calm in the face of the agitation of others. He must prioritize and respond to the problems step by step. She must be able to tolerate strong emotions in the clients, and stay with the clients as they experience their pain, longing, anger and sadness.

In order to do this work, the therapist must have or develop *good self-care skills*. All therapists experience vicarious traumatization. The therapist must use the team to help them through difficult times. Outside of work the therapist needs strong supports and connections in order to maintain a work/life balance.

A *sense of humor* is crucial for surviving and thriving in these jobs. *Self-*

awareness is also essential. The therapist needs to notice her responses to individual children and families, and use these responses to deepen her work. He can seek out and accept help in this area from his supervisor and his team. She can monitor her vicarious traumatization and know when she needs a break.

There are many skills and much knowledge that a therapist should have, but most of them can be taught in supervision or through workshops and training. When the therapist is eager to learn and grow, the agency has merely to provide the opportunities. In addition, the therapist must know or learn *writing skills* and have the ability to *document* and do *treatment planning*. Of course, the therapist must be responsible, come in on time, and be self-motivated in completing the job requirements. Often, some on-call duties will be part of the job.

It would be wonderful if agencies had the ability to pay this paragon what she or he is worth!

Developing the New Therapist

Many therapists begin work in congregate-care settings immediately after leaving graduate school. Even if they have had previous experience, often they have not received crucial training.

First, the therapist must be trained to understand trauma. The new therapist should receive foundational trauma training. He will learn the prevalence of trauma, how it affects people, how it relates to their current presentation and symptoms, and how they can heal. She will be alerted to the effects of vicarious traumatization, how she can protect herself and maintain the best possible work/life balance. He can incorporate into his work the elements that promote vicarious *transformation* (Pearlman, 2009) such as clinical consultation, self-care, practices to examine the effects of the work, and a spirituality component.

The new therapist may need to learn how to present a case succinctly and with meaning, in such a way as to enable case consultation or advocacy for the needs of the client (see an outline in Appendix G).

Many therapists do not understand the art of *formulating* a case, a process described in detail later in this chapter. Through formulation a therapist can lead the team in focused treatment and provide guidance for decisions within the case.

The therapist can be given opportunities to learn trauma-specific treatments that are appropriate for the program population, such as Dialectical Behavioral Therapy (Linehan, 1993), Trauma-Focused Cognitive Behavioral Therapy, (Cohen, Mannarino, & Deblinger, 2006) and others. Also she can attend training on subjects such as suicide assessment, diagnosis, and other specific areas of interest.

A new therapist may have to be trained in trauma-informed treatment planning. The treatment plan reflects the therapist's theory about what went wrong for this child and what will be the steps in his healing.

Of course the therapist must be taught agency-specific policies and procedures.

Support from a good clinical supervisor will help the therapist develop further in areas such as self-awareness, sophistication of interventions, time management, and addressing vicarious traumatization.

The Therapist and the Team

Now that this incredible person has been hired and is receiving ongoing training, what should his or her job be?

The therapist is the leader of the Treatment Team. The therapist must be truly integrated within the team. Ideally his office will be on or near the living unit. Her physical presence helps with her availability in times of need. All unit management decisions, such as what the responses to behaviors will be, what the bedtime rituals will be, how parents will be welcomed into the program, and how hygiene issues will be handled, will be made by a leadership team consisting of unit administration, childcare supervisors and the therapist(s), and include consultation with the childcare workers.

The therapist is the flag-bearer for considering the "why" of behavior. Whenever the team is concerned about a child's actions, it is the therapist's job to ask, "How do we understand this behavior?" In time, all team members will ask that question before deciding on a response to the child's actions. The therapist must articulate the case formulation and lead the establishment of a treatment theme for each child. A treatment theme specifies the main issue a child is working on right now and becomes the organizing factor for all responses and interventions. Examples of treatment themes might be:

- Dahlia is working on learning to trust adults and take help.
- Joseph is working on noticing when he is first starting to get upset.
- Mark is working on asking adults for help.
- Jennifer is working on making friends.

The child and family are involved in establishing their treatment theme. Of course, the theme will change over time as the child grows and changes. The theme helps the team remember what is important and gives them a starting point in understanding the child's behavior.

The therapist shares information with the team. In congregate-care treatment programs the assumption, explained clearly to the child and family, is that the line of confidentiality is around the team, not the individual client-therapist relationship. Most of the child's issues and events are shared with the team. When a child does not want a particular item to be shared (for example, that he is discussing early sexual abuse in individual therapy), the child and therapist can create a less specific way the information can be communicated. Jamika and her therapist Alison, for example, could tell the team that Jamika is discussing some hard things from her past right now and may need their support. In general, though, the entire team may know the child's history, her goals, and her plans for the future (discharge plan).

The therapist must also communicate events that are scheduled – such as family therapy – and communicate stressors that the child is facing, such as having to go to court. Then the team can be most supportive to the child. Similarly, the therapist will seek out communication from the team about the child's behavior in various settings and receive observations they have made about the child. Communication will be open and constant, and mechanisms (such as log books) will be employed to make sure that every team member is in the loop. This is one of the larger parts of the therapist's responsibilities.

At times disputes arise between team members about how to respond to a given child. The therapist will need all his/her clinical skills to make sure these disputes are resolved openly and respectfully. The best resolution is one that is not just a compromise, but a synthesis of the wisdom of both points of view. For example, a childcare worker feels that the team is not being strict enough with Annette, and points out that Annette's threatening behavior is upsetting the other girls and disrupting the unit. The therapist understands that Annette is feeling powerless and scared, and thinks she is doing the best that she can. Both of these ideas are true. After a discussion, the team arrives at a response that will help Annette feel safer and more in-control while protecting the other girls. They concentrate on giving Annette other ways to be leader on the unit with staff monitoring. The outcomes of such discussions will be better than either the therapist or the childcare worker could have thought of alone.

The therapist is physically present on the unit as much as possible. If the therapist can greet the clients when they come in from school, she will be able to gauge which clients are upset or need extra help and take pro-active measures. These youth cannot generally sit and talk about their problems at a scheduled time in a therapist's office. However, if the therapist is nearby they can often take advantage of his presence to talk when they need to. If the therapist participates in fun events with the youth such as celebrations, trips, and everyday activities she will be building the relationships that are so necessary for the child's healing.

In times of crisis the therapist will also be present whenever possible. The therapist should not participate in imposing physical restraints on a child unless it is absolutely necessary for safety. But she can play a large role in helping the youth and the unit to calm down. He can be a resource for the other children who will be feeling unsettled by the crisis. She can also be a resource for the staff that are also unsettled. The therapist has a key role in decision-making in a crisis. Through an on-call system, a therapist can assist by phone in situations in which there is no therapist on grounds.

Restorative tasks that respond to behavior that hurts others *can* be assigned by childcare workers. However, they are more likely to be both meaningful and powerful for healing when the team, led by the therapist, has considered possible tasks in advance. In a Treatment Team meeting, the group can review how they understand the child's behavior, what needs he/she is trying to meet, and what skills the child would need to be able to meet those needs in a more positive way. They can then design some possible restorative tasks that will give him/her practice in these skills. Then, when the child displays the behaviors, the staff will have a starting point to figure out the current response.

The therapist also has a role in maintaining the morale and hope of the treatment team staff. He can notice when people are feeling discouraged and defeated, and work with the other managers to create restorative events and discussions. She can initiate discussions of vicarious traumatization on a regular basis, and after major events or when the team is under stress. At times the therapist must represent the hope of the team, the determination not to give up on a certain child.

Through sharing his knowledge and her thinking process, the therapist is a teacher for the staff. The therapist also educates the team on the workings of the child welfare and court systems. Many childcare staff go on for further schooling and themselves become therapists, often because of the inspiration of therapists they have known.

With strong resources and good planning, the program will have more than one therapist, and therefore the therapists will be able to offer crucial support to each other. Within congregate-care treatment settings there is a strong pressure for the therapist to be a 'fixer,' the person who takes away a screaming child and brings him or her back calm. The therapist is called upon to change the child's behaviors, preferably immediately. When a child is creating major difficulties for a unit and is the problem of the week, the therapist also often feels blamed and incompetent, just as the child does. Therapists can help each other withstand these pressures and remember their actual job of treatment. They can also provide concrete support for each other such as in shift coverage and ideas. Most importantly, they can share the pain and stress of the job and offer each other comfort, encouragement, and laughter.

Individual Therapy

Individual therapy is an essential part of trauma-related treatment. It is one place where the relationship between the therapist and the child is built. During these times when they meet as a duo and the child is calmer, the therapist and child can together explore the patterns in the child's experiences. As the therapist repetitively conveys that the child has reasons for their behavior, some of the child's shame starts to evaporate. The therapist and the youth can collaborate on figuring out how the child might better meet their needs. The therapist helps the child see the good in themselves through their unswerving regard for the child. As the therapist is trustworthy, kind, respectful, and caring the child begins to imagine new possibilities within relationships.

Yet many of the children are not able to sit with a therapist in an office. They imagine that such an experience involves going over everything they have done wrong and will only make them feel worse. They do not want to discuss their past because it will only bring them pain, and they blame themselves for everything that has gone wrong. They are scared to get close to this experience because they expect the therapist to leave (an occurrence they have been through many times), and they expect the therapist to reject them. Relationships and caring scare them. Being in a room with the door closed, facing an authority-figure adult scares a lot of them.

So the therapist must be flexible and creative to engage the child. Maybe the child never comes to the therapist's office. Instead, they go for walks together or play games together. Or the therapist talks briefly and frequently with the child on the unit. If the child seems uneasy about being alone with the therapist, the therapist encourages him to bring a friend. The therapist may offer art projects or cook with the child. The therapist does not insist that the child do things a certain way. Instead, the therapist meets the child where he or she is, and concentrates on helping the child feel safer and more connected.

One of the hardest demands of trauma-informed treatment in a congregate-care setting is that the therapist must focus on exploration before even mentioning change. There are so many pressures on the therapist to change this child and fast! But the fact is that hurrying to force change does not work.

Luis assaults people when he doesn't get his way. Latasha cuts herself so badly she sometimes needs to go to the Emergency Room. How can we stop these behaviors? That's why people pay programs the big money after all.

And there is plenty of external pressure for change: at every review someone is asking why that child hasn't changed yet. Her parents, too, have suffered enough and want to see something different soon.

Then there is the internal pressure. Therapists' lives would be a lot easier if these children would stop doing these crazy things. Therapists judge themselves: "Do I really know what I am doing? When Luis hit his teacher yesterday is it because I am not a good enough therapist? I feel guilty about the pain the teacher suffered." Staff can start to blame each other: "Isn't it the therapist's job to take an angry child to his office and bring him back calm and happy?"

When the therapist feels compassion for the child, he or she starts to feel even more urgent about change. Luis's life would be so much easier if he could control his anger. He is in danger of being kicked out of this place, as he has been out of his last six places. It is so painful to see the blood stream down Latasha's arm, and the alarm on the faces of the girls on the unit and the childcare staff.

In this urgency for change the therapists themselves feel powerless, vulnerable, and even incompetent. They feel much like the kids they serve. So, like the children, they may turn to something that they think will give them more power and control: punishment. Surely if the team restricts Luis long enough he will learn that his life goes better if he does not hit people. Or, being more enlightened, they think about rewards: "Maybe if I promise Latasha that I will take her out to lunch if she can go a week without cutting ..."

It would be astonishing if Luis didn't already know that his life would go better if he controls his anger. Look at all the bad things that have happened to him already: he is on probation, he has been kicked out of six placements, and he is in residential treatment, just to name a few. When Latasha is calm she fervently wants to stop cutting, and she hates her scars. She does not need more motivation – she needs more skills.

This very urgency we feel to change the children gets in the way of effective treatment. It makes it harder to stop and think about what is really going on. How does the therapist understand this behavior? What is actually happening when Luis hits someone? What leads up to Latasha's cutting? What problems are they trying to solve? How does this behavior help them in the moment?

The therapist needs to take time to explore, observe, think, and consider. She needs time to help the child feel safe enough to share their experience. They will be able to do this when they form strong relationships. In collaboration with the child the therapist will discover the meaning and function of the behavior.

Then, the therapist must consider what skills the child would need in order to choose a different behavior, a new way to meet his/her needs. It will take time for the child to learn these skills.

Luis eventually formed a close relationship with his therapist. After a while Luis shared how scared he was that he is such a bad kid that no one will ever take care of him or meet his needs. He said he has learned that force is the only way you get anything you want. Staff started looking for the first signs that Luis was agitated and asking if he needed anything. In small steps Luis learned to trust them enough to ask for help. It was important that at the same time Luis discovered a flair for cooking, and became the star student chef of the school café. He got a lot of praise and recognition for sharing his skill and was generally feeling better and calmer.

Latasha connected with her therapist slowly. They began looking at the patterns that led up to her cutting. After a while, they identified several factors: not getting enough sleep, fighting among the other girls on the unit, and not hearing from her mother. They worked out several strategies, including putting together a crisis kit containing calming music (via an mp3 player and ear buds), a piece of fur to rub, and a couple of pieces of honey-sweetened hard candy. Medication helped with her disturbed sleep. This approach did not always work, and she continued to cut herself for a long time, but the degree of self-harm decreased in frequency and severity. She started telling staff when she felt vulnerable.

Note that these children did not change quickly. They did not change because of punishment or reward. But with individual therapy, time, safety, and positive relationships they did change.

The real take-home message with these children is that the therapist must explore and validate the child's current coping strategies and behaviors before he or she makes any suggestions for change.

Some therapists can add to the possibilities for healing by developing skills in bodywork, meditation, EMDR, yoga, neurofeedback or other body-related interventions. (See Appendix H for brief descriptions of complementary therapies.) More and more data are showing the importance of including nonverbal strategies in the path towards health.

And then the therapist looks for small changes and highlights them for the child, his family, and the treatment team. Change is slow and comes as a result of much repetition. The therapist can be the person who holds the hope and the vision for healing.

Family Therapy

The children in congregate-care treatment programs come with all sorts of families. Many have involved, committed families. Some have no one in the world. In between are many other configurations: families whom have some contact with the child but are not a long-term resource; relatives who offer some relationship; siblings who are in other placements; former foster and adoptive homes; and other friends and connections. The job of the therapist and the team is to facilitate any potentially positive connections the child has in the outside world. This includes outreach to the families and helping them overcome any practical and psychological barriers that get in the way of their visiting their child (such as transportation).

It is important for the team to remember that the parents themselves are often trauma survivors. Their early years, too, were most likely characterized by attachment disruptions, neglect, and traumatic events such as domestic violence and/or sexual abuse. Often they have received no treatment and may not have even ever talked with anyone about their lives. As trauma survivors, they distrust people and do not expect relationships to be a source of help. Parents can be living with a feeling of danger and have difficulty relaxing. They may be currently living in unsafe situations. Their own upbringings may not have taught them emotion-management skills. They may not have any reliable connections they can call upon for sustenance, even when the person is not present. Since the parents often blame themselves for the problems in their lives, they may feel ashamed and expect others to reject them. And they may never have learned how to recognize, name, or modulate their own emotions. All these trauma symptoms make being a parent very difficult. They also make interacting with their child's treaters difficult.

The best therapists form strong alliances with the families of the children in their program. They acknowledge that the parent is an expert on their own experience and on their child's. If the parent is wary, unreliable, angry, or difficult, the therapist looks for the adaptation in the symptom. What is the parent experiencing? Have the program staff unwittingly blamed the parent or made them feel unwelcome? What needs is the parent meeting? How can the team help them meet that need without alienating the program staff?

The therapist tries to understand the parents' life and respect the difficulties they face. Transportation, childcare, multiple appointments, financial stress, and lack of support can all be real impediments to the parents' participation in the program.

Another way that therapists can help parents is to offer psycho-education groups on trauma, how it affects people, and how they can heal. If the group can include teaching the parents the skills that are being taught to the children, it will be doubly helpful. The parents will be able to use this information to understand both their own lives and those of their children. The groups will be most successful if they can include childcare and transportation.

In addition, the program can offer opportunities for the parent and child to have fun together and reclaim the joy of their relationship. For example, family meetings that involve just throwing a Nerf ball back and forth can help build the brains of both parent and child.

Group Therapy

Group therapy is a powerful intervention for all ages of children. It offers the primary reassurance of discovering that one is not alone, that others have had the same experiences and the same feelings.

There are many types of groups, and the therapist is limited only by his or her own creativity. Skills Training in social skills, self-soothing, emotion management, and mindfulness are especially valuable for trauma survivors. Dialectical Behavioral Therapy (Linehan, 1993) offers a tested curriculum for such a group. There are many other curricula in such areas as anger management and social skills development. These groups have less emphasis on the child relating their own experiences and feelings and more closely resemble a class.

Children can gain a lot from activity groups with the official purpose of cooking, or art, or drama, or music, or any of many other activities. Through these groups children can have fun (not easy for someone who lives with a sense of constant danger), learn to cooperate, develop skills, and gain a sense of self-worth. Any occasion in which the group can present their efforts to others for applause should be embraced. For example, a boys cooking group made lunch for the president of the organization. Both he and they enjoyed this event greatly, and it led to a further event of the boys cooking for the Board of Directors meeting.

Psycho-education groups about trauma are important for the youth as well as their parents. In addition, there are many trauma-specific treatment group curricula such as TARGET (Brom, Horenczyk, & Ford, 2009), The Trauma Recovery and Empowerment Model (Harris, 1998), and Seeking Safety (Najavits, 2001), among others. A therapist trained in these models can add depth to the treatment offered to the children and their families.

Another group that programs can offer at appropriate ages is Healthy Sexuality. A curriculum such as *From Streetwise to Sex Wise: Teaching Healthy Sexuality to High Risk Kids* (Brown, 2001) is an excellent guide. These youth have been exposed to many forms of unhealthy sexuality, and offering them accurate information and a chance to examine their values in sexual decision-making is an important part of their growth.

Finally the therapist and other members of the team can call the community together for a spontaneous group. This might be done when there has been an upsetting event, when there is news, when someone announces they are leaving, or when as issue has arisen that affects everyone. Staff may be afraid that talking directly about the issue will inflame the clients and make things worse, but quite the contrary is true. If you don't talk about something openly, the conversation goes underground. The youth can be surprisingly serious and articulate when given the opportunity to explore their reactions.

Case Management

In some systems, the therapist and the case manager are two separate jobs; in others, both roles are filled by the same person. In either case, the case management and the therapy need to be closely connected. The therapist/case manager is the advocate for the child and family, helping them to navigate through the often confusing and frustrating child welfare system. To be most effective in this role, the helper must understand the system himself. Relationships that the helper develops with key players will maximize the possible assistance for a child. The helper must weigh (with the help of the team) which battles are worth fighting, and understand when a decision cannot be changed. The helper advocates for careful and well-planned transitions that give the child some power and some time to adjust. She must be able to articulate a trauma-informed explanation of the child's behaviors, and use this understanding to recommend the most helpful services for the child. The helper also interprets events to the child honestly, giving him or her the most possible input. When possible the child should be assisted in keeping a record of the events of his life, such as in a Life Book or a Goodbye Book with pictures. The helper may also need to persuade other professionals not to give up on the child.

Treatment Planning and Paperwork

While every organization has its own unique documentation requirements, the basic structure is similar within all. When a child is admitted to a program, the therapist uses past records and referral documents to develop a master treatment plan. The program then does its own assessment, and modifies this plan according to its observations. The *master treatment plan* states the *problems* that have brought the child to this level of care, and then describes their opposite, the *goal* of treatment for this child and family. This goal describes the functioning which when attained would allow the child to be treated at a lower level of care. The *objectives* are specific, observable steps toward the goal. Through the objectives the therapist is articulating his/her theory about what is wrong and what the process to fix it will be. The objectives include the *methods and modalities to be used* to reach them, *estimated completion dates*, and *the person responsible*. The goals and objectives include all domains of life, including any medical issues that may be present. The *interventions* include all the multitudes of ways the program will address the problems, from therapy to sports to music lessons to diet to medications. These interventions also include specific skills-development through a curriculum-based group or other means. This treatment plan is reviewed on a regular schedule, and comments are added about whether progress is being made on the objectives and goals. The treatment plan is revised as objectives and goals are met, new problems appear, or the team decides not to focus on a particular identified problem, perhaps because another is taking precedence. Between Treatment Plan Reviews, progress notes by all team members document interventions, progress or the lack of it, and all relevant events.

One effective tool for trauma-informed treatment is the Individual Crisis Prevention and Management Plan (ICPMP). This document is filled out at the time of the child's admission to the program and revised frequently. It describes what sorts of situations tend to upset the child, the first signs the child is becoming agitated, what helps them in these times, and what does not help. In addition, it contains any necessary warning or risk factors the child has, such as medical problems that must be taken into account during a restraint, or psychological realities such as flashbacks. The ICPMP utilizes information from the child, the family, past treatment providers, and anyone else who knows the child. Filling out the ICPMP with his/her therapist helps the child begin the process of knowing himself, understanding what upsets him, and learning how to self-soothe. It may help the child to choose from an initial list of interventions that the program can do, as children often have no idea what helps them (see Appendix I for a sample ICPMP).

One useful mechanism is an Assessment Meeting at a prescribed time after admission – a month is a reasonable time for some longer-term treatment, but time frames vary by program; the time should be long enough for a child to settle in and learn the program's routine. At this meeting all team members plus the family and any engaged outside professionals gather to discuss the goals for this admission, the methods, and to share information. By this time the program team will have reviewed the material and be aware of questions. The therapist and the family present the child's history. At this meeting the therapist will have a beginning formulation of the case. By the end of the meeting, the entire team has an understanding of how the child came to be in this situation, what they plan to work on, and how they are going to do it. The child is also involved in the meeting if possible.

Formulation

Trauma-informed care depends on clinical thinking, that is, looking beneath the behavior of the moment, and asking, "Why? What's going on?" Its basis is understanding that symptoms are adaptations, that behavior has reasons, that people are doing the best they can, and that their behavior is solving a problem for them. The job of the clinicians in a treatment program is to be the standard bearers for clinical thinking, to teach and train the team until this sort of inquiry is second nature to all members of the team.

A formulation makes explicit the clinician's best understanding of the child's history, their current circumstances, the effects these factors have on the child, how the team understands the child's current behavior in light of their situation, and what the team thinks will be the best path for growth and change necessary to develop healthier methods for meeting needs. The formulation is typically one to two paragraphs that provide a clear road map for understanding and for treatment. The formulation evolves as the team understands the child and family better.

In the Germaine Lawrence program in Boston, for example, every time they talk about a child, they start with a quick repetition of the formulation by the clinician, just to remind them of their road map and where they are on it.

Here are some examples of formulations:

> 1. Sarah suffered early neglect and abuse followed by repeated moves. Her siblings were adopted but the adoptive parents asked for Sarah to be removed because they did not think they could handle her aggression and property destruction. She struggled to maintain safety by keeping her fears hidden in oppositional behavior. She sees danger everywhere and over-reacts with physical and verbal aggression. Her processing difficulties contribute to this misapprehension of events. She responds to caregivers with suspicion but does accept limits. She can be warm and funny and the staff connects with her in play. She will need to develop safety and trust in order to be able to relax, to explore her past, and to decrease her conviction that what has happened to her is her fault.
>
> 2. Vanessa had early experiences with severe neglect and witnessing domestic violence because of her mother's drug addiction. She learned to take care of herself, which taught her resourcefulness and skills such as cooking. The loss of several family members combined with mom's addiction and unavailability sent Vanessa and her sister into a crisis culminating in their removal from the home. The family seems to now be on a positive track as the mother is in recovery and the girls have made improvements. However

Vanessa understandably still has difficulty trusting her mother and other adults, and does not let adults help or guide her.

3. Steven is a bright and insightful child who has suffered immense abuse and neglect in his formative years. He was witness to horrendous domestic violence, substance abuse and sexual activity. Steven was often the caretaker of his brother and biological mother while his own needs went unmet. As a result, he learned that it was not safe to trust adults to care for him. Upon his adoption to the Anderson family, Steven struggled to adjust. His adoptive parents appeared to accept his need to be in control and for a while went along with his behavior. However, over the last two years, the relationship between Steven and his adoptive mother deteriorated. Ms. Anderson did not have much support in raising this difficult child. Steven is now unsure what relationship he wants with his mother or with any other adult.

The formulation articulates the therapist's theories, his understanding of what causes problem behaviors and what helps to heal them. The formulation leads directly to the treatment plan. In the treatment plan the therapist describes the problem behaviors, their positive opposites, the behaviors the team would like to see, and the steps to get there. The treatment plan, again, is the implementation of a theory: it makes concrete the understanding of the steps that would help a child heal. Thus if Sarah sees danger everywhere, what will help her is experiences of safety and trustworthy people, positive relationships, and developing skills to master her own emotions. These steps will be clear in her treatment plan.

If Vanessa cannot trust adults and use their help, what will change is small experiments in trust: using her leadership and self-care skill to accomplish things positive, trustworthy relationships, an understanding of her past and its effect on her, and developing emotion-management skills to withstand the fears she experiences when she begins to trust.

If Steven and his foster mother are locked in a painful cycle, what will help? The relationship between the therapist and Ms. Anderson may begin to meet some of her needs for support, allowing her to relax with Steven. Perhaps the therapist can help her connect with a parent support group. Structuring positive experiences between his adoptive mother and Steven may begin to rebuild their connection. These interventions would be clear in the treatment plan.

So the clinician's job is to gather information respectfully and understand the experience of the child and family, then to use that to develop a formulation. The formulation articulates what has happened, what is going on now, how these factors produce these behaviors, and what steps may help move the client and family towards more effective meeting of needs. Then, the clinician must convey this formulation to the entire treatment team, including the child and family (in understandable and respectful language).

Then, and perhaps even harder, the clinician's job is to keep the formulation alive. Whenever a new behavior happens, or the four-hundredth repetition of the old behavior, or an accomplishment, or something bewildering, the team must return to the formulation. Is this still how they understand this child and family? Do they need to adjust their thinking? How do the new events fit into their theories? Where does this understanding lead them? What new interventions are suggested?

Measuring Change

The Treatment Plan must also specify how the team will measure change. How will the team and the child know when the child is different? Some obvious measures are fewer episodes resulting in restraints, less self-harm, fewer run-away attempts, less aggression, and decreased property destruction. Other more subtle changes include improved interactions with others, ability to play independently with peers, ability to ask for help, and other positive behaviors. (See Appendix J for a sample trauma-informed treatment planning system.)

Support for the Therapist

If therapists are to be thoughtful, caring and responsive and able to manage their complex jobs, they need administrative support. They need excellent clinical supervision. Clinicians need weekly individual supervision that is trauma-informed, includes attention to counter-transference and vicarious trauma, and includes in-depth review of treatment. Participating in a weekly Treatment Team meeting with the childcare staff and the teachers allows an opportunity for clinicians to convey their understanding of the child and his/her behaviors, and to communicate and receive information efficiently. They also need time with other therapists (such as a weekly therapist meeting) where they can share dilemmas and receive suggestions and support. They need access to ongoing training of many sorts. They need opportunities to replenish themselves and their work. If the clinicians are expected to respond to emergencies and stay late as necessary, the agency can reciprocate by allowing them flexibility in work hours.

The therapists must have reasonable caseloads that allow time to think about their clients. At the congregate-care level, six-to-eight cases are a reasonable expectation for a clinician who also is responsible for family therapy and case management.

With this support, the clinical leadership gradually develops a more knowledgeable and sophisticated team, in which all the staff assume the child is doing the best they can, routinely wonder what is behind a behavior, and seek ways to help the child develop new skills. This thinking will produce more creative and caring intervention possibilities. And this trend will lead to more deep and lasting healing for the children and their families.

Clinical Administration

Many administrative structures have been tried by various agencies. These structures can be divided into two basic categories. In one method, there is an administrative line of reporting and responsibility for all the childcare workers and supervisors in the various programs; that line ultimately reports to one administrator (typically the Residential Director). And there is another administrative line for all the clinicians and clinical supervisors which reports to a different administrator (usually the Clinical Director).

However, there is a second method that has some advantages. In this structure, a clinician is the Coordinator of a given unit or program. Both the therapists and the childcare supervisors report to that clinician. There can be a Childcare Supervisor and possibly an Assistant Supervisor to whom the childcare workers report. The Supervisor then reports to the Coordinator.

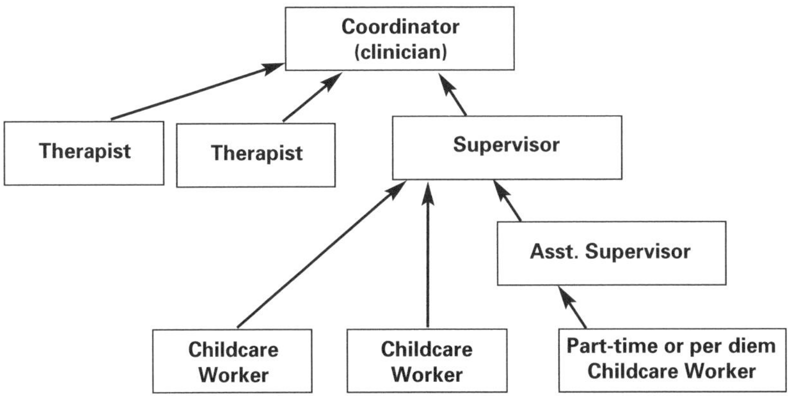

Therefore, this Coordinator is responsible for assuring that the team works smoothly together and that all team members have an active role in decision-making. The Coordinator is in charge of the treatment program of this unit. If there are disagreements between staff, he or she can make sure they are discussed openly and a mutually acceptable solution is reached. The Coordinator also monitors the compliance aspects of unit functioning, such as paperwork completion, cleanliness, proper supervision of the children, etc.

The Coordinator maintains constant vigilance to assure that the unit is providing trauma-informed care. He leads case discussions towards understanding symptoms and developing skills. She provides clinical supervision for therapists and for staff. He monitors progress of cases to ensure that they are proceeding toward discharge and that any difficulties are being addressed and communicated to the involved people. She encourages the unit in integrating sensory and bodily techniques as much as possible. He pays attention to the vicarious traumatization of his staff, and offers opportunities to discuss and address how the work is affecting staff. She pays attention to the needs and the development of the team, including promoting recognition and fun activities for team building. If possible, the team holds regular retreats.

The Coordinator is responsible for hiring and promotions, although the Unit Childcare Supervisor will also be central in hiring and promoting childcare workers. He oversees staff development. The Coordinator is also involved with staff or therapist performance issues, creating performance-improvement plans or progressive discipline when necessary. In the case of the childcare workers, this performance feedback is done through the Supervisor.

When necessary the Coordinator attends case meetings to support the team and advocate for the child and family. The Coordinator assures that families are welcome in the unit, and meets with families when any problems arise.

The Coordinator also uses data to evaluate treatment, including numbers of restraints and seclusions, staff turnover, and client treatment outcomes. The Coordinator is also involved with the administration of the entire agency, and is a conduit between unit and agency, acting as both an advocate for unit needs and as an administrative agent on the unit.

Chapter Eight

Trauma-Informed Care for the Family

One of the most significant reasons for treatment programs to move towards trauma-informed care is that it offers benefits for families. The method is easily applicable in a home setting, and provides healing experiences for both the child and the parents. For many years, professionals have recommended to parents that they create elaborate sticker charts with rewards for positive behaviors and punishments for transgressions. However, parents are rarely able to continue with these charts for more than a few weeks, as the method does not fit well into family life. The Restorative Approach offers an intervention that can be started while the child is in treatment and can then fit readily into family life after discharge.

Basic Principles of Working with Families

As discussed earlier, a basic premise of trauma-informed care is that children's contact with their families should never have to be earned. Programs tempted to use family visits as a reward to be earned by good behavior will find that this tactic is not helpful to the children or their families. The child's connection with their family is the greatest predictor of future success. There are usually many barriers to that relationship already, from the mundane realities of transportation, schedules, distance, and other children in the family needing childcare, to psychological issues and life problems. Treaters must not add more barriers; a child must be able to see his or her family whenever possible.

Of course, there may be safety issues that interfere with visitation. The child may be unsafe (unable to maintain emotional control in a triggering situation, and therefore likely to hurt himself or others), or suicidal in which case, the parent is welcome to visit on the grounds of the program. Or, the parent's behavior or home situation may be unsafe. In that case, again the parent can visit at the program, with supervision if necessary. When possible, the child can be brought to their home by a staff member who will stay with her. Programs can opt to provide warm, comfortable, private spaces where families can visit their children and have things there for them (and for any siblings) to do such as toys, books and games.

Of the basic principles of working with families in any treatment program, the first and foremost is respect. Too often the families have experienced blame and a judgmental attitude from treaters. The reality of their situations has been dismissed, and any difficulty in implementing the treaters' suggestions has been labeled as resistance.

Treaters can also help the family by paying attention to the siblings (if any). The siblings are also affected by the child's behaviors and placement. Some programs offer sibling groups. Inviting the siblings into family therapy and validating their experiences is important. The program may also provide fun activities for the child and their siblings, such as parties, celebrations and open house evenings. When possible the siblings can be invited into recreational activities. When the siblings are also in placement, considerable effort and the cooperation of other professionals is often necessary to enable sibling visits. All these efforts help the child maintain and strengthen the bonds with their siblings despite not living together.

An example of how a trauma-informed perspective can change the blame dynamic between staff and parents occurred in a day treatment program working with 10-year-old Joshua. His behavior was hard to manage and was causing program staff to tear out their hair. The staff had asked Jaquanda, Joshua' mother, to keep him from watching TV at home as a consequence for when he had a bad day in the program. They were angry and frustrated that she had not been following through with this requirement, and Joshua was still watching TV every night no matter how his behavior in the program had been. The staff felt that Jaquanda didn't care and was undermining their work. However, when they paid attention to Jaquanda's life they realized that she had two other younger children and a job as a nurse's aide at the hospital where she was on her feet all day. When she came home at night the last thing she could do was handle Joshua's running all over the apartment. She needed him and her other two children to watch TV so she could get dinner going. She had neither the time nor the energy for the fight that would start if she tried to stop Joshua from joining the other kids in front of the set.

When the staff understood Jaquanda's reality they could see that it was not lack of love or commitment that made her allow Joshua the TV. They were able to work more collaboratively with her to achieve their mutual goals for Joshua. They began letting Jaquanda know every time Joshua did anything good, however small. They invited Jaquanda and her children to have dinner with the program once a month. They included Jaquanda and her children in some play activities and donated various toys and games to the family. When the program staff created this more positive alliance with Jaquanda, Joshua's behavior began to improve.

Staff can remind each other to appreciate both the strengths and the struggles of the parents of the children under their (temporary) care.

Treatment programs must be safe places for families. Rather than strict visiting hours that limit the parents' access to their children, parents must be welcome at any time, even if it may create some inconvenience for the staff. Parents are always greeted warmly, and not just at admission meetings. They are included in what is going on. Parents feel that their views are actually appreciated by the staff. The staff are sensitive to how difficult it is for a parent to allow their children to be cared for by strangers, and at times to seem closer to these strangers than they are to their own parents.

One way to help parents feel welcome and included is to create opportunities for parents to share their skills with the group. A parent could cook a meal with the unit, teaching the youth some special dishes they know. Another parent could teach knitting. If a parent feels they have something to give, they will be more available to also learn.

Another way to help parents feel safe is to make sure they have reliable transportation to and from the program's facility. One mother did not attend her son's treatment review, although a cab had been arranged for her. Staff was angry at her lack of participation until they learned that the cab driver had told her he would take her the 45-minute ride to the program, but he would not be able to come back and get her and bring her home. She had other children coming home from school, so she chose to stay home.

It is essential that the program welcome any family members or caring others who are interested in this child (with appropriate permissions from the guardian). Children in treatment suffer from not having enough connections. It is very sad when you are 11 years old and the only people who care about you are professionals who are paid to do so. Families come in many forms, and programs also welcome different relatives, friends, former foster parents, pastors, teachers...whoever has a connection to that child.

The therapist can reach out to any known family and friends, invite them to visit the child, and help them overcome any barriers to such visits. Even when a person is not a placement resource for the child, they can still add something to the child's life.

Of course family members and visits may at times be disruptive. Just because a child becomes more agitated after a family visit does not mean that the visits are stopped, even though it might be more convenient for staff. It does not mean the family is harming the child. It may mean that it is hard for the child to say goodbye to them and have to stay in a treatment center. At times, either external mandates or staff observation will lead to a decision that visits must be supervised or otherwise supported. The goal is always to find some way that the child can have contact with people who love him.

When a parent is angry, disruptive or difficult, the therapist and the program staff examine this behavior with the same lens that is used for the children. How is this behavior adaptive? How do we understand this behavior? That perspective will lead them to possibilities for constructive intervention that will ultimately help the child.

Trauma Survivors as Parents

Once again, a crucial factor to remember when working with parents is that many of the parents of the children in treatment are themselves trauma survivors. Often they too experienced early neglect, abuse, and attachment disruptions. Many have never received any help; some have never even talked with anyone about their early trauma. Therefore, like their children, these family members have learned not to trust relationships. They relate to other people as a source of pain, not of comfort: they hurt you and then disappear. As a result of early and continuing trauma the parents may also have overly active nervous systems, an internal biology that experiences life as being full of constant danger. In addition, these adults may never have had reliable connections that live on in their minds and hearts. They may not be able to think of anyone who they can turn to for comfort and sustenance when times are hard.

Like their children, the families may blame themselves for the bad things that have happened to themselves and to their children. Their own understandable tendency in that direction has been given a push by the many professional and personal acquaintances that blame the parent for whatever is going wrong for the family and the child under care. And if the parents have experienced inconsistent and neglectful parenting themselves, they may have never have learned how to manage their own feelings, or to identify or modulate emotions.

How would these results of trauma affect being a parent?

Parenting brings you into contact with a lot of people: doctors, teachers, social workers, parents of your children's friends, and, in some cases, therapists and treatment providers. If your experience with relationships has mostly been painful, you will assume the worst of such people. You will be sure they are going to blame and dismiss you. If you are feeling defensive and scared of being mistreated, you may react with hostility and a difficult cycle begins. Furthermore, every parent needs help. Any parent can admit that they could not parent well without someone to call when the child has a fever to ask whether she should take the child to the doctor; someone to babysit; someone to pick the child up if the mother is sick; someone to share the concerns and the triumphs. If you cannot trust anyone and do not have good friends, parenting is a much harder job.

If your nervous system is over-active and you already feel constantly on edge, the crying of a baby can make you feel like you are going crazy. And if you already feel bad about yourself, you assume that the baby is crying because you are doing something wrong; if you were a better mother, surely you would know how to comfort them. This kind of thinking can start a quick downward spiral into despair.

Like their children, the parents can plummet quickly into intolerable feelings of despair, hopelessness, and fear. No one wants to feel this way, and so they do something to get away from these feelings. Unfortunately, the methods many people have learned to feel better immediately generally also result in long-term negative consequences.

So, for example, when 20-year-old Laura's two-year-old son Shawn is being defiant and resistant, she does not have a close friend or relative to tell her that this is normal and will pass. She already feels overwhelmed by other life stressors and Shawn's behavior is getting on her last nerve. Besides, Shawn's angry words remind Laura of when his father, Steve, used to hit her. Now she has another guy trying to rule her. Laura does not notice when she is beginning to be exasperated, and then all of the sudden she feels furious at Shawn. She wants to smack him, but knows she shouldn't. When she tells herself she is a terrible mother for even thinking such a thing, it just reminds her of her own mother, who always said she was no good. Laura feels that her life is ruined and it will always be bad. She reaches for a beer, then another, and gradually begins to feel calmer until she is finally able to sleep. Unfortunately she oversleeps the next morning and Shawn is already up wandering around outside when she wakes up.

Laura needs skills and support in order to be a good mother to Shawn. She needs trustworthy, non-judgmental relationships so that there is someone she has the courage to call when she is feeling overwhelmed. She needs to learn some concrete techniques other than self-medicating with alcohol for relaxing and soothing herself when life gets hard. She needs education about normal stages of child development. When she can begin to experience a feeling of competence in caring for her son, she will feel less despair and be able to give up the symptoms she needs now.

In offering help to parents, it is not enough for us to tell them to give the child a time-out or to help them establish sticker charts. The first, most essential thing we must do is to establish strong, trustworthy relationships with these parents. Like their children, the family members can only change within the context of a caring, reliable relationship. We can do this by constantly looking beneath their behavior to the frightened child inside. We can understand the parent's experiences in growing up and the legacy their childhood has left in them. When we convey that we understand that the parent is doing the best they can, and that we see their potential to do better, we help that parent feel safer and more relaxed, creating a climate in which learning and change are possible.

Helping parents incorporates the concepts of the brain's basic building blocks being formed in a child through attuned interaction with adults. Attuned interaction happens when parent and child are focused on one another, each affecting the other. E. Z. Tronick's (2005) "still face" studies have shown that when a child and parent are engaged in an attuned interaction, and then (at a signal from the experimenter) the parent freezes and becomes unresponsive, the baby's emotional stability immediately disintegrates. The baby may start crying and try other ways to re-engage the mother. Even the baby's posture and body tone deteriorates. Studies by Cohn, Campbell and Ross (1991) have shown a direct correlation between attuned play at six months of age and the child's attachment and relationship ability at 12 months. Through repeated attuned interactions, the baby's brain is built. Connections are formed between the sensory, feeling, thinking, and creative parts of the brain. Needs are perceived and met. Stress is calmed; difficulties are surmounted, all within the relationship. The need for attunement continues through all ages. Attuned relationships continue to be the main vehicle for growth and healing.

Attunement is also a major source of pleasure for both mother and child. It intensifies the bond between them and provides the fuel for handling the more difficult parts of parenting. Attuned interactions give both mother and child a sense of being good, competent, worthwhile, lovable people. With less time for attunement both can become more irritable and self-doubting.

If a parent has not received much attuned caretaking themselves it is more difficult for them to offer it to their child. In addition, attunement demands time and focus. If the parent is overwhelmed with life difficulties; if she is worried about getting enough food to eat; if he is sick, depressed or has other mental health problems; if she is in an abusive relationship; or if he is struggling with substance abuse, he or she will not be available to attune with the child. This lack of attuned attention has an impact on the brain development of the child, subjects the child to more unmanageable stress, and leaves the child with little assistance in meeting his or her needs.

Survivor Parenting as the Child Grows Up

It is also helpful to consider the unique challenges for trauma survivors as parents as their children achieve different developmental stages. A baby's complete dependence may terrify some mothers. The weakness and vulnerability of the baby may be uncomfortable for a survivor mother, because in her life vulnerability is associated with abuse. She may see the baby's actions as volitional, describing him as trying to manipulate her, or as always trying to get what he wants. She may feel she needs to toughen her up and not "give in" to her crying.

The defiance of a toddler can remind a mother of past abuse, especially if the child is a boy and reminds her of his abusive father (or of her own). In addition, the toddler stage begins the challenge of allowing the child to explore the world while also providing him/her a safe base. If the world has been a scary, dangerous place for the mother, she may keep the child close to her and not allow him/her the autonomy a child needs to grow. On the other hand, when the mother is overwhelmed with life demands, mental health issues, and/or substance abuse, she may give the child too much autonomy and not be present to provide safety.

As a child grows into the latency period, a parent is drawn into relationship with many others around her child's needs, primarily school personnel. When, due to trauma, the parents themselves had a difficult school history and have bad memories of school, it will be hard for them to interact positively with their child's teachers. They may assume that the teachers will be harsh and judgmental. Parents may feel inadequate in helping the child with homework or other school tasks. In addition, during the school ages the parent must continue to make many decisions about the child's safety and autonomy. Can the child have sleepovers at a friend's house? What media should the child watch? Can the child go to the park alone? The parents' experience of the world will of course influence these decisions and, in some cases, make them more difficult.

Parenting a child of any age is a very physical experience, as a parent must meet a child's bodily needs. A trauma survivor can be left with a complicated relationship with their own body, especially if sexual abuse or physical abuse is part of their history. Is my body my own? Is it worth caring for? Does my body exist mainly to meet the needs of others, despite what I may feel? Do I like being touched? Am I comfortable with the vulnerability necessary for self-care, such as being naked in a shower? All these complex feelings about one's physical self are activated by caring for a child's body, and by the intimacy and touching that are a part of parenting.

Teaching and modeling healthy sexuality are also a part of parenting, and also may be difficult for trauma survivors. Many parents never themselves received healthy messages about sexuality. In addition, early abuse may have interfered with developing ease and pleasure with their own sexual selves. A parent who has been sexually abused and never received any help may convey to their child that sex is a dangerous thing that people do to you and that you should try to avoid. In parenting either a boy or a girl, a parent will teach their own ideas of what a man or a woman is. Can a mother who was abused both as a child and as an adult teach her boy how to be a man who is strong and nonviolent? Can she teach her daughter to be positively assertive? Can a father protect and teach his daughter anything about sexuality other than to say no? Can a father speak openly about sexuality with a son despite his own experiences of sexual abuse, including accepting the possibility of his son's homosexuality?

These issues are all accentuated as the child becomes a teenager. In addition, the questions of autonomy and the decisions a parent must make become more difficult as the teenagers' scope widens. The questions around technology and social networks emerge with intensity at this time: how can a parent protect their child in the electronic arena? Protection demands vigilance, which is hard to maintain when facing other life pressures. In addition, the parent and child live in a society in which children are sexualized and pressured to consume. In the face of these demands, an overwhelmed parent may give up and withdraw from their child. A parent who themselves did not receive much guidance and support during their teenage years may wrongly conclude that their teenager no longer needs them. They may allow their child too much independence. On the other hand, a parent's past and current experiences of the world as a dangerous place may result in attempts to keep the child inside and safe. Taken to extremes this can result in rebellion by the teen.

It is essential to remember that in addition to reacting to internal models formed in childhood, the parent may also be accurately assessing the dangerous physical or electronic neighborhood in which the family lives.

Throughout all ages, parents who have had to handle adult tasks as a child may not know what is appropriate to expect from their child at various developmental stages. In addition, parents who have been disciplined harshly may not have models for effective discipline, may not know how to pick their battles, and may not have strategies for responding to behavioral problems. Boundaries between adults and children may have been confused in their homes, and they may have been involved in both adult problems and adult sexuality. Thus it will be hard for them to know what boundaries to set with their children.

One unique situation often encountered by treatment program staff is the parent who is in recovery and is trying to re-establish a relationship with their child. In these families, drug and/or alcohol abuse have resulted in the parent losing custody of the child. Often the child has had other bad experiences as a result of the parent's addiction, such as neglect, abuse, sexual abuse, and witnessing domestic violence. If the parent has achieved sobriety and is now trying to reunite with their child, the treater may have the task of helping to rebuild the relationship. The child is usually struggling with intense, ambivalent feelings of both love and anger. The child may be proud that the parent is turning her life around, yet worried whether she will sustain this change. The parent may feel such guilt that he is paralyzed in establishing effective parenting in the present. Discipline is difficult when you are feeling so worthless about what you have already put your child through. The goal for the treater is to facilitate the parent and child in speaking about as much of their experience as they possibly can at this point. Often both are afraid of talking about what is most real. The child may be afraid that if they speak their anger their mother will fall apart and relapse, or their father will become angry and relapse. The parent may avoid talking about the past because it is so painful. However, there is also often a tremendous amount of love and connection between them. If they can feel safe enough to share their deepest emotions with each other, they will be much stronger in solving the difficulties that face them.

When parents feel ashamed and inadequate because they have had to turn the care of their child over to strangers, they sometimes react by over-advocating. Although they are not able to care for their child at this time, they can be their child's watchdog. So parents may criticize the way the agency handles certain events, or disagree with general policies the agency observes. They may think the agency is too lax, not vigilant enough, or not strict enough, or in other ways inadequate. Agency staff can take this personally and become adversarial with the parent. Or, the parent and child who are estranged from one another may find the easiest way to feel connected is to join together in criticizing the agency. The staff then feels undermined by the parent. It is helpful when staff can remember what the parent may be feeling, how hard and scary and sad it is to have their child in the care of strangers, and how bad they may feel that they have not been able to be a good parent for their own child. In some cases the therapist may be able to acknowledge this reality with the parent. Through looking at the feelings beneath the actions, the parent and agency may be able to forge an alliance for the sake of the child.

Treatment programs may also be called upon to help families when children first disclose abuse. In this case, the trauma survivor parent's reactions are inevitably influenced by their own experiences revealing or keeping secret their own abuse. A mother herself may have been sexually abused, and is now learning that her daughter has been sexually abused: the one thing that she wanted never to happen to her child. If she told, and it did not go well, or if she kept her abuse secret, she may question why her daughter had to tell. Then there are the many real ramifications that may occur following a disclosure of abuse by a parent or step-parent, such as the mother's loss of relationship, physical help, and financial and emotional support. In addition the mother is likely to blame herself and question her judgment. In these situations, programs that primarily treat the child have to be especially vigilant not to get into an adversarial relationship with the mother. The treaters have to appreciate the intense and complex situation she faces and that it will take time for her to find her way forward. The program must offer her all the support and kindness they can.

Play and Joy

It is impossible to relax and play when you feel you are in danger. The over-sensitized, reactive nervous systems of both parents and children who are trauma survivors makes relaxation difficult and interferes with both sleep and with play. Thus, the parent and child miss some of the joy possible in their relationship. The joy of play strengthens the parent-child bond, and provides the energy to solve the problems of parenting. In addition, play is the major vehicle for children's learning. In play with their parent, children learn skills, social interactions, the concept of fairness, how to lose, how to win, and many other leisure skills. Therefore, one important role that treatment programs can fill is to facilitate play between child and parent. Instead of traditional family therapy, some families may benefit from a structured time to have fun together. Agencies can provide access to their recreational facilities. The therapist or childcare worker can participate and help assure that the interactions remain positive. In addition, agencies can regularly schedule fun activities for parents and children: parties, picnics, sporting events, and so on. They can also invite parents to participate in their children's recreation and field trips. One resource for learning more of the power of play and how to facilitate positive experiences between parent and child is Project Joy. Project Joy (www.projectjoy.com) is a grassroots nonprofit that uses the power of play to heal and strengthen children whose lives have been deeply impacted by trauma. Their mission is to ensure that nothing destroys the playfulness of children.

The Strengths of Trauma Survivors as Parents

Surviving trauma creates strengths as well as challenges for parents. Parents may have learned courage, resilience, and adaptability. They may have a keen ability to sense other people's emotions and needs. They may be self-reliant and strong. They may know where to find help and resources. They may have a deep sense of what they do *not* want to do as a parent. Their own history may result in their appreciating their child more deeply. It is important that treaters recognize and build upon these strengths. Identifying the positive results of difficult experiences can begin the slow process of transforming pain into growth, and creating a narrative of one's life. Sharing the positive aspect of a painful story with their children can help build appreciation and respect for all that the parent has accomplished.

Providing Effective Services for Parents

Recent discoveries about brain plasticity showing that brains can change and grow at any age offer hope for survivor parents as well as for their children. People of any age can change within caring, safe relationships. What can a program do to provide maximum effectiveness and healing for the parents with whom they work?

First, the program must collaborate with the parents and offer the families real choice. The essence of trauma is lack of control over one's own life. Programs must not duplicate that experience by being rigid in their expectations of parents. Rigidity would include specified inflexible visiting hours or meeting times, earned visitation requirements, blaming parents for not following the program's expectations, and cultural insensitivity.

Rigidity in a program is also characterized by treaters who are sure that they know what is best for a family and ignore, or don't solicit, the family's experience and knowledge. For example, the Johnson family has two children, Micayla and Torrence, in two separate treatment programs an hour's drive apart, plus twin two-year-olds, Frank and Francine, at home. Mrs.

Johnson is herself a trauma survivor who grew up both witnessing violence and being physically abused. Micayla's therapist has become aware of this background and is recommending that Mrs. Johnson seek therapy for herself before Micayla can start visits at home. Meanwhile Torrence's therapist is concerned that Mrs. Johnson is not attending all her weekly family therapy appointments with Torrence. And the state's caseworker has required that Mrs. Johnson attend parenting classes to help her with the twins. This treatment system is ignoring the fact that no parent could possibly attend all these appointments, raise a family, and hold down a job, much less learn anything from them. More change will be possible if all the involved systems hold a meeting together with Mrs. Johnson, ask her what she really needs, listen respectfully and do their best to provide it. Change will also be more likely if one central person forms a safe, lasting relationship with Mrs. Johnson through which all other requests can be filtered. This person can help her with both practical and psychological issues.

When programs are safe, collaborative, and respectful, it is possible for parents to grow and change. One powerful intervention is to provide the opportunity to connect with other parents. Through support groups, parents normalize their experiences and learn strategies. Parent groups help decrease the sense of isolation that is so pervasive for trauma survivors. Parents can also share strengths and resources, and become supports for each other.

It is helpful if programs provide specific information about normal child development and what to expect at different stages. Also, programs can teach strategies for behavior management, including the Restorative Approach. They can both help parents figure out how to respond to various dilemmas, and help parents explore what the behaviors evoke for them and what their own experience at their child's age was.

Psycho-education about trauma, its effects, and how people heal, can be helpful to parents on many levels. It can help them better understand their child's behaviors and not take them so personally. In addition, parents can use this information to better understand themselves and their own actions. When Michelle and her therapist reviewed the explanation of trauma provided in her daughter's treatment program, Michelle said: "I wish someone had known some of this and explained it to me when I was a child!"

When possible, it is helpful to teach parents specific emotion-management skills, which include identifying emotions, modulating them, and getting through difficult situations without making them worse. Again, this teaching can be done by having parents participate in programs, such as Behavioral Therapy skills groups (Linehan, 1993), that are teaching these skills to their children.

Any intervention that builds parents' self confidence will also help them be better parents. Such interventions can include recognizing progress they have made, allowing them opportunities to share their skills, and celebrating milestones. Parents could be involved in giving back to their community with their children, such as with food drives. Even more importantly, parents can be involved in an advisory group to the treatment program, be members of the Board of Directors, or participate in community systems improvement efforts. Having a real impact on the treatment system offers parents an opportunity to transform their pain into social action. And, of course, their voices are invaluable in designing effective programs.

Furthermore, participating in agency and systems management teaches parents the possibility of effective action. In their early experience of trauma children learn that no action is possible and there is nothing they can do to stop the abuse. With repeated abuse this assumption may generalize to all areas of life. Life happens. Feelings come and go. There is nothing I can do that makes any difference. Through offering opportunity for involvement, programs can teach parents how to act effectively and give parents experiences of success.

Families and the Restorative Approach

Programs using the Restorative Approach may want to develop a handout to be given to parents at admission that explains how they handle behavior problems in the program and why. Such an explanation may help decrease parents' confusion when programs decrease their reliance on consequences and implement restorative tasks. For years these parents have seen their children punished for misbehavior and have been encouraged to establish punishments themselves. Their own upbringing may have relied on punitive restrictions and physical punishment. They may understand that the child will make amends for harm caused, but often say, "And in addition, what will their consequences be?" Like many staff, the parents worry that their children are "getting away with" bad behavior, and wonder how the child will learn and change without experiencing negative results from harmful behaviors.

When the parents themselves are trauma survivors, that history may further complicate their reactions to the new approach. Perhaps a parent had to get through her own trauma by being silent and tough, and she feels that the program's "indulgence" will be harmful to her child. Their experience makes them feel that the child needs to just stop acting up and get strong, and they are afraid that an approach that they see as "too nice" is just unrealistic in this dangerous world. We must always remember that the parents are also doing the best they can out of their love for their child and their sense of the world.

In many cases the program staff will be able to help the parent create restorative responses to problems that occur in the family home. In doing so, they will give the parents a powerful tool that they can continue long after the child is discharged.

When a child is a ward of the state, or even if the state is involved in case supervision, the document explaining how the program handles difficult behaviors and why can be shared with their state worker, who may have many similar reactions to those of some parents. (See Appendix K for an example of an explanation of the Restorative Approach for parents and guardians.)

Crisis Planning

When a child is spending time at home or being discharged, crisis planning can be an important teaching tool. The crisis plan addresses the possibility of either the child or the parent experiencing a crisis and becoming emotionally dysregulated. It includes the factors and situations that tend to cause the person to be upset, the first signs, what can be done at that time, coping skills that help, what doesn't help, what to do if the crisis becomes worse, and people to call. The plan is developed collaboratively between the child and parent whenever possible, and with support from program staff. It is a living document that is revised and updated as events demonstrate what works and what does not. The value of a crisis plan is not just to help in this weekend's crisis. As it is examined, modified, implemented, and changed again, the process teaches both the parent and child how to manage their emotions. (See Appendix L for an example of a Crisis Prevention and Management Plan.)

Summary

Most of the parents of children in treatment programs are themselves trauma survivors. Therefore more effective change will be possible if family interventions are planned using trauma-informed thinking. The program must be as safe and welcoming for the families as it is for the children. Relationships are the most effective source of healing, so every effort is made to form a strong alliance with the family through understanding and respecting the realities of their lives, being flexible and thoughtful, and celebrating their strengths. All people who care about the child in care are invited into the treatment (when safe), and the program offers practical help to overcome barriers to the family's participation. The child's contact with family never has to be earned. All behaviors by parents are the parents' best way of meeting their needs in the moment. All behaviors are adaptive.

Before deciding how to respond to a problem with a parent, treaters must ask: "How do we understand this behavior? What needs is this person trying to meet?" Staff can then consider how they could help the parent meet those needs in a more positive way. The therapist can help the parent do two crucial tasks: to look at their own experiences as much as possible and how that history may be affecting their current parenting; and to open an honest discussion with their child. Through participating in their child's treatment, the parent can learn the effects of trauma and feelings-management skills. Through being part of the agency programming and management, the parent can build self-worth and offer valuable opinions. Through forming connections with staff, learning skills, and strengthening their connection with their child, true and lasting healing can take place for parents. (See Appendix M for an evaluation scale for use in examining the effectiveness of services for parents.)

Chapter Nine

Trauma-Informed Foster Care

Implementing trauma-informed care in foster care programs presents unique challenges. Foster parents are a precious resource in our child welfare system. They offer traumatized children what they need most: a loving family. The best thing that could happen to a child who has been wounded is to live with a family that loves him, accepts him, and sticks with him. Foster parents come into their role from all walks of life and for every possible reason. Every family constellation is represented. Some foster parents are relatives of the child, or have known her in some previous capacity. Many have experienced their own traumas and see providing foster care as their way to give back.

Being a foster parent to a trauma-surviving child is quite different from being a staff member in a treatment facility. A foster parent is in her own home, and may or may not have immediate backup. Other members of the immediate family, such as a partner or the biological children, may be present. The foster parents are trying to integrate the child into their actual life, their extended family, their neighborhood, and their favorite activities.

Childcare staff in treatment programs are taught a method of interacting with children – the Restorative Approach, using trauma-informed treatment principles – that is significantly counter-intuitive, and is usually completely unlike the way they were raised. But they have a team, other workers, treatment professionals and policies to help them maintain these strange practices. Foster parents do not have any of these supports readily available. Instead, they have a chorus of extended family members and friends telling them they should be stricter and not let the child get away with so much. It is much harder to change one's style of parenting in one's own home where one may have successfully raised one's own children.

The most important gift that a foster family can give a child is permanency. The children are damaged by disrupted attachments and being moved over and over again. The education and support that agencies give foster parents is primarily aimed at increasing their stamina to *stick with the child.* Keeping these children is often very difficult, as they put the family through such extreme behaviors, based on their own prior experiences of relationships. Yet the foster parent has the most power to heal the child, by helping the child to experience pleasure and associate it with other people; and by building the child's brain through rhythmic, repetitive, rewarding activities.

One of the most powerful determinants of how a family responds to behaviors is how they define them. For example, Natalie, age 12, has severe difficulties at bedtime. When she was placed with the Bruce family, they defined her bedtime behaviors as defiance. They had told her to turn out her light and go to sleep, and she kept getting up. The Bruce's case manager asked them to sit in her room, read her a story, and talk with her, and to give her a nightlight. Mrs. Bruce thought this was just being too indulgent; she would never let one of her own kids get away with this defiance. Did Natalie have no respect for her? Besides, Mrs. Bruce said, she could tell that Natalie was enjoying her presence in her room. This coddling was just rewarding bad behavior. The placement disrupted.

Then Natalie was placed with a single mother, Mrs. Harris. She immediately connected Natalie's bedtime behavior with her having been abused and left alone. She started using music to help Natalie fall asleep, and gave her a nightlight. They developed a bedtime ritual they both enjoyed, which included reading a book and then singing a good night song to each other. These interventions did not make everything perfect, and there were still many other behaviors to deal with, but Natalie gradually began going to sleep more easily.

When agencies train foster parents in understanding trauma, how it affects children, how it relates to their current behaviors, and how they can heal, they offer a new framework for explaining their foster child's behavior. The theory helps them not to take the behaviors so personally. The training must stress that these behaviors are adaptive and reflect what has happened to the child. The child is doing the best she can, and will do better when she is happier, feels seen, heard and connected, and when she feels safer. All training efforts are directed towards this end. (See Appendix N for a tool for assessing trauma-informed foster homes.)

Trauma Training for Foster Parents

There are usually two types of training offered to foster parents. In prelicensing training, offered to parents before children are placed in their home, parents are still in a decision-making period. With all that they learn about the type of children that are in foster care, do they still want to take on this role? Many agencies used a standard training curriculum for this pre-service training, such as the Parent Resources for Information, Development and Education (PRIDE) curriculum (http://www.cwla.org/programs/trieschman/pride.htm). It is possible to weave information about trauma into this curriculum.

Secondly, most states require some amount of ongoing training for foster parents after children are placed with them. The number of hours per year differs between states and programs, and is typically higher for the therapeutic level of foster care. This is an area where training can focus on understanding trauma.

In designing training it is essential that the foster parents and the social workers who support them receive the same training. The parents may learn something from the formal training, but its real impact will be when the caseworkers use the concepts in the moment to understand the behavior of an actual child.

In the best-case scenario, foster parents are invited and welcomed and encouraged to attend any trauma training that the agency offers its staff. However, certain revisions may make the training more accessible to foster parents.

The practical considerations of the training must be designed to make it possible for the parents to attend: providing daycare and transportation, offering food, and holding the training on a schedule that fits into the lives of people who are working and caring for children. An evening supper meeting once a month for 2-3 hours may work. Having the dates for the year scheduled in advance helps the foster parents plan.

Foster parents (and actually almost everyone else) respond best to training that is concrete, practical, and does not contain long lectures on theory. Good training includes multi-media presentations, small group activities, applications to the children they know, and much discussion. Remember, the goal of the training is to change the parents' definition of the child's difficult behaviors. When the training is successful, the next time their own foster child is being particularly non-compliant, the parent will remember that this may be more about the child's past than about her. She or he will be able to consider what needs the child is meeting and what he may be afraid of. This reframing of the behavior will enable the parent to be flexible and collaborative in solving the problem. It will also help Mom or Dad find the patience for the long process of change.

Like childcare staff, foster parents are concerned that understanding the results of trauma will lead to giving the child an excuse for not attempting to change their behavior. Instead, the theory can provide more effective methods to change their behavior. Foster parents may emphasize that the child needs to take responsibility for his behavior. The training can help the parent understand that the child's deep hopelessness and shame make that difficult, but that as the child feels happier and safer she will become more able to look at her own actions.

Handling Problem Behaviors in Foster Care

Like all staff, foster parents come to their role with experience and ideas relating to handling children's problem behaviors. These ideas have evolved from how they were raised and how they have raised their own children. With a little flexibility, a wide range of parenting styles can accommodate trauma-informed foster parenting. Foster care support staff does not need to focus their energy on persuading parents not to ground or restrict a child. As long as the disciplinary response is not too excessive or punitive, it probably will not hurt the child. Foster program staff trained in trauma-informed care focus their efforts in two main areas: enhancing the relationship between the foster parent and the child, and changing how the foster parent understands the behavior. These two intertwined efforts together will contribute to the overriding goal: increasing permanence.

Enhancing the Parent-Child Relationship

The relationship is the most powerful tool that the foster parent has to change the child. The program must use every possible means to strengthen and celebrate these relationships. One way the caseworker can be particularly helpful is by pointing out any evidence he sees of the child's connection to the foster parent. The parent may miss these initial subtle signs in the midst of all the chaos. Also, the foster parent can be taught that it is just when the child feels most close to them that the child also feels most vulnerable and scared. It helps if the parent expects some acting up when she has been particularly close to the child. She can see that behavior not as a rejection of her but instead the child's fear of getting his hopes up and being disappointed again. The case- worker can suggest specific activities the child and parent can do together to strengthen their bond. She can also help by sharing with the parent what she knows about the child.

The program can also help with the relationships by offering positive events for groups of the foster children and parents of one agency, such as picnics, trips, ceremonies, holiday parties, etc. These events have the dual purpose of enhancing both the particular foster parent-child bond and creating a community of children and parents who are connected to each other and to the program. They are then more able to turn to each other for help in difficult times. It is also good when the program can make funds available for the parent and child to enjoy special fun activities together.

Changing the Understanding of the Behavior

As mentioned above, changing the way a behavior is defined has a powerful effect in changing the way it is approached. The concept that symptoms are adaptations is one of the most useful things foster parents can learn. When a parent understands that a child is doing the best they can to meet their needs, then they can approach a problem by trying to understand the child's needs, and by wondering what the child has to learn in order to meet their needs in a less harmful way.

Response to Behavior that Hurts Others

Many foster parents find the concept of *making amends* useful. When the child hurts someone in the family, or disrupts the whole family, what can he or she do to make that person's life better? It is sometimes difficult to understand that this task is not a punishment; it is a way to teach the child how you mend relationships that have been torn. Therefore, it does not have to be aversive or unpleasant for the child. If the child broke something, can he mend it? If she kept everyone up late, can she cook dinner? Can he do an extra chore (such as making breakfast or tidying up the bathroom) to allow mom a little extra sleep? Oftentimes the making-amends tasks are not as major as the behaviors the child did, but they are a token of reconciliation. It is probably not a good idea to require the child to apologize. If the child is sorry, he or she may do so spontaneously; otherwise the parent/foster-parent would be ordering the child to lie. Remember that whether or not he or she shows it, the child will be experiencing this problem behavior as one more piece of evidence of how horrible he or she is. He will be expecting to be kicked out of the foster home. So concrete tasks that allow him to contribute also may help build his self-esteem by a small but incremental amount. Encourage foster parents to try this approach, to see how it fits for their family, and report back to the group. If some parents see that this approach works for others, they may try it. (See Appendix O for Guidelines for Behavior Management in the Home.)

Interactions with Biological Family

In any gathering of foster families, the subject of the children's contact with their biological families always starts an emotional discussion. Foster families are being asked to co-parent with their child's biological family. This hard work brings up so many emotions for all parties. The foster parent may experience the child being disappointed by planned visits that do not happen, or visits that happen but do not go well. The foster parent is left to manage all the behaviors that result from the child's experience. The child may fear that as she starts to like the foster parent she is being disloyal to her biological parent, and some biological parents explicitly convey this belief. It is very hard for a biological parent to know how to react to the mother who is doing what she could not do: parenting her child. Her guilt and sadness may lead her to be overly critical or demanding. The biological parent is very likely a trauma survivor herself, and struggling with the same issues of shame, physical dysregulation, and distrust that her child exhibits. It is a complex emotional nexus for all.

The most important thing a support worker can do is not attempt to fix or dismiss the feelings, but to validate how difficult and painful the whole situation is for everyone involved. Whenever possible encourage the people to talk about what they are feeling, preferably together, as much as they can. And don't try to make it better. Acknowledge. Validate. People can find extraordinary reservoirs of strength and patience when they are understood and appreciated.

It is important to note that the foster parents' biological family also plays a role in this intricate dynamic. If the foster family has biological children, the relationship between them and the foster children can be complex. The foster child inevitably feels like a second-class citizen, and the agency workers are alert for anything that reinforces that perception. For example, in one family the foster children called the mother "Miss Noreen" while of course her own three daughters called her "Mom." The foster children's jealousy of the bio children can be acted out in various ways, some of which are dangerous for the bio children. This dynamic is one of the primary causes of placement disruption. A parent cannot stand by and see their children hurt. Some parents worry that just the time and attention they give to the foster child combined with the chaos that has come to their home will hurt their own children. Siblings of foster children do report resenting their foster brothers and sisters, and many also report that they learned and grew from the experience. A child learns compassion, generosity, and giving from having a foster child join their home, and may form a rewarding and pleasurable relationship.

The foster parents' own parents and extended family can be a source of stress or support or both. Foster parents report feeling isolated from family and friends, as no one understands why they do this difficult work or why they "let the child get away with" such strange behavior. In this regard, their experience replicates that of their foster children. The agency can help by welcoming all extended family into both the training and the celebratory events, and once again by validating the reactions of all.

Role of Agency Support

The social workers (or case workers) in a therapeutic foster care agency have a crucial role in increasing the likelihood of successful placements. From initial screening and training, through careful matching, through obtaining and coordinating services, through responding to crises, to thoughtful and conscientious discharge planning, the worker is a central resource for both the parents and the child. Agencies utilize various divisions of labor, and if one worker is primarily the parent support and another the child support, it is essential that they communicate constantly and both give the same message.

The first step is to make sure all staff is trained in the effects of trauma, how they relate to the child's current behavior, and how the child can heal. It will also be helpful if they can attend the training when it is offered to the foster parents, so that they can enhance the training with specific examples known to the parents. But this training is just the beginning of the work.

When the foster parent calls to discuss how to respond to a behavior, whether it is an emergency or an everyday matter, the worker first asks how the foster parent understands this behavior. What need is the child trying to meet? Can they figure this out, by noticing when the behavior happens and when it doesn't, what the child says, what they know about his history, and what in fact actually happens as a result of the behavior? If they understand the meaning of the behavior they will have many more options about how to respond.

For example, Mrs. Grayson called her worker Lenny because she was exasperated by the mean things Joseph said to her following every visit with his biological mother. She assumed his mother was putting these ideas in his head. Since the visits were supervised, Lenny checked with the state worker who assured him that nothing had been said about the foster mother. The conversations had been about the progress the mother was making on her issues and how she hoped she would be able to get Joseph back soon. So Lenny and Mrs. Grayson considered other possibilities. From some other comments Joseph had made, Mrs. Grayson began to speculate that when Joseph saw his mother and she talked about his returning to her, his growing affection for Mrs. Grayson seemed to him to be disloyal. Maybe at times he even found himself wishing he did not have to return to his mother because he appreciated the regular food and peaceful home he had with Mrs. Grayson. He immediately hated himself for these thoughts. This conflict was particularly intense after a visit, and he hated Mrs. Grayson for "keeping me from my mom … and making me like her."

In a traditional parenting model, Mrs. Grayson would punish Joseph for the mean and inappropriate things he said to her, and would no doubt include a lecture about how Joseph should not treat people this way or he will never get anywhere in life. This would do nothing to strengthen their relationship and would confirm Joseph's negative ideas about himself. He would be more alone and confused than ever and probably would lash out more.

What if instead, after Lenny and Mrs. Grayson talked, she gently brought the subject up with Joseph at a time far from a visit. She could say, "You know Joseph, I have been thinking about how hard it must be for you to see your mother and then come back and live here. I know you love your mother and hope she is getting better. I know that it is hard to be here and wonder how she is doing." Maybe Joseph would take that opening, maybe not. But he will hear it. If he is able to tolerate a conversation, Mrs. Grayson could mention that many people love more than one mother, and give some examples from people they both know. She could ask him what would be best for him when he first gets back – being alone, some cocoa, a game of basketball with her older son? Of course, even if they make such a plan there is no guarantee that Joseph will do it the first or even the seventh time. But Joseph will notice this kind of validation. And he will be a little less alone in the world.

The support worker has a crucial role in changing the conversation and thus the response.

The agency can also offer practical supports such as respite care to get foster families through bad periods. And they constantly point out and celebrate any relationship gains that are made.

Vicarious Traumatization

At a recent foster parent training Lillian responded to the discussion about vicarious traumatization. "I've been a foster parent for sixteen years" she said. "And this is the first time anyone has ever asked me how the work is affecting **me**." This discussion rapidly expanded to descriptions of being unable to sleep, of agonizing when children ran away, to the heartache of biological families, to worry about bio kids, to isolation from family and friends, to never being able to do anything fun.

Just as treaters are negatively affected by work with trauma survivors, so are foster parents. They experience intimately the pain of their children's lives and the symptoms that express it. Vicarious traumatization can affect all aspects of the foster parents' life: their sense of safety, their spirituality, their sense of hope, their physical selves, their sexuality, their ability to have fun and play. Vicarious traumatization (VT) is not the fault of the client, and it is not a sign of weakness in the foster parent. It is an inevitable part of caring for a traumatized child.

Agencies have a crucial role to play in combating VT. First, they can offer the parents concrete help, such as respite care for a weekend off. Activities and programs for the child can decrease the pressure on the parent. Support groups can be meaningful if conveniently scheduled for the parents. Anything the agency can do that allows the parents to continue their own personal interests and enjoyments will help prolong the placements.

The antidote to vicarious trauma is connection. It is meaningful to foster parents to hear this concept named, explained, and normalized. The discussion also includes a focus on the benefits and personal growth the foster parents have experienced from doing the work. Learning that other parents have the same reactions helps the parent not feel so alone or so crazy. Some aspect of how the work affects the parents as people is included in every training event offered.

The Contingent Life

Things were not going well in the Morris home. The parents were arguing and there was talk of Mr. Morris moving out. Mrs. Morris was crying a lot and staying in bed all day on some days. The agency was wondering if they should remove the two foster children placed there, Lisa and Danny. The social worker, Mark, was talking to Lisa. "How is this all affecting you, Lisa?"

"It isn't. I don't care about these people. I just live there."

"Well, Lisa that isn't quite true. You have been there for nine months; I know you have had some great times with Mrs. Morris. It must be hard to see her so sad."

"No it isn't, and I don't know why you keep saying these things. I just stay in my room. I do not care at all. I have my homework to do. I am trying to get on the honor roll."

Two days later Mark got a call from Mrs. Morris. They had to come get the children right away. Mr. Morris had threatened her last night and the police were called. It was no longer safe for the children to be there.

On the way to the Morris home Mark thought about what Lisa had said. At the time, he had been trying to get her to admit she cared. But now he thinks that Lisa knew the right strategy after all.

In working with foster children, staff might imagine what it is like to live a contingent life, a life in which at any time you might have to pack up and leave your home. And you cannot predict what will cause this displacement. It might be something you do – but maybe not the worst thing you do, but just the thing that particularly upsets this foster mother. Or it may have nothing to do with you. You will often be blamed and you certainly blame yourself. But there you are again, another new home, new community, new school, but the same old self.

What would be the best emotional strategy in this life? It certainly would not be to form intense emotional connections quickly with these foster parents. It might not even be to unpack your bags. It might be to close up deep inside yourself and watch.

The more that both the staff and the foster parents can deeply empathize with this experience, the more they can validate all of the child's actions, and have the patience to stay with them long enough to create a different experience.

Summary:

Understanding trauma can be a powerful tool for foster parents. If foster parents attend training that covers how trauma affects children, the biological changes, the skills children need to learn, the concepts of symptoms as adaptations and what children need to heal, they will understand the child's behavior in a new way. They will be less likely to interpret the behavior as defiance to take it personally. This helps the foster parent to keep the child. Anything that the foster parent and the team supporting them can do to enhance the relationship between child and parent will increase the child's healing.

One stressful part of the relationship is interaction with the biological family. The support worker can assist by encouraging every person to talk about their experience and by validating their complex emotions. Agency support is also crucial in managing difficult behaviors by defining symptoms as adaptations and by figuring out what need the child is meeting and helping them to meet that need in a more positive way. Vicarious traumatization is an inevitable part of being a foster parent. Agencies can help by teaching foster parents about this concept, giving them opportunities to talk about it, and by helping them to care for themselves and each other. All parties will be more compassionate when they imagine for themselves what it is like to live a life that can be disrupted at any time.

Chapter Ten

The Trauma-Informed Agency

The Perils of the Traumatized Agency

Sandra Bloom has been a leader in describing how organizations, themselves living systems, can experience trauma and demonstrate trauma symptoms, which, if unnoticed and unaddressed, can destroy the organization. In her 2006 paper for the National Association of State Mental Health Directors, Dr. Bloom explains the parallel between the effects of trauma on the clients, the staff and the organization as a whole.

Just as clients have developed their feelings and difficult survival and emotional adaptations in response to trauma, so do staff who work in "chronically stressed organizations." Bloom continues:

> Likewise, in chronically stressed organizations, individual staff members – many of whom have a past history of exposure to traumatic and abusive experiences – do not feel particularly *safe* with their clients, with management, or even with each other. They are chronically frustrated and *angry*, and their feelings may be vented on the clients and emerge as escalations in punitive measures and humiliating confrontations. They feel *helpless* in the face of the enormity of

the problems confronting them in the form of their clients, their own individual problems, and the pressures for better performance from management. As they become increasingly stressed, the measures they take to "treat" the clients tend to backfire and they become *hopeless* about the capacity for either the clients or the organization to change. The escalating levels of uncertainty, danger, and threat that seem to originate on the one hand from the clients, and on the other hand from "the system" create in the staff a chronic level of *hyperarousal* as the environment becomes increasingly crisis-oriented. Members of the staff who are most disturbed by the hyperarousal and rising levels of anxiety institute more *control* measures resulting in an increase in aggression, counter-aggression, dependence on both physical and biological restraints, and punitive measures directed at clients and each other. Key team members, colleagues, and friends leave the setting and take with them key aspects of the *memory* of what worked and what did not work and team learning becomes impaired. *Communication* breaks down between staff members, and interpersonal *conflicts* increase and are not resolved. Team functioning becomes increasingly *fragmented*. As this happens, staff members are likely to feel *overwhelmed*, *confused*, and *depressed*, while emotional exhaustion, cynicism, and a *loss of personal effectiveness* lead to demoralization and burnout.

And how are these parallel processes manifest in organizational culture? Under these circumstances, the organization becomes unsafe for everyone in it. Emotional intelligence decreases and organizational emotions, including anger, fear, and loss, are poorly managed or denied. The crisis-driven nature of the hyperaroused system interferes

> with organizational learning. When the organization stops learning it becomes increasingly helpless in the face of what appear to be overwhelming and hopelessly incurable problems (p. 39).

Further exploring this process in *Destroying Sanctuary* (2010), Bloom & Farragher apply trauma theory and knowledge to the life of organizations, demonstrating how traumatic experiences and their subsequent symptoms result in organizational stress and decline.
Through the Sanctuary Foundation, Bloom and Farragher are creating a new operating system and restoring "sanctuary." Their method relies on the "Sanctuary Commitments," which are commitments to:

- Nonviolence
- Emotional intelligence
- Social learning
- Open communication
- Democracy
- Social responsibility
- Growth and change

These commitments are universal and apply to all members, employees, and volunteers within the organization.

Becoming a *Trauma-Informed* Agency and Not a *Traumatized* Agency

When agencies begin to implement trauma-informed care, they soon learn that all aspects of the organization's functioning are affected. Providing excellent trauma-informed services has implications for the agency's mission, administration, culture, supervisory structure, and physical plant. Every area of the consumer-client experience must be considered, from first call to post-discharge. Consumer involvement in agency management is helpful. Boundaries between staff and clients must be strong, clear, and flexible. And, since a central tenet of the Restorative Approach is that the staff cannot provide healing relationships to the clients unless they themselves feel cared for, the staff experience at work must also be examined.

Mission and Values

An important part of emphasizing and solidifying an agency's commitment to trauma-informed care is to imbed these principles into their mission statement and/or value statement, as well as into their strategic planning process. The principles to emphasize can include the importance of relationships; the commitment to a respectful, collaborative approach; the focus on clients' strengths; the understanding that all behavior is adaptive; and a sense of hope for growth and healing. Roger Fallot and Maxine Harris (2001) have identified these core values of trauma-informed care: **safety, trustworthiness, choice, collaboration, and empowerment.**

Administration

The actions of the agency administration will determine the success of its transformation to trauma-informed care. The administration must truly understand and support this approach, or it will not have a chance. Staff is keenly attuned to what is actually expected and rewarded within an agency. Mere lip service will not convince them to make this difficult change toward more effective healing.

How can administrators demonstrate their support? First, they can arrange financing for training for all staff on trauma, how it affects people, and how they can heal through attuned relationships. Key members of the administration can attend at least a portion of trauma training themselves (rather than sending designees in their places). The agency must make provisions for the staff to be released from their regular duties to attend the training.

Then, it is helpful to create a Trauma-Informed Care Task Force to oversee the transition. A competent person with administrative skills and organizational credibility is the best candidate to lead this task force. Administration supports the recommendations of the trauma task force and follows through on their plans as completely as possible.

Expectations are conveyed in many ways throughout an agency. Does the administration value control and lack of disruption more than anything else? Can the administration tolerate a certain level of organizational chaos in making the transition, including such things as staff confusion, conflict within the treatment team, resistance to change, and increased property destruction? Trauma-informed practice encourages staff to be flexible and to offer choices to the clients, even when the result is that the client is not immediately brought under control. Can the administrators support this approach?

In one agency, trauma-informed care champions had been working with the staff to be more flexible. They were teaching staff to ask upset clients what is wrong and to listen and to validate the clients' feelings before discussing consequences or solutions. Then Maggie, age 16, had just learned that her mother had relapsed. She was screaming in the main hall on the afternoon of the Board Meeting. The CEO was wondering what Board members would think if they walked in the door and heard a girl yelling about running away and killing herself, and heard staff empathizing with how bad she was feeling. So he took a staff member aside and said he knew she was upset but could they please get her to go back to the unit or at least into one of the meeting rooms?

What messages are sent in this two-minute interaction? Here are three: that not upsetting the Board is more important than what is happening to Maggie; that in fact what Maggie is feeling and saying is unacceptable and shameful and should be hidden; and that the job of staff is to get Maggie to quiet down and stop bothering people. Those two minutes can on one hand undermine months of training and on the other show how important administration support and understanding is to establishing trauma-informed care.

In programs implementing trauma-informed care, the administration looks for every opportunity to praise staff members for their patience and kindness. They express their sadness about what the children are going through, and acknowledge how real and important the stressors on these children are. A response of compassion to both the child's and the staff's experience in an incident will have a very powerful effect in reinforcing the staff's flexibility with the child.

This example also points out that it is important to share the principles of trauma-informed care with the Board of Directors. They need to know why the agency is making this change and how it will affect agency's functioning. Both possible positive and possible negative ramifications must be shared with the Board. If possible, Board members can be invited to attend some portion of the trauma training, or even participate in the transition and oversight committees.

Staff members want to do a good job. They want to be seen as competent and successful. If the administration makes them feel bad or incompetent about the children's emotional outbursts, they will try to stop these outbursts. If the administration helps them feel proud of their kindness and flexibility with the children, the use of this approach to difficult behaviors will increase.

Fundraising is a key function of the CEO of any agency. Implementing trauma-informed care can help with fundraising. The agency can become a leader in an advanced and forward-looking treatment modality. Developing sophisticated treatment skills will help the agency survive current economic stressors. Emphasizing the trauma histories of the clients served helps donors understand why they need assistance. Also, using research such as the ACE Study (Center for Disease Control, 2008) will demonstrate the economic benefit of helping people heal from trauma.

Another function of agency administration is managing the many aspects of compliance, licensing and accreditation that are part of present-day mental health treatment provision. This function includes monitoring all the many types of documentation necessary for current standards of care, and responding when an incident results in an investigation by licensing or accreditation agencies. One helpful measure is to invite key members of regulatory and financing agencies to attend the trauma training, and alert them in advance to the changes that the agency plans to make.

Serious incidents include a child getting hurt, a parent complaint, a sexual incident, an increased number of runaways or restraints, or any of the myriad of other things that can go wrong in congregate care. In a few cases these incidents might be the result of obvious misconduct by staff. But many times staff was doing the best they could with the limited resources and multiple demands of the moment. In these situations, the response of administration is crucial in determining both the progress towards the implementation of trauma-informed care and the general staff morale. If the agency is under pressure from outside reviewers, does the administration scapegoat and blame individual staff? Is the message that if they had just done their job right this bad thing would never have happened? In fact, there is no possibility that staff can prevent bad things from ever happening. When an agency develops a culture of blame, the staff begins to focus on avoiding mistakes and covering up those that do happen. Their increased caution interferes with their ability to be creative and flexible with the clients.

Instead, problems can be treated as an opportunity for all staff, administration through line staff, to learn together and improve their practice. Any positive things that happened as part of the incident are acknowledged and praised. Definitely, improvements can and should be made; yet it is also important to appreciate there are limits to what people can do. Most important is that administration conveys that the team is in this together and this is not one person's problem.

Administrative leaders can further set the tone for trauma-informed care by celebrating both staff and client achievements. Their concern, kindness, and compassion toward issues affecting both staff and clients model the response needed from staff. Their heartfelt joy when a client wins an award or a staff member gets their professional license reminds everyone of the purpose of this difficult work.

Administrative Structure

Trauma-informed care is fundamentally based on clinical thinking, thinking beneath the behavior to the "why," and using this understanding of the adaptive function of the behavior to determine the most effective and healing response to the behavior. Furthermore, delivering trauma-informed care necessitates closely-knit, well-functioning teams with the ability to openly work out differences of opinion. As previously described, the administrative structure that best maximizes these conditions is placing a clinically trained person (a coordinator) in charge of a treatment unit, and both the childcare staff and the clinicians assigned to that unit report to the coordinator. There may also be a childcare supervisor who reports directly to the coordinator. The leadership group consists of the coordinator, the therapists, and the childcare manager that meets regularly to create and implement the treatment model in support of the vision.

The ideal treatment team to implement trauma-informed care has the characteristics described below.

Clinical thinking (asking "why" and "what needs are being met," along with "how can we meet these needs differently") is integrated into every moment of the work – through every daily activity, every assignment of consequences for actions, and every structural decision.

Relationships are emphasized at every level. Staff is encouraged to form strong relationships with the children, and given time and mechanisms to do so. Close and supportive relationships form among members of the treatment team from all disciplines: childcare workers, teachers, therapists, psychiatrists, nurses, and others. These relationships hold the children in a safety net. They also provide the humor, sustenance, honesty, caring, and support for each other necessary to provide the stamina to do this hard work.

The treatment environment belongs to all, and decisions are made together by the team. Should bedtimes be later? How can staff get the youth to brush their teeth? What should they do about this recent bunch of runaways? How do they react to the kids' attempts to split them? What should they do about anger developing between the first shift and the second shift? All these questions are everyone's business and everyone's responsibility.

The team develops the ability to discuss hard questions with each other. They are able to accept help when a team member offers to take over a difficult situation in which the involved staff appears stuck. They ask each other for help. They are able to discuss whether a given response to a child was too harsh, or too lenient. They feel safe enough to discuss their individual reactions to certain children: those they want to kill and those they want to adopt. They talk about how the work is affecting them personally.

The model for the provision of therapy is a flexible response when the clients need it or are having a crisis, not through once-a-week appointments in the clinician's office. The therapist is regularly present on the unit and in the clients' lives, and takes advantage of opportunities when the client is receptive to connecting. They may also have appointments in their offices for those youth who can accept this structure, but many discussions are held on walks, or while playing a game, etc. The therapists participate when they can in unit fun events like celebrations and some activities.

Information about the child is shared within the team, and the child knows this fact. If the child wants the therapist to not share a certain item, the therapist can honor this confidentiality request while hoping the child will be ready to share with a few team members soon. This approach communicates to the child that the entire team is part of her treatment and is there for her.

Everyone on the treatment team has regular opportunities to *talk and think* about the work, i.e., they are not expected to be interacting with the children every minute they are at work. These opportunities for thought and conversation include individual supervision (weekly for clinicians and full-time childcare workers), treatment team meetings, staff meetings, etc. In these forums they have a chance to learn about the child, his background, his issues, his plans, and current happenings in his life. They have a chance to explore their own reactions to the child. They share things they have observed, learned, and found helpful. They participate in setting the course of treatment, as all understand that every minute of the day is part of the treatment.

The reporting structure is clear and organized. Every staff member knows who his direct supervisor is, what her job description is, and what his own and other team members' responsibility is. The direct supervisor is responsible for guiding the professional development of his or her supervisees by handling performance issues, providing needed training, encouraging and praising, and helping staff members to reach their own goals.

This structure puts into action what is known about healing from trauma: it is not only, or even particularly, what happens in the therapist's office that produces healing. The everyday, care-taking moments have strong potential for deep healing. In these moments the child forms new templates for relationships and learns that other people can be helpful, can be trusted, and are a source of comfort. The child learns that he or she is worthwhile and deserves care. The child internalizes these relationships and can use their representations to handle life's difficulties. The child observes and practices feeling-management skills. The fun, repetitive, rhythmic activities build the child's brain and help him or her to associate other people with positive emotions. So, it is essential that all of the people who care for the child understand that they are providing treatment, and develop the ability to offer healing relationships. All staff members must be included in both understanding the child and in using that understanding to shape their interactions with the child.

Culture

How is an agency culture created? One part of the creation of culture comes from the administration. What do the agency representatives inquire about? What makes them happy? What problems do they tolerate, and what difficulties result in swift action to terminate an employee? How does the administration interact with employees? Is the CEO open to employees who wish to talk with him or her?

The administration enhances the culture by where they spend time and attention. Do they attend the children's ceremonies and activities? Do they celebrate staff achievements? Do they talk with the youth?

Key elements of an agency culture that supports trauma-informed care include (Harris & Fallot, 2001):

- Putting the clients first.
- Attention to the clients' quality of life.
- Honoring relationships between staff and clients as the key source of healing, and relationships between staff as equally important.
- Attention is paid to clear and reasonable boundaries.
- Compassion and kindness are primary approaches that are honored and praised.
- An expectation that employees will treat each other well.
- Differences of opinion and problems are handled openly.
- Staff at all levels is invited to, and do, make suggestions and contribute to improving the treatment process.
- In relationships with administrators and supervisors, staff members feel supported.
- Staff members feel comfortable bringing their clinical concerns, vulnerabilities, and emotional responses to clients to team meetings, supervision sessions or a supervisor.

- The emotional safety needs of all staff, including support staff, are attended to.
- Mistakes are discussed openly and solved as a team.
- Attention is paid to addressing vicarious traumatization.

All employees create the agency culture. For example, the advice that longer-term employees give to newcomers conveys their understanding of what kind of children these are and what is expected in this program. Do the older (in length of service) employees brag about physical abuse by clients that they have endured without reaction? Do they say things like: "You can't trust these kids" or "Always watch your back around these kids"? Or do they relate successes, or particularly moving experiences of connection with a child? In the first instance, the new employee may get the impression that toughness and being like a rock are the traits that are required in this place. Often senior childcare staff recommends to new staff that they "start tough and become lenient later." There is an assumption that toughness and caring are opposites. Is it possible to create a culture in which senior staff teaches new staff a strong, respectful, caring, and structured response to the children?

When two employees or groups of employees are angry at each other, the supervisory staff has an important opportunity for culture creation. For example, at one agency the childcare staff and the therapists were very separate. The childcare staff thought that the therapists did not understand the children; after all, they only saw them one hour a week. The staff saw the therapists as unrealistic, too soft, and as creating treatment plans that they could never implement. Meanwhile, the therapists despaired among themselves about the childcare staff being so harsh, and never following through with suggestions that the therapists made.

With this background, Carrie, a childcare supervisor, approached Joe, the director, with a complaint. Mary, the therapist for her unit, kept making family therapy appointments just when the unit had scheduled activities. This conflict caused major difficulties for the unit, as they had to leave a staff member behind to watch the child until the session was over, and thus often they couldn't do the activity at all because they would not have the required staff-child ratios. Joe, who had been promoted from childcare to a supervisory role, was incensed by this situation. He and Carrie talked about how clueless Mary often seemed. They decided to announce in the next staff meeting that certain standing times for family therapy would be established, and if the therapist wanted to meet outside of these times she would have to discuss it with the Unit Supervisor first. Their solution seemed very reasonable to Joe and Carrie.

This very common scenario illustrates many team problems. The therapists and unit staff are not talking. They are not learning from each other. They do not understand each other's realities.

What if Joe responded to Carrie's complaint by asking if she had talked this over with Mary? Then, he could schedule a meeting to figure out how to meet both the unit needs and the family needs for flexibility in scheduling. A next step might be a retreat to bring childcare staff and therapists together, with exercises to build trust, have fun together, get to know each other as people, and then explore ways to increase team cohesiveness.

In a trauma-informed care agency, a supervisor presented with a problem between employees remains calm and does not assume blame. In fact, in most cases he assumes that all parties were acting in good faith and were doing the best they could at the time. Whenever possible she expects the parties to talk to each other directly before bringing the problem to a third party. His interventions center on increasing communication and cooperation between the parties so that they can form stronger relationships, understand each other's need and thus find their own solutions. When relationships are strong on a team, mistakes can be tolerated and worked through, and very few rules are needed.

Working with children who have experienced severe trauma is hard work. Only a culture that emphasizes strong, caring relationships between staff can provide the safety and the energy necessary to continue and to feel hopeful. An agency in which staff treat each other and the children with compassion and kindness, and handle disputes openly; in which staff are encouraged to discuss their personal reactions to the clients and work; and in which all members participate in creating and improving the treatment services, is an agency that can offer the most powerfully healing experiences to clients.

Physical Plant

The physical space of an agency of course affects the experience of both those who receive services there and those who work there. Many child-serving agencies are housed in old buildings, some of which started as orphanages. There may be little that can be changed in the basic structure. However, within that structure there may be some flexibility in the allocation, decoration and use of space. Looking at the space with an emphasis on creating safety for trauma-survivor clients can suggest some feasible changes.

Here are some aspects to consider:

- Is the waiting room comfortable and welcoming?
- Is there ample space for each person without crowding?
- Are the restrooms accessible and marked?
- Are there private spaces for discussions?
- Are the decorations multi-cultural?
- Are there private spaces for family visitation that are comfortable and include things to do?
- Are the living or program space nurturing (e.g., colors, plants, music) and affirming (e.g., display of child art/work, culturally competent)?

- Do the clients have privacy and opportunities for quiet and retreat?
- Is the space in good repair and well cared for?
- Are there precautions to prevent unauthorized access to the client's space?

Many other such questions will suggest themselves. Asking staff and families about their experiences with the space will also suggest possible changes.

It is also important to consider how the space supports the staff's needs. Are there private spaces for discussions between supervisor and supervisee? Does the staff have a place for peace and quiet during breaks? Does staff have private secure storage spaces for personal belongings? Is there opportunity for staff to eat meals away from the clients? Are the grounds and parking areas safe and well lit, especially for third-shift staff?

It may not be possible to accomplish every one of these ideals. However, looking at the physical space with an eye toward how it supports or impedes trauma-informed care may suggest some creative improvements that are possible.

The Consumer's Experience

The "consumer" in this context is the child or youth, the parent or foster parent, other friends, relatives and providers who are involved, the guardian, the child welfare agency, and sometimes the courts. The consumer's experience with an agency begins with their first inquiry call. Do they feel welcomed and understood? Is the process flexible enough to meet their needs? Does the staff help them surmount the inevitable system requirements and barriers? Do they feel a sense of compassion for their situation?

Similar characteristics are part of the intake process. Particularly in residential treatment, staff makes it clear that they understand what a difficult step this is for both the parent and child. Although there is always an intake process, it may need to be altered for certain clients. A family may want to come and see the program before the official intake. A child may be too scared to participate on the first visit, and may need to come back several times before a meaningful intake can take place. Although this kind of flexibility takes extra time, it sets the tone for the entire treatment: we care more about you and your experiences than we do about following pre-defined procedures.

Often treatment programs are concerned about implementing formal trauma-screening protocols at intake. They rightly worry that the questions might be both intrusive and triggering for the client. For this reason, use of the instruments must be conducted with sensitivity. However, asking about trauma at intake does begin the process of considering symptoms as adaptations. It conveys: we don't want to know what is *wrong* with you; we want to know what *happened* to you. The process also includes an investigation of the client's strengths that have allowed him or her to survive. It is important that the screening is relatively brief, not overly complicated, and avoids unnecessary detail that would increase likelihood of triggering traumatic memories.

The specifics of the treatment milieu are covered in detail in other parts of this book. It is worth emphasizing here that both the physical and the social environments can contribute to a feeling of safety for the clients. In the physical arena, safety can be created through privacy, personalization, choice, and protection. It is easy to underestimate how important locked doors can be to clients who have been harmed. Many agencies are in old buildings: are the clients hearing unexplained sounds at night? Lighting in rooms and passageways can help with safety.

A youth who has been neglected, molested, and/or physically harmed learns to be acutely aware of the nuances of his social environment. This perceptivity is necessary for survival. So when this youth enters treatment, he or she carefully monitors the social signals of the staff and clients. Even relatively minor episodes of sarcasm, harshness, or meanness tend to confirm the child's fears about the potential of these people to hurt him/her.

The youth is likely to encounter threatening or scary interactions with peers. He/she will also experience episodes of dysregulation by peers, and possibly restraints accompanied by screaming and anguish. Staff tries to eliminate as many unsafe experiences as they can. Those that remain are acknowledged and validated.

The physical attractiveness and repair of the environment sends a message to the children about their worth. These youth are often accustomed to getting second-best and broken things. One agency built a new, beautiful school. Staff was saddened when Mark, on his first tour of the new school, said: "This is for us? This is too good for us. The kind of kids we are, we will just ruin it." Effort (and money) spent to repair damage and replace worn items will be repaid in increased self-esteem of the clients, and of the staff. No one wants to work in a broken, chaotic environment any more than any one wants to live there.

Choice and collaboration can be woven in to every aspect of the agency experience. Food is one example: are there choices? Does the food reflect the culture of the clients? Do staff help the children find food they can enjoy, or is the attitude more "eat what you have and be grateful?" Is the food presented in an attractive manner? At one agency, Jaquan was newly admitted and very anxious. He was presented with a salad and began to scream. "I HATE red lettuce!!!" he yelled. Patiently, Laura, a childcare worker, picked all the pieces of red lettuce out of the salad. Laura didn't tell Jaquan that red lettuce tastes just like green lettuce. Instead, she helped him feel heard and cared about, and provided the opportunity for Jaquan to think, "Maybe this new place might not be so bad after all."

Client participation is solicited in every area from deciding tonight's activities to treatment planning to agency management. One good strategy is to appoint former clients or parents to the Board of Directors. Another is to have a Parent Advocate who reaches out to parents, helps with any issues they have, and brings the parent voice to agency management decisions.

The most important thing is to regularly look at the treatment experience through the client's eyes. This perspective can be attained by various forms of soliciting feedback from the clients themselves, and also by walk-throughs with this purpose. Look for every instance of safety/danger; inclusion/authoritarian decision making; respect/ judgment; encouraging effective action/encouraging passivity; flexibility/rules before people. Ask the clients for suggestions to improve.

Boundaries

When they begin to acknowledge the power of relationships in the healing process, many personnel are afraid that more boundary violations will result. How can an agency emphasize relationships and still maintain clear, flexible boundaries?

People may assume that because the Restorative Approach emphasizes relationships and speaking from the heart, there are no boundaries. Quite the opposite is true! For relationships to be safe and healing, the boundaries must be reliable and trustworthy.

Because abuse is in its essence a violation of boundaries, it is especially important that staff pay attention to boundaries when working with abused clients. The children have experienced major boundary violations, such as sexual abuse. They have also experienced many other chronic, less obvious boundary problems. Many of the children have had to handle responsibilities far beyond what is reasonable for their age, such as an eight-year-old being responsible for her two-year-old sister. They have been over-involved in adult issues, such as being worried about the rent or finding food. They have been exposed to adult sexuality and to relationship worries. They have had to parent their parents, care for a sick mother, listen to parental problems, and help ease a parent's depression.

Oftentimes while handling these inappropriately adult responsibilities, the children have found great satisfaction and even a sense of competence. Janeese is proud that she kept her two-year-old sister safe. Louis feels good about having been the man of the house while his mother was sick. Darlene felt special when her mother confided her problems with her latest boyfriend.

Also, being aware of adult issues and taking on adult responsibility is a survival strategy. Many of the adults that these children have known were not capable of protecting them. If the children didn't do it, no one would. So when Jackie asks her therapist fourteen times if she has called her DCF worker to approve a visit, and also places a call to the worker herself, it is because she has no experience that adults will do what they promise to do, and she has had lots of experience that if she wants something done she has to do it herself.

When adults come along and say: "It's okay, we will take care of everything, you can relax and be a kid now," the children's answer is "Yeah, right." They don't have any good reason (yet) to believe the adults, and they don't want to give up the sense of competence and strength that they have developed on their own.

Trauma-surviving children expect boundary violations. They are eager to become a staff member's best friend. They may try to engage with staff sexually because that's what they're used to from adults. They continually test, asking with their behavior: "Who are you to me? Can I trust you? Are you really who you say you are?"

It is up to staff, as adults, to maintain the boundaries. They are professionals, and their relationships with the children must be primarily to meet the children's needs, not to meet the staff's.

In a trauma-informed system staff are encouraged to speak from the heart. We can all recognize there is a big difference between saying: "You ran away last night and I was worried about you. I was wondering if you were safe." And saying: "You ran away last night and I was worried about you, and I haven't been sleeping anyway because of my financial problems and the fact that my grandmother is sick, and I can't believe you added to my stress."

Some boundaries are obvious and clear cut: Do not have sex with the clients – or with members of their families.

But within the social service field there are a lot of gray areas, and a lot of disagreement among treaters. Many boundary issues arise out of good intentions when a staff member, teacher, or caseworker wants to do something extra for a child or feels an especially strong sense of compassion for a particular family.

Here are some examples of the many issues that can arise.

Margaret is a teacher, and one of her students, Rachel, is having an especially hard time as her mother has disappeared and no one knows where she is. Margaret plans to come in and take Rachel to lunch this Saturday to help her through this.

Danny's mother, Darleen, felt that his teammate Seth was particularly kind and sensitive to her during a recent episode when Danny ran away and was missing overnight. She brings Seth a $30 gift certificate to a local restaurant as a thank you.

Doug, a staff member, recently bought his son some new expensive sneakers, and his son wore them once and didn't like them. It is too late to return them, but he knows that Jarell is just the same shoe size as his son so he brings the sneakers in for Jarell.

Sarah is a therapist and is seeing Anita's family. They can't concentrate on their issues with Anita because they tell her they do not have any food in the house and do not know where to get any for that night. Sarah wonders if she should just give them $20.

Melissa, a program resident, approaches Juanita, a part-time third-shift staff member. Melissa says that Juanita is the only staff who understands her, the only one she can talk to. She has an important secret she must talk with someone about, but first Juanita must promise not to tell any of the other team members.

Many other dilemmas arise. The issue of staff/child touch is a particularly sensitive one, and different agencies have different policies around this concern. Other complications arise when a staff or a child leaves the agency.

Amidst this morass of complexity, how is a staff member to know what to do? The answer is simple: **talk about it**. First, staff must know and follow their agency's boundary policy. Yet no policy can cover all the decisions they are faced with. So if a staff member is considering doing anything outside his/her job description, before saying anything to the child or family, he/she discusses it with the supervisor and/or the team. What would be the effect of this action on the child? On the group? On other staff? Is he making any implicit unrealistic promises about his role to the child? How will she feel if she does this extra thing and then the next day the child is mean to her? There are many sides that must be considered. Supervisors and team members must be alert to boundary issues on their team, and challenge any decisions that seem problematic, even at the risk of seeming like the Scrooge of the team.

In general, any extra gestures such as money, presents, donations to a child or family should come from the agency, not from an individual staff member. No treats (lunches out, presents, extra attention) should be available only to the child that someone particularly likes. That partiality will result in certain less engaging children not getting any goodies, a situation which replicates the rest of their lives. Extras should be decided by the Treatment Team in a way that is fair to all and reflective of the treatment process. There should be no secrets kept between a child and one team member that are not shared with the rest of the team. The question of physical touch between clients and staff should be openly discussed within the agency, and guidelines developed that meet the children's needs and help the staff feel comfortable. When a child or a staff member leaves the agency, the staff should make no promises to the child about ongoing contact. The child and family can be encouraged to have ongoing contact with the agency, not with an individual. No staff member should talk with a child about adopting them or becoming their foster parent. Instead they should talk to their supervisor and explore thoroughly whether this is a possibility and whether they really want to do it before raising the child's hopes.

No matter what treatment system is being used, boundaries are crucial in creating healing relationships. Supervision and team discussions are our most powerful tools to sort through the complexity and do what is right for the children. The children cannot grow and change unless they feel completely safe in the strong, clear relationships staff offers them.

Language

The Restorative Approach encourages staff to speak from the heart, and to use I statements: "When you ran away, I was so worried about you. I couldn't sleep because I worried that something bad would happen to you." Or, "You just hit me. I am not ready to give you a hug. I feel hurt and upset right now. I'm sure we can work this through later but right now I need some time to calm down before I can reconnect with you."

Some objections to this approach include people's worry that staff will be emotionally out of control, and will be too intense/vehement/dysregulated in their response to the clients. Will the staff be using the clients to meet their own emotional needs? Will the staff emotion be overwhelming to the kids? Will the staff forget that they are the professionals and being paid for the work?

And there is also some concern that staff expressing distress or hurt, worry, or other personal reactions will interfere with giving the kids unconditional positive regard.

Staff members' emotional reaction to being hit, kicked, bitten, kids being mean to them or running away, is always a part of what is happening in the treatment. If staff has no direct way to express those emotions they will act them out, through excessive harshness, through distance, through over-involvement. No one ever really feels always unconditionally positive about anyone; it is dishonest to act as though a staff member feels completely positive about a child who has just physically hurt them. Better to have the real feelings in the open in a controlled way, to be worked through and transformed, and to model the positive possibilities.

Children learn emotional regulation through relationships with emotionally regulated adults. How better can a child learn what to do when something goes wrong than through a close connection with a staff member who is deeply affected by an event, but then mends the relationship? Authentic relationships are the source of healing. How can a relationship be authentic if one person is not allowed to make I statements?

There is always the possibility that there will be emotionally dysregulated staff, staff with poor boundaries, staff with over-intense reactions either positive or negative. That is true no matter what system is in use, no matter what instructions administrators give them. This reality becomes first of all a team issue, because a well-functioning team allows staff to confront each other directly on such matters. It also becomes a supervision issue to be handled directly and vigorously by the unit manager.

If administration doesn't trust the staff to have real, straightforward relationships with the clients, how can they leave the clients in their care? Agencies have to teach people how to speak from their hearts, while maintaining good boundaries and emotional regulation. If staff does not learn and model authenticity, they lose the most powerful tool they have: themselves. They rob the children of the reparative experience of good, flexible, calm relationships.

The Staff Experience

Remember the trauma-informed care principle that staff cannot treat the children any better than they themselves are treated? In order for the staff to heal the children through warm, genuine relationships, the staff must feel safe, cared about, and cared for. In implementing trauma-informed care, it is essential to pay attention to the quality of life experienced by those who work in the agency.

Just as for the clients, safety is a prerequisite for every form of relationship. This includes both physical and psychological safety. What can the agency administration do to provide that safety?

Training and supervision are important prerequisites. No one can do trauma-informed care well if they are expected to be working with the clients every moment they are at work. Everyone needs time to process and reflect on the events. Initial, pre-employment training must include an introduction to trauma-informed care, and a clear description of the approach used at this agency. New employees are immediately taught to understand symptoms as adaptive, and that each client is doing the best they can at the moment. They are taught the agency's position that the relationship is the most powerful tool of change, and that this agency heals through helping clients feel better, not through punishment. Then, every staff member needs ongoing clinical supervision, including and especially the direct-care staff. More than administrative supervision, it must be a safe place to explore how the staff can understand the client's behaviors, and how to use that understanding to create interventions. It is a place that staff can vent and feel safe. It must include attention to both counter-transference reactions and vicarious traumatization. The supervisor will then have an opportunity to encourage good self-care.

All staff must learn about the children, and reading the record is not enough. Staff needs time to meet with the therapist and come to understand the child's background and how it is currently influencing the present. Staff needs to know the goals, objectives, and proposed discharge path for this child. They need a clear sense of the formulation of the treatment: how does the team understand what is going on with this child and what is the current focus? What problems is this child trying to solve with his behaviors? What self-capacities does she need to develop? What social supports does he have? What are her strengths? In most cases in intensive treatment, it is not a good idea for the therapist to keep secrets from the rest of the team. The line of confidentiality is outside of the team. If everyone is expected to think clinically about the meaning of behaviors, everyone needs the information to do so.

Each staff member needs an opportunity to discuss current issues and dilemmas with the team and develop strategies based on the formulation. What have others found that helps? What can the team add to the child's Individual Crisis Management Plan? What are the early signs of distress that staff should watch for – and what helps at those times? Who is doing well with this child and can become more involved? Who is struggling?

The daily routine of staff can either increase or decrease their stamina. Is staff able to take breaks and have meals away from clients? Are spaces available for them to talk and relax? Is staff encouraged to take vacation time they have accumulated? Administration must guard against the temptation to take advantage of the good hearts of their best, most responsible staff by over-working them.

Staff has a voice in decisions that affect their work. Every effort is made to solicit staff input; to have staff members on decision-making committees; and to have an open door policy by administration. Many excellent treatment improvements arise when an individual staff member is given permission to explore their own passions. For example, Michael was staff member on the girls' unit who loved horses and had close ties with a local stable. He developed an entire therapeutic horseback riding program for the girls, including soliciting funding and obtaining the necessary permissions. For some girls this was the most important part of their treatment.

Relationships between staff sustain them as they do this difficult work. They cannot offer good trauma-informed care without respectful relationships among the team members. Also, the clients learn from observing how the staff interacts with each other, and these clients have learned to be very astute observers. Therefore, the agency must promote good relationships between staff members. One necessity for relationships is time: staff need time to talk, to joke and laugh, and to share personal stories, as well as to discuss work.

Making time for staff to have fun together helps create and strengthen the relationships that will help during a crisis. This relationship building can be through potluck lunches, sports teams, wellness activities, celebrations of personal milestones, etc. Recognizing and celebrating staff achievement also helps in creating a culture. Many units have recognition boxes in which staff (and clients) can put in notes about good things they observe each other do. One note is pulled out and the staff member who is praised gets a small gift, like a gift certificate to a coffee shop. All the notes are read aloud in a staff meeting. Many other ways of recognizing staff success have been tried. All are important.

It is important not to neglect the support staff when implementing trauma-informed care. Administrative assistants, receptionists, maintenance people, and kitchen staff all interact with the children. Anyone can provide a relationship that counteracts the child's early experiences with unreliable or abusive relationships and teach them that people can be trusted. Because support staff also observes painful events and learn sad stories, it is essential that support staff also understand trauma, the adaptive nature of behaviors, and the importance of relationships, boundaries, and vicarious traumatization. They also must have a place to talk when the job is affecting them. They must understand that they should bring information back to the team and not keep secrets. And they too need relationships and celebrations with their peers.

Summary

Trauma-informed care is not something that can be implemented in one small part of an agency. It does not just involve substituting restorative tasks for traditional consequences. It involves a profound change in the way the work is conceptualized and delivered. All aspects of the agency are relevant to the program's ability to create lasting healing. The mission and values of the agency must emphasize the power of relationships. The administrative structure must support both accountability and connected teamwork. A culture of caring must be present in all aspects of the work. Even the physical plant can enhance or detract from the work, and must be evaluated for safety and comfort. From the first contact with the agency, the consumer will experience respect, flexibility and understanding. They will develop relationships that are trustworthy and safe, including clear boundaries. All staff use the language of relationships and emotions when speaking. In order to provide these relationships, the staff experience in the agency must also be safe and respectful. They must have a voice; receive supervision and support, and have time to reflect on their work. Fun and recognition are also crucial in sustaining staff. Through attention to these areas agency leadership can create an environment that transforms both staff and clients.

Chapter Eleven

Cultivating a Trauma-Sensitive Staff

The key to success in trauma-informed treatment is attracting, hiring, and retaining excellent staff. Every agency realizes how hard this process is to do well, and how difficult it is to keep good staff once they are hired. Fortunately, anecdotal reports suggest that many agencies experience a significant decrease in staff turnover after implementing trauma-informed care. This new way of working produces jobs that are both more interesting and more important. Because every person who has direct contact with the child and family is an agent of healing, and those who are with the child day-to-day have the most powerful opportunity for change, finding the best people for these jobs and training and treating them well are essential.

Staff Management

Job Descriptions

The descriptions of the jobs in the agency and the competencies that are required to do them should reflect the principals of trauma-informed care.

Some core competencies include:

- The ability to form and maintain healing relationships with the client.
- The ability to actively listen.
- The ability to avoid power struggles and not to take things personally.
- The ability to utilize an understanding that the clients are doing the best they can and their symptoms are adaptive.

- Flexibility in handling behavioral outbursts.
- Ability to function well in a complex multi-disciplinary team.
- The ability to ask for and accept help.
- Willingness to self-reflect.
- Self-care skills.
- Articulating these characteristics clearly will help both in the selection of personnel and in supervising them.

Hiring Practices

One way agencies have discovered to determine whether a candidate is comfortable working in a relationship-based approach is through the use of scenarios. (See Appendix P for some possible hiring scenarios.) In some cases agencies have developed a statement that describes their treatment approach and then asked candidates to read, decide if they can work that way, and return the statement signed if they want to proceed with the hiring process. It is useful to ask candidates how they deal with stress and what self-care practices they find helpful. Other options include:

Ask a candidate about a time when he or she was successful in making a change and what helped him or her.

Ask a candidate with prior work experience to describe a client that they felt especially connected to, and one they found it difficult to connect with, and why. This question looks for self-awareness of differing response to different clients.

Ask a candidate about a time when someone helped him or her, a teacher or a mentor or anyone significant in his or her life. What did that person do that was helpful?

Ask, "What do you think might be the most difficult time of day for clients?"

Ask what can staff do to make clients feel safer/more comfortable around bedtime and/or shower.

Offering the candidate an opportunity to observe in the milieu can clarify both for the candidate and for the employer whether or not there is a good fit.

Supervision

The foundation of a trauma-informed approach is the ability to think clinically about the clients, looking behind the immediate behavior to the why; to understand what needs the child is trying to meet. When agencies want to develop this ability in staff, one of the most powerful tools is supervision. Every staff member receives individual supervision, including childcare staff and clinicians, and ideally teachers, nurses and staff in other disciplines and roles. Supervision is an opportunity to help the staff member learn and grow. Merely asking the staff member how they are, or talking with them about administrative requirements or meeting with them when they have done something wrong is not enough. Supervision is a place to share struggles, look at the clients one is having a hard time with, and also to share triumphs and successes. When a staff member's performance or actions are problematic, supervision is the place to discuss the specific changes that must be made and to review progress, using a progressive discipline system when necessary.

Supervision also includes an emphasis on identifying and addressing vicarious traumatization: how is the work affecting the staff member at this time, and how is he taking care of himself? In supervision, a staff member can vent all their frustration and discouragement, and gradually begin to consider how to move forward. The supervisor can call attention to the elements of vicarious transformation and encourage the staff member to include in their work practices that promote positive personal transformation. Supervisors often review specific topics of trauma-informed care that are relevant to a given discussion. Although it is hard to schedule time for supervision in the treatment world of constant crisis and understaffing, it is a crucial part of employee retention and growth.

Promotion

Internal promotion of the staff that are most skillful in trauma-informed care is one of the surest ways to move the agency forward. This process develops a skillful work force and sends the message that the agency is serious about these practices. It is important to remember to offer training to staff who receive promotions. It is easy to fall into the trap of assuming that because a person has worked for the agency she already knows all she needs to know. She doesn't. A star childcare worker who is promoted to supervisor will need training in the agency personnel policies as well as education in how to offer clinical guidance and how to confront problem behaviors.

Employee Problems

It is inevitable that when an agency first transforms its practices there will be some employees who resist or try to subvert these new methods. These employees can be influenced in many ways, both in groups and individually. The supervisor can point out parts of the employee's performance that are relationship-enhancing, while also being specific about areas that need to change. A written performance-improvement plan that is devised with the employee, contains detailed information and goals, and is reviewed weekly can be a helpful tool. The supervisor can explore the employee's concern and fears about the new methods.

It is essential that employees' resistance be addressed. Other employees will be watching and will see the resistance as a test of the agency's seriousness about the new way. Some employees in fact leave, which can be a good thing. Others become converts and can be some of the most persuasive advocates of the method.

Staff Training

New Employee Orientation

New employee orientation (NEO) is an opportunity to establish the organization's philosophy, beliefs and methods at the beginning of an employee's tenure. Most organizations have found that the best approach is to include an introduction to trauma-informed care in NEO. This introduction includes the importance of the relationship in healing, the adaptive nature of symptoms, the collaborative and empowering approach to clients, and the effects of the work on the treater. New employees arrive with differing levels of previous experience in the helping fields, and some have had none. Others may have worked in agencies that emphasized control and punishment. Everyone also arrives with ideas about how to treat children based on their own upbringing. This introduction establishes the organization's commitment to the principles of respect, flexibility, and connection.

Basic Trauma Training

Within two-to-three months after beginning employment the employee is required to attend a basic training in trauma. The previously mentioned Risking Connection (Saakvitne, Pearlman, Gamble, & Lev, 2000) program is an excellent three-day training that includes many small group activities, personal reflection, connections with other employees, and practical guidance.

All employees in all direct service jobs should attend this basic training. The training is as useful for those providing outpatient therapy, in-home services, education, nursing, and foster care as it is for those in more intensive programs. Some agencies also require that all the support staff attend the training, as they also interact with the clients. Others have developed a one-day training for support staff. Educators in special education schools also need this training. It may be modified in their case to include a greater emphasis on the results of trauma on learning and memory.

Refreshers

Offering regularly scheduled refresher training meets many needs. It enables the agency to combat the inevitable drift back into a control-oriented approach. It provides an opportunity to explore topics in more depth, or discuss areas or strategies that are a struggle to implement. An employee who is having trouble working in a trauma-informed way can be referred to a refresher. Refreshers can be offered on a monthly, quarterly, or every-six-months schedule. The Traumatic Stress Institute (2009) has developed modules on specific topics that can be used as refreshers or within regularly scheduled staff meetings.

Agency Trainers

The Risking Connection training program (Saakvitne, Pearlman, Gamble, & Lev, 2000) offers a method for agencies to develop internal Associate Trainers who are licensed to offer Risking Connection training within their own agencies. To participate in this program, an agency must meet certain requirements. The trainers are chosen within specific criteria. They must pass a knowledge test and then attend a three-day Train-the-Trainer training. Having in-house trainers enables the agency to offer ongoing training and refreshers to new and current employees. The trainers are then eligible to participate in an ongoing learning and development program offered by the Traumatic Stress Institute.

Additional Skill Development

There are important skills that are necessary to provide treatment through relationship. It is easy to forget to teach these fundamental techniques, but they are woven into every intervention.

Skill Development for All Staff

Liking the Clients

Central to a positive relationship is that both sides experience the other as liking them. Do the people that work in the agency convey delight in the clients?

Clients often get the feeling that the staff does not really like them or enjoy being with them. They feel that staff wants to get away from them and have breaks from them. They feel that staff is at times involved in their own interests and not willing to be interrupted by them. They notice staff sitting and talking together. On the other hand, they describe how much it means when staff participates in games and activities with them. They feel close to staff that listens when they speak, remember what they said, and ask them about it later. They are quick to blame themselves for staff not wanting to be with them, because of the way they acted. But they describe acting better around staff who genuinely care.

What the clients need, and have never had, is someone whose face lights up when they come into a room. Think of children in "good-enough" homes, who are celebrated in so many ways! Their pictures are on the refrigerator, their events are attended, their performances little and big are applauded. But more than that, they constantly receive feedback that they are delightful. Someone loves them, wants to see them, wants to hug them, and wants to hear about their day.

Some research has shown that a critical factor in school success is the proportion of positive to negative comments a child hears during a day. How many times do clients hear their own name used in joy, as in, "Stephanie, I am so glad to see you!" or "Stephanie, what a wonderful math paper!" In contrast, how often is their name used as a warning: "Stephanie, stop that!" or "Stephanie, don't do that!" In the clients' lives it has mainly been the later.

Martha Holden of the Family Life Development Center's CARE project (Holden, 2009) teaches staff that their main job is to make sure that the child they are caring for has a marvelous day. What if everything staff does was organized around that goal? What if all staff saw that their goal is to help the children be happy?

The children in treatment are marvelous. Every day they demonstrate strength, courage, intelligence, wit, creativity and humor. Of course, they can also be obnoxious and even scary. But if staff don't see the marvel in them, who will? And how can they possibly change and grow if they have no one who is delighted by them?

What would it take for each staff to become that staff which listens, which joins with the children in games and activities, who laughs with them, who creates positive memories? How can staff become the people who show the child that she is worthwhile by looking forward to their time together, seeking her out and obviously wanting to be with her? This engagement can't be faked. But it is what makes treatment jobs meaningful and what heals the children.

Active Listening

Active listening is a skill that many people are taught at the beginning of their careers, and later forget. It consists of listening to what the person is saying and then either repeating their exact words or paraphrasing what they have said, and checking for accuracy. It then moves on to validation; expressing that the listener understands how the person could be feeling that way, it makes sense. It does not include giving advice on how the person should handle their problem.

When helpers talk to each other about a problem, this is what they want. For example, Kate comes into work feeling dragged out. When Naomi asks her what's wrong, Kate replies: "Last night I was over at my elderly father's house. You know he lives alone and he has been sick recently. I am so agonized about whether I should move him or get him more help or what. And to make things worse, while I was there I ate three stale donuts that he had!"

If Naomi said, "Well, Kate, that is not a good coping skill. Think what will happen to your future if you keep eating so many donuts. Next time you are going there, bring one of those bags of baby carrots," would Kate experience this as helpful? Not likely. Kate might even want to slap Naomi. Even if Naomi said, "I know a good assisted living facility in the area. Why don't I set up an appointment for you?" Kate would most likely not find that helpful.

What does Kate need from Naomi? A simple, "That must be difficult. I know how hard it is," is what people need from friends, and that is what the clients need from staff. There may be a time later in the conversation when Kate says, "Didn't you tell me you found a good place for your mom? Where was that?" and *now* she is asking for advice. But starting one's response with advice is not helpful.

Skills Development for Clinicians

Many professional training programs do not focus at all on the effects of trauma, although this is slowly beginning to change. In the meantime it is a mistake to assume that a new clinician comes to a program with an understanding of trauma and how victims heal. In addition to the basic training required of all staff, the agency may wish to send clinicians to specific, focused treatment about trauma and some of the evidence-based interventions. Trauma-Focused Cognitive Behavioral Therapy (Cohen, Mannarino, & Deblinger, 2006), Seeking Safety (Najavits, 2001), Motivational Interviewing, (Naar-King & Suarez, 2011), and the Trauma Recovery and Empowerment model (Harris, 1998) are just a few of the models for treatment. Clinicians can become specialists in a method that fits the client population the agency treats.

New staff clinicians may need specific training in formulating their cases. As mentioned in Chapter 6, it is important to teach this skill specifically, as the formulation organizes the treatment plan and thus guides all aspects of the intervention. The clinician's case formulation is shared with all team members, and revisited and revised when significant events happen in the case.

Skills Development for Childcare Staff

What Treaters Say About the Children Matters

Skill development begins with how staff understands what is going on with the children they serve. This understanding is reflected in how they speak about them when the children are not present. Training and vigilant correction/reframing of staff conversations can gradually begin to change the culture.

It is important to teach the theory of what happened to these children, and to stop and challenge negative, dismissive, or shaming staff statements. One comment can lead to an attitude that will infect the staff's response to the child and interfere with the child's healing.

For example, a staff member was discussing a client and said: "We had a girl named Megan who was cutting to be manipulative. She was doing it to get discharged and go to a place like detention where she wouldn't have to work on her issues."

What are the assumptions behind this statement? How does it differ from this statement?

"Megan has been working on some difficult issues recently. This has brought up some painful feelings and she has begun cutting for relief. Sometimes she doesn't even want to work on her issues and wishes she were in a place like detention where she wouldn't be in treatment."

Same facts, different assumptions, leading us to different responses.

In another instance, staff may make statements about how bad the children were, for example, "You'd better watch out putting that in your pocket. These kids will steal it from you in a minute."

Or, consider a staff member talking about a child who says mean things: "Jesse just likes making other people feel bad. He admits it."

Someone describing the cutting of a foster daughter: "She just wants the foster mother to feel sorry for her." The phrase "feel sorry for her" implies that staff should resist feeling sorry for her, and by extension resist coddling her, fussing over her, or being sympathetic. Yet some cuddling and caring may be just what she needs.

Treaters make these casual comments constantly in their many discussions about the clients. Yet by each comment they are expressing a theory, an understanding of why the children are doing these things. And at times it is a theory that blames the child and implicitly accuses him or her of doing the behavior deliberately to annoy the staff.

When treaters make these comments they forget that the child is doing the best he can, that her fears and needs are legitimate to her, and that he is using the only means he has to meet them. He will be able to change only when he feels safety within committed relationships, and when he gradually learns new skills.

Try monitoring the conversations in the staff office, and see what assumptions are expressed in the casual comments about the children.

Speaking from the Heart

Childcare staff may need specific training in using themselves and building relationships with the children to create healing. It is a very different approach from what they have been taught both personally and professionally.

The use of self is central to a relationship-based approach. Staff and therapists speak from their hearts. Instead of saying, "If you run away you will be restricted for a week and lose your privileges," staff say, "If you run away I will be scared, I will worry about your safety. I will have to keep you closer to me because our trust will be broken."

Staff is encouraged to evaluate their work by what *they* do, not by what the kids do. The program can utilize The Attitude, described by Daniel Hughes in *Building the Bonds of Attachment* (Hughes, 2006). The elements of The Attitude are: Playful, Accepting, Curious and Empathetic. PACE. Staff explores what these elements mean to them, which are easier, which harder. Any day in which staff has approached the children with the Attitude is a successful day. It is up to the adults to structure an environment around the children that maximizes their chance for success: organized, predictable, reliable, calm.

Using Calming Techniques in a Crisis

Any crisis management curriculum used by an agency, such as the Therapeutic Crisis Intervention System (Cornell University Residential Child Care Project, 2012; Nunno, Holden, & Leidy, 2003) or the Crisis Prevention

Intervention CPI (Crisis Prevention Institute, 2011; Nunno et al. 2008)) will offer staff techniques to help calm a person who is emotionally escalated. It is important to emphasize and augment those elements, because crisis management is one of the most difficult and important staff tasks.

As previously described, no one can think well when emotionally dysregulated. When a youth begins to escalate, the childcare worker can become scared. Both the youth and the childcare worker become more and more dysregulated, begin expecting the worst possible outcome, become frightened and respond to their own fears by becoming controlling and threatening. The youth talks about hitting people and hurting himself. The worker talks about consequences of increasing severity. This can only get worse.

Youth workers need to specifically be taught skills for calming someone down, starting with active listening and validation. Depending on the safety of the situation, they can include taking a walk, shooting baskets, or listening to music. They could involve sensory interventions such as rocking, fur, or weighted blankets. If a pet is available, stroking the pet can help. The child's crisis management plan suggests things that are uniquely calming to this child. Contact with a special person can help. Calming skills do not include the worker telling the child the consequences he is earning, giving them advice for how to live his life better, or giving orders; instead, the worker is as flexible and patient as possible.

To accomplish this calming response, workers must know the specifics of how the emotional brain hijacks the thinking brain in times of perceived danger. Thus, neither the child nor the worker has their best thinking available while dysregulated. Once both have calmed down, problem solving will again be possible.

Skills Development for Supervisory Staff

When a skilled childcare worker is promoted from within to become a supervisor, it is easy to assume that because she is a great person in her previous role, she will be a great supervisor. But being a supervisor requires different skills, and internal promotions to being a supervisor of former peers present particular challenges. The supervisor's success will be enhanced by specific ongoing training in the agency's personnel policies and disciplinary process, as well as how to enhance the growth of supervisees and to confront problems.

Skills Development for Support Staff

Support staff from maintenance, secretarial, business and other agency departments interact with the clients on a regular basis. At times one of these people becomes the most important connection for a child. Every relationship the child has within the agency has the potential to form a new template about people and thus create powerful healing, Furthermore, support staff experiences are affected by all manner of client symptoms, such as aggression, property damage, and self-harm. Therefore, it is helpful when they can be included in basic training about trauma, its effects, and how survivors heal. Whether the agency chooses to have support staff attend full three-day trauma training, or to develop and regularly offer a separate one-day training for support staff, their training needs should not be neglected.

Vicarious Traumatization

No staff development effort can afford to neglect the inevitability of vicarious traumatization's impact on its staff. Because trauma survivors are hurt within the context of relationships, they must heal within relationships: this principle is the bedrock of trauma-informed care. But, all therapeutic relationships have two sides – the client and the helper or treater. For therapeutic relationships to be truly transformative, they must consider the health of *both* the client and the treater. While there are now libraries full of books on helping traumatized clients, only recently has there been more discussion of *also* taking care of treatment providers.

At the root of vicarious trauma (VT) is a complex interaction of factors in both the *person* doing trauma work (their own family history, current life stressors, self-care strategies, etc.) and factors in the *context*, especially the workplace (nature of the clientele, choice and flexibility about the work, agency awareness of VT). While both areas are important, agency systems (primarily context) can embed attention to VT within the fabric of their culture.

Paralleling the isolation and shame experienced by trauma survivors, there are powerful forces pushing against treaters knowing about VT; noticing it in themselves and talking with peers and supervisors openly about it. Treatment providers have been socialized to "tough it out" and cover their vulnerability for fear that they will be viewed as weak, thin-skinned, or incompetent if they reveal that they are deeply impacted by working with traumatized clients. Self-care strategies, while important, only help so much when an agency culture reinforces these isolating messages. To truly shift the culture, it is clearly not enough to mention VT during training or have an occasional retreat when staff seems burnt out. To change culture, agencies *must embed* awareness and attention to VT in the very fabric of the agency, into the mortar between the bricks.

So, what are the messages agencies want to give employees about VT? How best can trauma-informed care build an agency culture that recognizes and supports staff and addresses their authentic reactions to working with traumatized children? What kinds of embedded interventions can counteract the prevailing sentiment that having strong feelings about the work is bad and a sign of incompetence? How can the agency promote practices that encourage positive personal transformation?

Messages. Trauma-informed Vicarious Traumatization interventions communicate the following messages: VT is simply part of doing this challenging work – it is less a question of *if*, than *when* VT will affect you; noticing it in yourself is *a good* thing and makes you better at what you do; sharing your feelings with others reduces isolation and shame – yours *and* theirs; maintaining a self-nurturing work-life balance is critically important; and the more you can find *hope* and *meaning* in your work and life, the less

VT will impact you, the longer you will be able to sustain yourself in your job, and the more useful you are to clients.

Embedded Agency Interventions

Mandated Staff Training. Staff is introduced to the concept of VT in staff orientation, and discussion of VT is a part of *all* mandated staff training. For new employees this matter-of-fact inclusion in training serves as an *inoculation* against the inevitable VT they will experience. They can begin to plan for self-care strategies that will sustain them in this work and learn of agency supports that will assist them in managing the stress.

Supervision. All staff that work with clients, including direct-care staff, receive regular supervision. That supervision is focused on exploring clinically related issues. Supervisors can model talking about VT: "With everything that's been happening, I'm finding that I can't stop thinking of work at home." They can ask direct questions about VT: "How are you noticing work seeping into your outside life?" "How were you feeling during that restraint?" "I notice when I'm stressed, I dream about work, does that ever happen to you?" In addition, talking about specific cases using a trauma focus will help the staff understand the client's actions, not take them so personally, and develop a road map to guide future interventions.

Regularly Scheduled VT Groups. Rather than gathering people only after a crisis, a regularly scheduled group sends the message that this is an ongoing aspect of our work that we need to address. Using an outside facilitator can help staff feel safe to talk about any and all contributors to their VT including ones within the agency. In their book *Trauma and the Therapist,* Pearlman and Saakvitne provide many exercises and ideas for exploring VT with staff (Pearlman, and Saakvitne, 1995).

End-of-Shift Debriefings. While sometimes difficult logistically, even a short check-in among staff about how the shift went can provide an outlet for venting feelings, and send the message that it is okay to talk about these feelings. This exchange can also be an opportunity for staff to search for positive meaning in their day.

Rituals Addressing VT. Building in ritual helps keep staff conscious of VT and the continual need for self-care. Rituals can demark the separation between one's life inside and outside of work. A team can begin or end meetings with a quick go-round about what feels challenging and gratifying about your work; at the end of a shift, have staff literally do the motion of brushing off what they want to leave at work and depositing it in a container of some sort; have staff quickly write down what they want to leave at work, and what they are looking forward to about being off work, and leave it in a ritual container.

Retreats. Annual or semi-annual retreats are opportunities for staff to be with each other outside of work, eat together, learn together, and have fun together. Integrate a VT exercise into every retreat. There are resources available for exercises and about how to lead activity-based learning. (See, for example, Project Adventure in References.)

Celebration and Recognition of Success. These celebrations can include: monthly commendations for staff who demonstrate excellence or go above and beyond; invitation to lunch with CEO for recognized staff; annual staff appreciation event; holiday parties; client/staff day; unexpected thank you or recognition emails.

Formal Program Structures. One example of a formal program structure comes from the Devereux treatment program in Massachusetts, which created a forum to respond to employees who experienced difficult events as the result of ideas generated during a Risking Connection training. Based on the Critical Incident Stress Debriefing literature, their response offered a voluntary forum for staff to talk with a trained peer about a difficult incident that occurred. Referrals can come to the response team via the staff him/herself, a colleague, or a supervisor. While not meant as psychotherapy or an investigation, the purpose of a team meeting is to listen supportively, validate feelings, teach about VT and self-care, and provide hope and exploration of meaning.

Over time, embedded interventions like these convince staff that agency attention to VT and self-care is not just lip service, but rather a deeply held agency value. Gradually, staff will internalize these messages and, as a community, share the weight of this incredibly demanding and challenging work. What previously felt like overwhelming feelings endured alone, can feel more manageable and worth the struggle when weighed against the great benefits of this honorable endeavor.

Working with traumatized clients can also offer helpers the opportunity to positively transform their lives. Caring about clients with such courage and resiliency changes the person of the helper. Dr. Laurie Ann Pearlman (2009) has named this positive change *vicarious transformation*. This she defines as: the possibility of being personally and positively transformed by the work. Dr. Pearlman states that: "Opening the self to the darker aspects of human experience can contribute to personal and professional perspective and growth." She suggests some conditions that promote such transformation: strong social support; access to and use of consultation; spiritual renewal; and social activism. She entitles these practices "working protectively." Dr. Pearlman suggests "radical self-care" which means "intentionally and frequently creating opportunities for respite and replenishment." This rest and replenishment includes all often-mentioned forms of self-care such as play, rest, healthy habits, relationships, and exercise. It also includes such deliberate practices as writing and talking about the work, which assists the helper in making some meaning of human cruelty and evil. Staying connected to personal physical and emotional experience and including the treatment framework in one's awareness is important. Accepting the inevitability of vicarious trauma and the limits of therapy can help. The therapist is responsible to manage the boundaries of the relationship even while "listening with respect and an open mind and heart." And just as trauma is best healed through connection, vicarious trauma is healed within strong connections both in the workplace and in one's personal life (Pearlman, 2009, pp. 214-221).

Agencies that cultivate this possibility will develop strong, committed and effective staff.

Celebrations

Celebrating individual and team excellence can be a significant vehicle for creating culture. There are many options in how to build in celebration:

- In programs, a celebration box can be created into which staff put notes about good things that they observe their peers do throughout the week. All cards are read out at staff meetings, and one is selected at random for a prize.
- Employee of the month programs work in some agencies, although there may be a problem when more people are excluded than recognized.
- A memo in a person's personnel file is more significant than it might seem.
- Publish particular staff achievements through a newsletter or on a website.

There are many other possibilities, but the main thing is to do something to recognize the hard work that the staff does every day and how often they do it superbly well (Brown, 2010).

Summary

As described above, the tasks involved in finding, developing and maintaining an excellent, trauma-sensitive staff is complex and ongoing. They include:

- Job descriptions that specify the skills of trauma-informed treatment.
- Hiring practices that evaluate the potential for these skills.
- Supervision to develop the best in staff.
- Addressing problem behaviors.
- Formalizing the relationship focus at New Employee Orientation.
- An intensive formal training in the effects of trauma, its relationship to present behaviors, how people can heal, and how treaters can take care of themselves, such as Risking Connection.

- Ongoing refresher training available to all staff.
- Developing internal trainers.
- Specific skills development for all staff in liking the clients, speaking non-judgmentally about them, what creates change, active listening, validation, and perseverance.
- eaching clinicians about formulation and specific evidenced-based interventions.
- Teaching staff relationship formation, and speaking from the heart crisis de-escalation skills.
- Offering specific training to new supervisors.
- Recognizing and addressing vicarious traumatization, and encouraging practices that promote positive transformation.
- Including support staff in trauma training.
- Celebrate special efforts and successes.

However complex, training and skill-development are the keys to excellence in trauma-informed care.

Chapter Twelve

The Process of Program Transformation

The Impetus to Change

Often the impetus to change to trauma-informed care starts when the agency experiences difficulty in carrying out its mission or in achieving success with its treatments. The clients being referred are more severely damaged, they have more frightening symptoms, and the traditional approaches are just not working. The agency experiences an increase in restraints and in emergency negative discharges. Staff injuries go up. Staff turnover also rises. The treatment teams confront problems they have not seen before, such as sexual acting-out or severe self-harm. A feeling of hopelessness and cynicism may develop among the staff.

Sometimes change is mandated by an outside body, such as the state Child Welfare Agency, perhaps following a severe incident in which a child got hurt or one child sexually attacked another. The licensing agency can mandate a corrective action plan that includes more training in the effects of trauma.

At times change starts with one or two people discovering trauma-informed care and realizing that their agency needs to change. The advocacy from these people draws the attention of the leaders, and a commitment to change begins growing.

Wherever the push for change begins, once the decision is made, it is imperative that top leadership strongly supports this transformation. They must articulate both their commitment to change and the reasons for it. Changing an agency culture is not easy, and requires significant resources. Leadership must be willing to persist in the change process for a significant period of time.

Administration must clearly explain to all agency staff what this change is and why they are making it. They must articulate the problems with continuing as they are. The time period during which staff have heard that there will be a change and before they know exactly what it will be is a period of high anxiety for staff. When childcare workers – who have experienced firsthand the injuries they can receive from these youth – fear that their disciplinary tools are being taken away, they are frightened. Administration must articulate the vision of a better treatment process that results in fewer staff and client injuries. It may be helpful to cite examples of other agencies in which this change has been successful, and perhaps exchange visits with those agencies. Staff is more likely to believe that this change is possible when they hear it from other childcare workers, not just from administration.

Trauma-informed care is a national trend, supported by the federal government through the National Child Traumatic Stress Network (www.nctsn.org) and many other initiatives. Extensive research supports the efficacy of trauma-informed care. It is helpful for the agency administration to become aware of and connected to the national movement. It can also be important to send staff to national conferences. Such collegial and educational gatherings help staff understand that this change is not just one person's crazy idea; it is an imperative in today's treatment environment.

The administration can articulate its vision for the future. This vision can communicate hope for a better treatment environment for both the children and the staff. The vision can include renewed pride in their agency as a center for excellence in the treatment of children and families who have experienced trauma.

Another part of administrative buy-in can be motivated by the financial advantages of making this change. There is no longer an economic niche for residential treatment programs that admit mildly hurt children and are kind to them until they are better. With the development of supportive services in the community, residential treatment is reserved for children who exhibit such serious behaviors that they cannot be safe despite much support and help. Funders are looking for places with sophisticated treatment skills and evidence of measurable results. Treatment programs are required to do more in less time. A program that has a specialty, has demonstrable skills, and can accept any child will be the program that thrives financially.

The administration can honestly represent to the staff that developing a trauma-informed agency will result in more effective treatment for children and families, a better place for staff to work, and a stronger financial position for the agency.

Beginning the Transformation

As mentioned in Chapter Ten, the first step is to create an agency Task Force to lead this change. The Task Force should consist of representatives from all areas and levels of the agency, including childcare, clinicians, nursing/medical, support services, education, and administration. Individuals who are eager to begin this change should be included when possible. Staff members who are influential with their peers are an additional possibility. If the agency has staff trainers, they should be included. The Task Force may be large, and since scheduling is such an issue in 24-hour programs, sub-groups can be formed and meet separately to consider specific topics then report back to the group. There should be a clear path for recommending Task Force decisions to administration and then implementing them when appropriate.

A first step for the Task Force might be to take an agency self-assessment (see Appendix Q for self-assessment designed for child-serving agencies), which can be completed either by the members of the Task Force or by a larger group. It will be helpful to have all respondents indicate their role in the agency. Areas in which there is strong disagreement among Task Force members often produce the most interesting results of the self-assessment. Does this disagreement align along role divisions? What could result in some members of the team having such a different experience than some other members?

An early step for the Task Force is to arrange training for the staff. It is necessary that all staff in the agency receive training in understanding trauma, how it affects people, how it relates to their current behavior, how trauma survivors can heal, and how treaters can take care of themselves and each other while doing this difficult work. It is not enough that the clinicians attend a trauma workshop. This culture change involves a paradigm shift, all treaters, whatever their job, are not going to be able to act differently day-to-day until they begin to think differently. It is necessary that when that child is holding a chair and about to throw it that the childcare worker understands what is happening in a new way.

The Risking Connection training offers organizations a pathway toward system-wide change to trauma-informed care. Through the Risking Connection Train-the-Trainer, agencies can gain the capacity to provide ongoing RC training within their organization. By doing so, they receive ongoing continuing education support for their credentialed RC trainers and join an international network of agencies using RC to create trauma-informed services.

When contemplating a change in agency culture, there is a tendency to rush to change everything at once. However, the most effective transformation combines mandate and process. It must be clear to everyone that this is the direction the agency is moving, and there will be no hesitation. At the same time, workers must have a voice in the details of how trauma-informed care will be operationalized in their specific program area. If administration mandates a change before workers are ready, there will be underground subversion of the new methods, and nothing will actually change. However, if administration relies entirely on a process approach, the discussing will go on forever, and nothing will change. One good option is to set a deadline that is several months away (such as, "We are opening the school with the Restorative Approach this September"), and to use the intervening time to discuss and plan for the specifics.

Another option is to create a pilot project in one area of the agency: one unit, one classroom, one campus. This unit can stop using points and levels, begin using restorative tasks instead of restrictions, and start talking more about the meaning of behavior. If this approach is used it is best to choose the unit with the most enthusiasm, the most committed leadership. Then leadership must work closely with this unit to overcome the inevitable obstacles. When the change is moved to the larger agency, the people from the pilot program can serve as teachers and models.

Early Steps in the Transformation

Before making any structural changes (such as changing the behavior-management system) members of the Task Force can lead subtle changes which will prepare the staff to move towards trauma-informed care. They can begin **modeling behaviors on the floor; such as when a child is upset ask them what is the matter.**

Don't talk about consequences. Don't talk about better ways they could be handling it. Don't try to get them to take responsibility for their actions.

When youth are asked what is the matter, staff must be prepared that the child's response will be about something that someone has done wrong at this "stupid place" (that's if they are putting it mildly). Staff does not argue or tell them why the person was right to do what they did. Staff paraphrases what the child said: so you are very angry about being sent up from school? It doesn't seem fair to you? Emphasize any feelings they impart, especially any besides anger: you are discouraged, you are sad, you are frustrated, or you were hurt.

Staff asks what else is upsetting them, and they stay for as long as they possibly can at the exploring and paraphrasing stage. No suggestions of how they could have handled it better, no mention of consequences that will happen, no taking responsibility for their action, just explore what they are upset about.

During all this interaction staff must keep their breathing slow, their voice calm, and themselves regulated. And this takes patience. They may have to keep doing this for a long time. When (and only when) the treater notices some de-escalation on the child's part, some slowing of breath, a reduction of yelling and a willingness to talk, then start considering where we can go from here. The child is upset and wants *this*, the adults think *that* is necessary, how can they both go forward? Wherever possible, compromise, be creative, use unique solutions.

Once the child has regained some sort of regulation, it is often surprising how easily the next steps can be figured out.

The next important step agencies can take to increase their readiness to make this change is to **increase the likelihood that staff will consider what is behind a behavior that a child is displaying before taking action to respond to that behavior.**

Remember the key concept of trauma-informed care: symptoms are adaptations; people do things for a reason. The behaviors the children do that are problems for those around them are solutions for them. Behaviors such as aggression, self-harm, destroying property, bullying, screaming, running away, throwing chairs all serve an immediate purpose for the child, and what's more, they work. The purpose is usually to escape some sort of intolerable feeling inside. Because the child has no reliable attachments to help him calm down, his emotions overwhelm him. Because she has a changed biology and a sensitized nervous system, a small problem feels like a catastrophe to her. And because he doesn't know any feelings-management skills, he does not know how to identify or handle the feelings, does not believe anyone cares, and does not think he is worth the trouble anyway.

So instead of staying with overwhelming feelings of fear and hopelessness, the child does something. And the problem is temporarily solved, even though there are long-term negative consequences.

Every behavior is adaptive. And when staff understands the benefits a child is getting from a behavior, they open up many more ways to help the child. This process is much more powerful than just trying to punish the behavior away.

How can an agency develop a culture in which the adaptive function of a behavior is routinely considered and discussed? The clinicians take the lead here. Shortly after a child is admitted (within two-to-three weeks) the team holds a meeting in which members of all disciplines (teachers, childcare workers, nursing, etc.) are present. The therapist conveys a beginning formulation of the case: a theory of what happened to the child and why they are acting the way they do. This formulation could be summarized in a treatment theme such as "learning to trust adults" or "learning to manage feelings" that highlights the most important thing the team will work on. The child will also be part of determining the treatment theme when his or her participation is appropriate.

Then for every behavior that occurs the therapist will lead the questions: Why is he doing this? Why now? What problem is she trying to solve? What has happened recently? How do we understand this? After a while this kind of thinking can become so pervasive in the program that everyone starts asking the same questions.

So when a boy often has a tantrum before bedtime, staff are wondering what it is about bedtime that is hard for him, and they are considering nightlights, staff presence outside his room, soft music, rather than thinking about punishing the tantrum.

Programs can begin by thinking about what meetings, what occasions, what communication channels can be used to explore ideas about the meaning of behavior. After a while it will be automatic for staff members to ask these questions and use theories to determine responses.

During this period of change, administration can be especially careful to notice and reward any change toward using the new model. They should praise staff for being flexible, kind and understanding. If there is an episode of dysregulation in the front hallway, they single out for praise staff that were exploring and validating what the child was feeling. When leadership attends a meeting about some episode of difficult behavior, they are sure to ask how the team makes sense of this behavior, and what needs the child was trying to meet.

Changing the Behavior Management System

At some point after the initial training, the Task Force or a sub-section of it will begin considering the behavior-management system. What should staff do day-to-day to help children move forward in their treatment? How should their progress be tracked? How should the team respond when a child hurts others?

In considering revamping the behavior-management system, one important conversation is to discuss the team's theory of change. What went wrong in these children's lives? What are likely to be the most powerful sources of change? Several exercises to explore this question are included in Appendix R.

The Task Force should establish some basic parameters for behavior management. A sample list of these parameters can be found in Appendix S.

One question that must be discussed early in this process at agencies that have more than one unit, program or campus is whether the various units will all use the same system, or whether general principles can be articulated and variation within them by individual teams encouraged. One factor here is how often staff move around and work in several programs. Related to this question is whether all programs will make the change at one time, or whether changes will be phased in gradually. Will the clients be involved in creating the new system? How will the changes be communicated to the children and their families?

When a unit or the whole program is ready to make a change, ceremony and celebration are maximized. There is a lot of publicity and acclaim. The treatment team can expect setbacks and trials during the transition. One challenge will be when a child does something seriously wrong. There will be an immediate push to return to punishment. The team will need support to maintain an interest in understanding the behavior and responding in a way that would help the child learn new skills to prevent it happening again.

Involving the Families

It will be crucial to communicate these changes to the children's families. Most of the children have been in many treatment programs over the years, most of which have used points-and-levels systems. The families may be suspicious because this program is doing something different. Some families are relieved; others feel the program is being too soft on their misbehaving child. Influencing the parents' reaction is the fact that many of them are also trauma survivors and are reacting on the basis of what was or wasn't done to help them.

It is helpful to create a document to give to families on admission explaining the philosophy of this program. (See a sample in Appendix K.) Such a document begins the task of family psycho-education regarding trauma and its effects. It explains to the parent what their child is experiencing, and may have the added benefit of explaining the parents' own experience to themselves.

Another important point to convey is that the Restorative Approach was designed to be usable in family settings, and they can use it with your help when their child visits home and ultimately when he or she is discharged. The clinician can support this broader application by demonstrating the approach in therapy and by helping the family create the possibility for the child to make amends on a home pass for any ways he hurts members of the family.

Other Stakeholders

It is also advisable to share the change process with other prime stakeholders including the agency Board of Directors and the various funding and licensing/accreditation bodies. Invite key stakeholders to the training, even if they can only attend part of it. The administration can make a presentation to the Board, listing all the reasons for the change, including the financial ones, what resources it will need, and their vision of the post-change future. Board members should be included in celebrating the milestones of change. The materials developed for families can be utilized with some modifications for other stakeholders.

Supporting Employees Through the Transition

Some employees will take naturally to this new approach, and will feel that their deepest instincts about how to do this work are being vindicated. These people can become champions, leaders of the change from whatever position they hold. Others will be reluctant and scared at first, but will gradually grow in their enthusiasm as they watch the approach work. Then there are still others who will resist this change and not want to work this way.

Spend the most energy celebrating successes and praising and promoting the champions. At each staff and agency meeting emphasize everything that has gone well with the new approach.

Some employees are scared. They have been bitten, punched and threatened by the youth. They feel that their control and their ability to punish is all that stands between them and chaos.

A combination of group and individual supervision is most effective in moving employees forward in this learning. When an employee remains resistant to this approach it must be made clear to him/her that the agency is moving in this direction and adopting these practices is not optional. In some cases a combination of supervision, specific feedback, praising any skills in relationship building and flexibility, and open discussion of fears and doubts is sufficient to help the employee change. In some cases stronger progressive discipline may be necessary. Some employees leave, being unable or unwilling to work in the new way.

Any splits or dysfunctions in the team (therapists vs. child care workers, first shift vs. second shift, staff vs. teachers) will emerge as this change moves forward. Open discussion among all team members is crucial. The change will have the best chance of success if all team members are encouraged to voice their concerns, and if resentments that have built up are aired and (hopefully) resolved.

Staff members that are champions of this new approach can be enlisted in training others, both inside the agency and for outside groups. This will increase their pride and job satisfaction, and solidify their commitment to the approach.

New Employees

Trauma-informed care will affect both the hiring and training of new employees. They must receive an orientation to this philosophy before they start to work, and a more in-depth training shortly afterward. Supervisors specifically instruct them on how behavior is to be handled on this unit. Any disagreement or reluctance is confronted immediately. In some cases, hiring a new employee gives the agency a chance to teach these methods from the beginning, but in many cases new employees have worked in other systems that emphasized points and levels, rewards and punishments. Explaining trauma-informed care at the beginning of their tenure is essential.

Later Steps

As the agency is successful in its transformation to trauma-informed care, the Task Force can work on solidifying the change. This strengthening includes making sure that all the policies and forms reflect the new way of thinking. It means looking at the process of intake and discharge to see if they can be more relationship-based. It may include changing the treatment-planning process to reflect a new understanding of what promotes and facilitates change, and what the steps are. It is essential to imbed trauma-informed care in these areas, so that it is not dependent on the presence of any few people at the agency.

Communication

As the transformation process continues, communication is essential. There must be regular feedback to all staff, families, board members and external stakeholders using every method of communication that the agency has: newsletters, websites, meetings, press releases, etc. All successes are celebrated. Writing articles for external publications can solidify beliefs and enhance the agency's reputation. Data on such things as reduction of restraints and seclusions decrease in staff turnover, and positive discharges will reinforce that the change is working and are to be widely shared.

Stages of Change

This recommended change process parallels the stages of change developed by John Kotter in *Leading Change* (1996).

Kotter's Stages of Change	What's Happening at the Agency	What to Watch Out For
Establishing a sense of urgency. 'Disconfirming' the status quo. Making clear that the current performance is not good enough; change is needed – and needed now. Communicate vision of better treatment and a better place to work. Communicate financial urgency of change.	Understand current environment & realities, including federal mandates to reduce restraints and seclusions. Identify crises, potential crises, & major opportunities, and make sure managers understand. Distribute performance & financial performance data more broadly throughout the organization, such as restraint and seclusion data, and discharge outcomes. Solicit information from clients and families. Use outside facilitators to force more relevant data & discussions. Stop management "happy talk" – communicate issues & problems. Attend national conferences, become aware of national trends. Thoroughly educate staff on future opportunities & organization's problems in pursuing them. Develop clinical team through workshops, conferences, and supervision.	Allowing too much complacency. If 75% or more of management team is convinced that current situation is acceptable & major change is not needed, change won't happen. Low overall performance standards. Internal measurement systems that focus on wrong performance indicators. Lack of performance feedback from external sources. "Kill the messenger, low confrontation" culture. Too much "happy talk" from management.
Create a guiding coalition to help set, validate and elaborate the strategy. Start with a small team committed to the approach and perhaps a small pilot project.	Pick guiding coalition members, balancing position, expertise, credibility, & leadership skills. Make sure members at all levels of organization are represented. Create teamwork through established common goals & planned off-site activities.	Failing to create a sufficiently powerful guiding coalition.

Developing a vision and strategy. Setting a clear and appropriate direction to orient and guide the change efforts. A picture of the future with implicit or explicit commentary on why people should strive to create that future.	Develop and articulate a vision of what trauma-informed care will look like. What are the guiding principles? Develop change strategy. Pilot project? Whole agency? Process? Timing?	Underestimating the power of vision. Staff will not 'sacrifice,' even if unhappy with the current situation, if they don't believe that the change proposed is achievable.
Communicating the change vision. Messages about change can never be over-communicated. Acknowledging the difficulties in the change is also important.	Use every vehicle possible to constantly communicate the new vision & strategies. The guiding coalition should be the role model for trauma-informed behavior. Use key elements in effectively communicating a vision of change: Simplicity Metaphor, analogy, & example Multiple forums Repetition Leadership by example Explanation of seeming inconsistencies	Under-communicating the vision.
Empowering a broad base of people to take action.	Get rid of obstacles to management & staff implementing change vision. Change systems or structures that undermine the change vision such as revising treatment forms & policies, re-writing handbooks and parent/child manuals. Encourage risk taking & nontraditional ideas, activities, & actions.	Permitting obstacles to block the vision. Formal structures make it difficult for staff to act. Lack of skills. Managers discourage actions aimed at implementing vision. Personnel policies. Information system functionality.

Generating short term wins. Generate and celebrate visible wins.	Plan for visible improvements in performance, or "wins." Create those "wins." Celebrate all instances of using trauma-informed approach. Use agency newsletters, etc. to highlight changes. Visibly recognize & reward people who made the "wins" possible. Concentrate energy on people who 'get it.'	Failing to create short term wins. Without short-term wins (& celebrations), the 'supporters' of change join the opponents.
Consolidating gains and producing even more change.	Use increased credibility of "wins" to change systems, structures, & policies that don't fit the transformation vision. Hire, promote, & develop people who can implement the change vision. Supervise and possibly replace staff who continue to resist. Develop teams. Implement more supervision. Implement forums for addressing vicarious traumatization. Reinvigorate the process with new projects, themes, & change agents.	Declaring victory too soon. Don't declare 'victory' (or the end of urgency) too early – results in loss of momentum.
Anchoring (institutionalizing) the new approaches into the culture.	Culture change occurs at the end of change process – when it is clear that the "new" system is superior to the old. Create better performance through new ways of interaction, better leadership, & more effective management. Revise HR systems (competencies, evaluations, promotions, etc.) to reflect the change.	Neglecting to anchor changes firmly in the corporate culture. Sometimes, staff turnover is inevitable to make lasting change. Leadership development & succession planning key for long-term success.

Summary

The transformation of an agency to trauma-informed care is a complex process that takes a long time. The initial impetus may be external or internal. Administration can begin by articulating their vision of the goal. Then, creating an agency Task Force can be helpful. The next step is training all staff in understanding trauma. Teams can start emphasizing understanding behavior before reacting to it. Then the Task Force can lead a re-examination of the behavior management system. It is important to involve all stakeholders, including families, the Board of Directors, and funders. Employees will have a great deal of anxiety as the transition begins; administration and task force members must support them through using increased and focused communication. The agency can create a plan to train new employees. These steps follow the blueprint of change articulated by Kotter (1996).

Chapter Thirteen

Sustainability

Sustaining trauma-informed care requires as much thoughtful and careful planning as implementing it in the first place. If an agency were to decide that they were finished implementing trauma-informed care and could now turn their attention to other matters, they would soon find erosion: they would begin to hear more punitive remarks from the staff; soon time-based restrictions would be used; and they would discover that new staff knew nothing about a relationship-based approach.

What makes it so hard to sustain a trauma-informed approach? In the first place, most people are raised with consequences and punishments, and they naturally turn to this response when a child does something that hurts others. And the surrounding society operates from a philosophy that the most effective remediation for criminal behavior is punishment. The strength of this belief produces the need for even more jails. Just as in the larger society, fear often drives the regression to a more punitive response by agency staff. Childcare staff fears that without strong punishments, chaos will break out, and they will be physically injured. Responding with compassion and hope to someone who has just hit you feels like making excuses and letting the youth off too lightly. A person's natural anger at being hit, feeling of powerlessness and urge to retaliate, can result in an emotional application of punishment. Asking staff to understand the youth's actions as fear-based is asking them to do the unnatural, to do the opposite of what they have learned throughout their lives.

Another factor that complicates sustaining trauma-informed care is the high turnover rates typically experienced by child treatment agencies, especially in direct-care positions. Strong training and culture are necessary to indoctrinate new staff into a relationship-based approach. The intense and crisis-driven nature of treatment programs is so hectic that the need for ongoing training may be overlooked, opening the door to the re-emergence of punishment and control as reactions to misbehavior.

Developing Policies to Support Trauma-informed Care

When trauma-informed care is first introduced to an agency, there are often a few leaders who have a deep commitment to this change, and who promote the new methods through both training and modeling. These people use staff meetings, treatment teams, training opportunities, and supervision to encourage a relationship-based approach. They are alert to any backsliding, and confront it quickly and directly. As long as these leaders remain, the organization may believe that it has implemented trauma-informed care and will never turn back. However, it is a mistake to let a major agency initiative depend on one or two people, no matter how sincere or charismatic. Even the most loyal employees have babies, or move away, go on medical leave, or retire. If the agency has not formalized its new philosophy into policy, those beliefs may disappear.

Policies that can be written to support a restorative approach include:

- Behavior management
- Treatment planning
- Individualized Crisis Prevention and Management Plans
- Guidelines for use of restraint and seclusion

Behavior Management

The program policy includes a list of what responses to rule breaking and other negative behaviors are and are not permitted. Are time-based consequences permitted? If so, are there any limits on their use? Points-and-levels systems are prohibited. Longer-term level systems may be used if based on treatment goals and if the child has not dropped levels. There can be an administrative review process of any consequences that continue beyond a certain specified time period or reach a specified threshold. The behavior management system is designed to reflect the agency's theoretical beliefs about what creates change. (For a sample behavior management policy, see Appendix S.)

Treatment Planning

Treatment planning is at its essence an expression of a theory. The clinician, with input from the team, the child, and the family delineates what problem behaviors are keeping the youth at this level of care. He or she then defines their opposite, the goals. The objectives are the steps that lead to the goals, and the interventions are the actions by staff that will facilitate achieving the objectives. When a clinician establishes a goal of less aggression against others, for example, and then writes an objective that the client will learn to express his emotions in words, he/she is basing this objective on a belief that people who can express themselves in words are less likely to hit others.

Therefore, it is important to examine the commonly used goals, objectives and interventions to see whether they reflect trauma theory. The agency can develop a series of possible goals, objectives and interventions that are based on their trauma-informed clinical theories. The treatment plan guides the interventions of the clinician and of the staff. All notes by both clinician and staff refer back to the goals and objectives. (For a sample of trauma-informed treatment planning, see Appendix J.)

Individualized Crisis Prevention and Management Plans

The Individualized Crisis Prevention and Management Plan (described in Chapter Seven) is an essential policy to operationalize trauma-informed care. The ICPMP is required as the child enters the program, based on what has been learned from family and previous treaters. It is reviewed and amended at every treatment review, with input from the child and family. It is easy to simply write the ICPMP and keep it in a notebook, but it is only effective if it is a living document, known and used by all. Administration develops a system for reviewing use of the ICPMP, and refers to it when debriefing crisis occurrences.

Guidelines for Use of Restraint and Seclusion

Guidelines for use of restraint and seclusion make clear that these interventions are used only in situations of imminent physical danger. Staff is educated about the potential for re-traumatization of the child during physical control. The ICPMP specifies situations the individual child may find particularly difficult. An example would be a child who has been sexually molested by a male and experiences flashbacks when held by male staff. Restraints and seclusions are reviewed regularly to determine what contributed to their necessity, with particular emphasis on environmental and staff factors. Tracking times of day that physical interventions occur may give valuable information about the need to adjust programming.

Training

Training is a key mechanism to ensure the sustainability of trauma-informed care. As discussed in more detail in Chapter Twelve, trauma-informed care should be integrated into the agency's orientation for new employees. After working two-to-three months the staff member can attend a full training. Refreshers help staff keep this new way of thinking alive, and also provide an option for retraining staff that are having difficulty.

It is also important to deliberately integrate trauma-informed training with whatever crisis-management training the agency uses. Building the bridges deliberately for staff helps avoid any confusion or any worries that they are being given contradictory directions.

Vicarious Traumatization

Management can demonstrate its commitment to trauma-informed care by imbedding consistent attention to the vicarious traumatization (VT) of its workers, as previously described. Some agencies develop peer teams to respond to serious incidents such as a long restraint or a staff injury. These peer teams reach out to the affected staff, inquiring about their feelings, reactions and thoughts. Agencies who have established such teams report that it takes time to create a culture in which staff takes up this offer. Initially, people tend to say they are fine and do not need any help. There may be a staff emphasis on being tough, on not being affected by the kids, on being strong and able to take abuse. However, over time this attitude can be changed into one of valuing help and understanding that every human reacts to crisis situations.

Challenging Times for Trauma-informed Care

Certain events can challenge an agency's commitment to trauma-informed care. These events include times of great turnover of either staff or clients, and times of especially severe behaviors.

Turnover

When management is aware that a certain unit or program is experiencing turnover of a large percentage of its members, management can take specific steps to recreate the team. These steps can include a team-building retreat, social events such as lunchtime potlucks, and lots of praise and celebration of any positive events. A simultaneous turnover of many of the clients in one program calls for similar steps: team-building activities, an increase of fun, active, connecting strategies by staff, and specific interventions to rebuild a caring culture.

Measure and Celebrate

A key method of sustaining trauma-informed care is to measure its results. In the next chapter some specific measures will be suggested. These measures are compiled regularly and reported to staff. All success is widely celebrated: a pizza party, praise for particularly skillful interventions through the agency's staff recognition system, newsletters, email, websites, blogs, staff appreciation boxes for peer recognition. All these avenues are ways of developing an awareness of the staff-child interactions that the agency is looking for, and increasing their prevalence. They underscore the message that the staff members who are valued at this agency are compassionate, flexible, available, empathetic and playful. Client successes are also to be celebrated, and when possible the team asks the client what made a difference for him.

When Devon left a treatment program not long ago, he was asked if he had changed, he said: "Yes, my anger fuse has gotten much longer." When asked what made the difference, he said: "Help was always available. Whenever I needed help, it was there."

Now *that* is something to celebrate.

Spread the Word

When someone teaches something, they learn it much more deeply. Plus, as they promote their new approach, they become more committed to it. For these reasons it can be very helpful to involve staff in training others how to do trauma-informed care. This training can take place between programs in the agency, or it can be for other agencies that are interested in this new method. One method is for staff to create a before-and-after skit. Start with a common problem (a youth refusing to go to his room, not following directions, something relatively minor), and in the "before" skit demonstrate how an increasing escalation of compliance, demands, and refusal can lead to a restraint. In the "after" skit, the staff models sensitivity to what may be going on with the client, and a collaborative approach to problem-solving which de-escalates the incident.

Involve the greater world in understanding the transformation that the agency is making. Invite significant stakeholders to attend the trainings, including Board members, funders and regulatory agencies. Share with the outer world successes that come as a result of the change, such as lower numbers of restraints and less staff turnover. Use agency newsletters, blogs, Facebook pages, Tweets and websites to share the achievements far and wide.

Learning collaboratives (Markiewicz, Ebert, Ling, Amaya-Jackson, & Kisiel, C., 2006) are a very powerful structure for strengthening and enhancing a change process. In the learning collaborative several agencies join together to receive training about a new practice. Then, as they attempt to implement it, they have continuing contact in which they share both their struggles and successes. They share relentlessly and steal shamelessly, and each reinforces the other's efforts.

Speak at some of the many national child trauma treatment or congregate care conferences that are eager for enthusiastic and knowledgeable presenters.

Write and publish an article, including research, in a peer-reviewed professional journal. Or, it could be more descriptive and be published in an agency trade journal or even a local magazine or newspaper.

The more the agency shares its commitment to trauma-informed care with the outside world, the harder it will be to allow it to fade away. And the success of one agency may inspire another to investigate these new ideas. Thus, gradually the world of child trauma treatment will change, and the children who have been wounded will get the excellent treatment they deserve to live much more fulfilling lives.

Summary

Sustainability of trauma-informed care requires active management by agency personnel. Developing policy that mandates the practices is essential. Ongoing training and attention to vicarious traumatization can be imbedded in agency practices. There are certain times, such as severe behavioral crises, when special attention must be paid to avoid slipping back into a punitive approach. Measuring, publishing, and celebrating the changes further solidify them.

Chapter Fourteen

Evaluating Trauma-Informed Care

Why Measure?

Agencies begin their transformation to trauma-informed care for many reasons. For some programs, it is a growing frustration with their inability to treat the more difficult population that is being referred to them. For others, it is a desire to reduce the use of restraints and seclusions. In some cases, a painful event such as a child being hurt in a restraint has brought negative attention to the agency, prompting external demands for change. In some programs, presentations or stories of success from others fuel the wish to change.

Each of these reasons to change, points to a reason to measure. The agency needs to know if the intervention is working and is achieving the desired goals.

Changing a culture is long, hard work. Measurement and the demonstration of success can help provide the stamina to continue the work. It also provides a language to use when explaining to stakeholders what the agency is doing (and why the agency is spending all that money on training). Board members, for example, understand a reduction in the use of restraints and better discharge outcomes. Sharing the results with state agencies and other referrals sources will enhance the agency's reputation, which may lead to more referrals, better results in obtaining grants, and more respect when dealing with problems.

Almost every grant application now requires some measurement of outcomes, whether it is a state, federal, or private funding source. Accrediting bodies such as the Joint Commission and the Council on Accreditation also have an outcome measurement requirement.

Measuring results has intrinsic value for the agency. Administration needs to know what is working and what is not. Where do they need to make changes in the initiative? Where are they achieving the best results, and could that program or unit, perhaps share their process with other agency departments? What does the consumer think about these changes, and what alterations would they suggest? Measurement results can be shared with administration and staff, examined closely, and ideas generated from the discussion can be used to improve the change effort.

What to Measure

At the beginning of the change process, the administration and the Task Force should articulate clearly why the agency is changing its treatment model. If this change is completely successful, in what ways will the agency look different in three years? What results will they see? How will they know it has been worth the effort?

Changes can be expected in three areas: process improvements, staff changes, and improved client outcomes.

The committee's vision of the outcome of this change can be circulated widely among the staff members, and their feedback incorporated. The vision can be extreme, describing what total success will look like.

Then, working from the vision, the committee can generate ways to measure change. How will the administration know if they are making progress towards this vision? What are the measurable indicators that can demonstrate this change?

Whenever possible it is helpful to use as measures information that the agency already collects for themselves or for regulatory bodies. The chances of continuing to collect, look at, and learn from the information are enhanced by using systems already in place. In general it is not necessary to add too many new, complex data collection processes, which may just produce resentment in the staff that is trying to change.

Process Improvements

Reduction of Restraints and Seclusions

Decreasing the use of physical control is often a primary goal of trauma-informed care implementation. If this goal is central to an agency initiative, it is important to specifically say so to all staff. Restraints and seclusions often start with a power struggle over a simple directive. Many agencies have experienced a reduction in their use when moving toward trauma-informed care. The method is designed for more flexibility and fewer power struggles. However, it is helpful to include specific focus on reducing the use of restraint and seclusion within the change effort. Strategies and materials to use can be found at the National Association of State Mental Health Program Directors (NASMHPD) website. There is also a useful Substance Abuse and Mental Health Services (SAMHSA, 2006) publication "Roadmap to Seclusion and Restraint Free Mental Health Services" which provides an entire curriculum for restraint reduction training.

Collecting a baseline indicator of the number and duration of restraints and seclusions prior to any change will be helpful for comparison. The duration of restraints and seclusion is an important change measure. One restraint that lasts two minutes is a very different experience for both staff and client than a restraint that lasts an hour and a half.

Reductions in AWOLs and Arrests

Running away and aggression which might lead to police involvement are two common symptoms of youth who have experienced trauma. As the youth feel safer and more connected, improve their biological regulation, and learn new skills of feelings management, they will have less need to resort to these extreme coping strategies. Like restraint, runaways and aggressive episodes often begin with power struggles over a rule or a child's demands. As power struggles decrease, these incidents may also decrease. Again, duration of absence in runaways can help differentiate events that have different risks.

Client Injuries

Decreases in restraints, runaways, and aggressive episodes also may result in a decrease of client injuries.

Length of Stay

Programs are under ever-increasing pressure to reduce length of stay, especially higher-level programs such as hospitals and residential treatment. Reducing length of stay is a complicated measure for trauma-informed care. In fact what children who have experienced both trauma and repeated attachment disruptions need is longer lengths of stay, and fewer disruptions and moves between programs. However, given the current environment agencies need to remain aware of the effects of any changes on lengths of stay. In fact, it has been noticed that with more effective and focused treatment, lengths of stay do decrease.

Youth and Family Satisfaction Surveys

Many agencies currently administer satisfaction surveys to both the youth and families that they treat. It is worthwhile to re-examine these surveys and add questions specifically inquiring about the methods an agency is trying to implement. Sample statements to include in a youth survey (with a point scale of agreement/disagreement) could be:

- Staff listens to me when I am upset.
- Staff is flexible.
- I feel staff care about me.

- Staff enjoys being with the clients.
- Staff understands me and helps me understand myself.
- For families some questions could be:
- I feel welcome to visit my child at any time.
- Staff helps me overcome any barriers to my involvement.
- Staff treats me with courtesy and respect.
- I am involved in decisions about my child.
- Staff understands me and helps me understand myself.
- See Appendix T for sample satisfaction surveys.

Staff Measures

Implementing trauma-informed care often feels scary to staff members. However, as the new methods take hold there are many advantages for staff. Because of the emphasis on daily relationships in healing, the staff understands the importance of their job in a new way. The new findings in brain science encourage programs to rebuild the children's brains by having fun and enjoying relationships, which is possible only if the staff are also having fun and enjoying relationships. The emphasis on flexibility and connection over compliance can result in few restraints and fewer staff injuries. Over all, the staff's responsibility becomes both more important and more interesting.

Therefore it is important to measure these things to gather information about the effect of the change on staff.

Some measurement options include:

- Staff turnover
- Staff injuries
- Number of staff sick days taken

In addition management can create surveys for staff about their experience in the organization, and track the results over time.

The Traumatic Stress Institute has developed two staff-related measures. One, entitled "Staff Behavior in the Milieu" asks about staff perceptions of whether the milieu behaviors of their team reflect the principles of trauma-informed care. The second, "Staff Beliefs," asks staff to agree or disagree with statements that reflect the beliefs that underlie trauma-informed care. (See Appendices U and V.) (Brown, Baker, Wilcox, in press.)

A standardized instrument that measures both job satisfaction and job burnout is the Professional Quality of Life Elements Theory and Measurement (Stamm, 2002), which measures compassion satisfaction and compassion fatigue, burnout, secondary traumatic stress, vicarious traumatization and vicarious transformation. Compassion satisfaction and compassion fatigue are two aspects of professional quality of life. They encompass the positive (compassion satisfaction) and the negative (compassion fatigue) parts of helping others who have experienced suffering. Compassion fatigue breaks into two parts. The first part concerns things such as exhaustion, frustration, anger, and depression typical of burnout. Secondary traumatic stress is a negative feeling driven by fear and work-related trauma. It is important to remember that some trauma at work can be direct (primary) trauma. In other cases, work-related trauma can be a combination of both primary and secondary trauma. If working with others' suffering changes you so deeply in negative ways that your understanding of yourself changes, you are experiencing vicarious traumatization. Learning from and understanding vicarious traumatization can lead one to vicarious transformation.

Client Outcomes

It is more difficult and also more important to measure the effect of trauma-informed care on client outcomes. It is great to have few restraints, satisfied customers, few runaways and arrests, and happy staff members. But are the children and their families actually getting better? One of the complications to achieving measurable outcomes is that the treatment environment surrounding the agency constantly changes. The referred population may change (and usually gets more severe). Programs may open and close. Still, it would not be ethical to attempt comparisons by offering only some clients trauma-informed care and others punitive, controlling care. Some outcome comparisons can be made over time, and/or comparisons can be made between units that have changed their approach and those that have not.

Some possible comparison points are:

- Number of negative, emergency discharges.
- Discharge destinations: what percentages of the clients are discharged to a lower level of care?
- Change in Global Assessment of Functioning (American Psychiatric Association, 2000) scores.
- Changes in scores on standardized instruments such as the Ohio Scale, (Ogles, Melendez, Davis, & Lunnen, 2000)
- The Child Behavioral Check List (Achenbach 1991, 1992) and the Trauma Symptoms Inventory (Briere, 1995).
- Number of goals and objectives achieved.

An even more important effort, if possible, is to do follow-up studies at some period after the child is discharged. To get reasonable returns from follow-up requires advanced planning. For example, the expectation of follow-up can be mentioned at admission. Families can be asked for the name of someone who will know their ongoing whereabouts, and be asked to sign releases to that person and to the state agency with which they are involved. The returns can also be increased by entering those people who respond in a raffle drawing, or inviting alumni to a dinner and surveying them at that time. Follow-up surveys can be simple and ask about specific signs of a life worth living, including:

Has the child:

- Been hospitalized for psychiatric problems?
- Been arrested?
- Been pregnant/fathered a child?

Is the child:

- Attending school?
- Holding a job?
- Involved in positive recreation?
- Using drugs or over-using alcohol?
- Again, these results can be followed over time.

Learn from and Share the Results

After progress has been measured, analyze the results. What is working well? What can the program improve? What areas are not being addressed and could be added? For example, one program discovered on follow-up questionnaires that many things were going well for their clients, but there was a high rate of early pregnancy/fathering. This led them to add healthy sexuality and pregnancy programs to their treatment.

Then communicate! Share the results with all staff, all Board members, funders, local media, trade organizations, and professional associations. Display the results in easily understood, graphic formats. Present the findings at conferences. Write and publish papers. Be proud of the difficult but wonderful transformation the program has achieved.

Summary

Measurement of outcomes is required by many external agencies, and is also the method for agencies to examine what is working and what isn't. The effects of transforming the agency to trauma-informed care can be seen in the process, staff, and client arenas. Process improvements may include reductions in restraints, seclusions, runaways, arrests, injuries and lengths of stay. Satisfaction surveys can reveal the opinions of the clients and families about the change. Staff measures can include decreases in staff turnover, staff injuries, and number of staff sick days taken. In this arena, too, surveys can be helpful. Possible client outcomes include positive versus negative discharges, discharge destinations, standardized test scores, GAF scores, and goals and objectives achieved. Post-discharge follow-up, although more difficult, can reveal even more important information. Once the results are collected and analyzed, the agency can publicize and celebrate its achievements, and make changes and improvements as needed.

Appendices

A. Exercise: Taking Responsibility

B. How to Assign a Restorative Task

C. Task Planning Worksheet

D. Creating Restorative Healing Tasks

E. Examples of Tasks for Healing

F. Restorative Tasks for Making Amends

G. Outline for Case Presentation

H. Complementary Therapies for Trauma-Informed Programs

I. Sample ICPMP

J. Goals for Trauma-Informed Treatment Planning

K. Sample Handout: The Restorative Approach for Parents and Guardians

L. Sample Family Crisis Prevention and Management Plan

M. Team Self-Evaluation: Effective Services for Survivor Parents

N. Assessing Trauma-Informed Foster Homes

O. Guidelines for Trauma-Informed Behavior Management in the Home

P. Scenarios and Questions for Hiring Interviews

Q. Trauma-Informed Care in Youth-Serving Settings: Agency Self-Assessment

R. Theory of Change Exercise for Staff

S. Sample Behavior-Management Policy

T. Sample Satisfaction Surveys, Family and Child

U. Indicators of Trauma-Informed Care: Staff Behavior in the Milieu

V. Trauma-Informed Care Belief Measure

Appendix A
Exercise: Taking Responsibility

Four volunteers are needed for this exercise: one reads what staff is thinking, one reads what staff says, one reads what the child is thinking, one reads what the child says.

VERSION ONE:

Child is sitting playing electronic game; staff walks into room.

Staff: **Thoughts**: Oh, there is (name). I heard she had a hard time in school today; I'd better talk to her to see what happened.

Child: **Thoughts**: Oh, here comes (name). I know she heard I screwed up AGAIN in school today. I know she's mad at me. I hope she doesn't see me. I'd better hide.

Staff: **Thoughts**: I am really getting discouraged, (name) doesn't seem to be changing, I wonder what I am doing wrong.

Says: Hi (name). Let's talk about what happened in school today. Can you tell me what went on?

Child: **Thoughts**: I knew it, she hates me now, I never should have started to like her, I bet they are getting ready to kick me out; nothing is ever going to work out in my life.

Says: It's those stupid teachers. They are no good. I want to get out of this dumb place and go to a place with a real school.

Staff: **Thoughts**: This kid will never take responsibility for her own actions. If she never learns to accept what she has done she is going to end up in jail. We have to make her understand that her actions are her own choice. Maybe she is right; maybe she doesn't belong here. We do not seem to know what to do to help her.

Says: But (name) you must have done something to get yourself into a fight. It can't all be the teacher's fault.

Child: Thoughts: See I knew it! She blames me for the whole thing. And she is right, I will never be smart enough to learn math, I am such a loser, and when Kristi made fun of me I just could not stand it. And now (name) hates me too I have to get out of this place!!!

Says: I hate all you f***ing people and if you get any nearer to me I am going to hit you, so leave me alone!!!!

Staff: Thoughts: She is really just impossible I cannot have a simple conversation with her. She really has to learn that she cannot talk to me that way.

Says: That's threatening. You have to go to your room now if you are going to be so disrespectful.

VERSION TWO:

Child is sitting playing electronic game; staff walks into room.

Staff: **Thoughts**: Oh, there is (name). I heard she had a hard time in school today; I'd better talk to her to see what happened.

Child: **Thoughts**: Oh, here comes (name). I know she heard I screwed up AGAIN in school today. I know she's mad at me. I hope she doesn't see me. I'd better hide.

Staff: **Thoughts**: I know (name) has so much trouble in school, especially in math. We have been working on how to ask for help when she is confused but it is so hard for her. And I know that Kristi, the girl she had a fight with, can be so mean and pick on people's weaknesses.

Says: Hi (name). How are you? I heard that this weekend you made that beautiful bulletin board over there, it really adds color to the unit.

Child: Thoughts: I know she is going to talk about school and she is mad at me, but at least she noticed the bulletin board I made. Might as well get it over with.

Says: Yeah but today really sucked.

Staff: Thoughts: I'm glad she brought up what happened. I know this kind of discussion is really hard for her because she always feels so hopeless.

Says: Yeah, I heard you had a problem with Kristi in math. That staying calm thing and asking for help thing didn't work out as well as we hoped today, but I also heard you calmed down and did well in art afterwards.

Child: Thoughts: Well, maybe she doesn't hate me, but I know I screwed up big time. I wonder if they are going to kick me out of here now? I never should have trusted these people.

Says: So I suppose I'm kicked out now, right, and that is fine with me because I hate this f***ing place anyway and this is a stupid school that doesn't know how to teach kids.

Staff: Thoughts: Is that what she has been afraid of all day? It's even more amazing she was able to calm down. Maybe she is making progress.

Says: Oh no, (name), we are not kicking you out! Far from it! We see the progress you are making. You and I just have to figure out what went wrong today and how we could come up with some better ideas for next time.

Child: Thoughts: That's surprising. Well, I would like to know how to keep that Kristi from aggravating me so much – I know she was glad she got me going.

Says: Well, you can start by getting rid of Kristie.

Appendix B

How to Assign a Restorative Task

Every restorative task should contain two components: **learning** and **reconnecting.** Learning would be anything that helps a child gain skills or knowledge necessary to prevent the behavior in the future. Reconnecting includes making amends for any harm done and repairing any damaged relationships.

The learning component is complete when the assigned task is done in a serious way by the child. The reconnecting component is done when those involved feel the child has participated in a meaningful process with them.

When you are deciding on a restorative task consider these questions:

Who was affected by what the child did?

How can the child make up for the harm they caused? (Do nice things for staff or unit, play positively with child hurt, apologize, do chores.)

What led up to the child's behavior?

How can the child examine and become more aware of what triggers, signs, and incidents lead up to outbursts? (Collage, writing assignments, discussion, etc.)

What skills would help a child avoid this problem?

How can the child learn/practice/remind themselves of these skills? (Make a sign, do a role play, explain it to someone else.)

What life issues are interfering with the child's coping?

How can the child explore these issues more? (Writing, collage, explain to people, talk about how to cope with disappointments, ask others how they cope.)

Restorative tasks reflect treatment themes and the basic issues a child is working on. General themes and guidelines for restorative tasks should be pre-determined in Treatment Team discussions.

Appendix C

Task Planning Worksheet

To be used in Treatment Team discussions to pre-plan possible restorative tasks:

Name of Child____

Date of Plan____

Disruptive behavior commonly exhibited by this child:

Formulation of issues contributing to this behavior and skills needed to decrease this behavior:

Restorative tasks to teach skills and build positive ways to meet needs:

Appendix D
Creating Restorative Healing Tasks

Question to consider	Example
What was the problem behavior?	Jason hit his peer Sammy.
What led up to the behavior?	Sammy made fun of Jason's errors in reading aloud.
What was he or she feeling? What need was the child trying to meet?	Jason was feeling stupid; sure he would never learn or be able to read right. He was angry with Sammy for making fun of him. He was trying to feel strong, powerful, and to hurt Sammy.
What would we want the child to do when he or she feels this way or has these experiences?	We would want Jason to tell an adult, or walk away, or do something else to help himself stay in control.
What skills and/or beliefs would the child need in order to be able to do this alternative behavior?	Jason would have to trust that adults would help him. He would have to notice that he was starting to get mad. He would have to feel enough okay about himself that he wasn't as reactive to instigation. He would have to know some skills for calming himself down.
What tasks can we create (preferably with the child) that will help him/her strengthen the positive beliefs and learn and/or practice the needed skills?	Jason can do a project with his teacher (build connection and trust). Jason can write a letter, draw a comic, make a collage about the first signs in his body when he is getting mad. (Build feelings skills.) Jason can teach a younger child a skill he is good at, or read to the elementary classes, or tutor someone in sports. (Build a sense of competence.) Jason can make a poster "what I can do when I get mad" after interviewing several people to get ideas about what one can do to stay calm. (Develop feelings skills.)

Appendix E

Examples of Tasks for Healing

What do we want the child to learn from his or her mistakes?

1. Patterns that will reveal what leads up to an episode of dysregulation, times when he is most vulnerable, pre-disposing factors.
2. Skills that would help her not do the same thing again.
3. How to recognize emotions when they are small and he has more options as to what to do about them.
4. How to meet her needs in more positive ways.

Therefore, it is important to think about what needs the child was meeting, what problem he was trying to solve. How was this behavior adaptive for her?

Using the formulation to guide the selection of restorative tasks.

If the child's behavior is in response to or an attempt to escape shame and low self-esteem:

Goal of tasks: Develop sense of achievement, self-worth, earn praise from others, learn that it is possible to work out problems and rebound from them.

Characteristics of tasks: Observable achievement, worthwhile, service to others, learn/practice useful skills, work out a difficulty with someone, solve a problem.

Examples:

- Cleaning
- Repairs
- Making and serving food
- Making sign telling steps of a task or giving instructions
- Helping staff or child with task

- Sorting a closet
- Teaching a skill to another child

If the child's behavior is a result of being unable to ask for help, unable to trust others, being fearful of close relationships:

Goal of tasks: Increase sense of trust; explore barriers to trust.

Characteristics of tasks: Connection with others, reliability, exploration of trust and barriers, require sharing of thoughts and feelings.

Examples:

- Read books about friendship and trust.
- Make poster, write essay on "what is a friend?"
- With staff make lists of "people I trust and why, people I don't trust and why."
- Write or talk about subject of "am I trustworthy?"
- With staff talk about "ten things that make it hard for me to trust people."
- Talk or write about "how I decide how much to trust someone."
- Ask if child feels they have a wall built around their heart. If so, talk about what it looks like, how thick, does it have doors and windows, draw a picture of the wall. Make no attempt to judge wall or to say it should be more open. Make it clear that wall was developed for a good reason.
- List: promises made to me and kept; promises made to me and broken.
- Talk with another child (with staff) about what you were feeling in a situation.

If the child's behavior is characterized by quick escalation, and is a result of an over-active nervous system and being unable to notice when he/she is first becoming angry or feeling other intense emotions, and not knowing how to respond to strong emotion:

Goal of tasks: Learn self-observation and distress tolerance.

Characteristics of tasks: Contain opportunities to learn/practice self-monitoring skills and distress tolerance skills, repetition desirable.

Examples:

- Develop scaling card for emotions, practice using.
- Develop list of ways to handle emotions.
- Make poster for room of these skills, practice using one of them.
- Explain to another child how to calm yourself down.
- Keep a mood chart for a week.

If the child is quick to anger over little things, look for fear, confusion, and a sense of vulnerability beneath the anger:

Goal of tasks: Learn and practice anger management, explore causes of anger, develop ability to share vulnerable feelings with others.

Characteristics of tasks: Contain opportunities to develop and practice (through role play) specific skills, exploration of reasons for anger, increased comfort with vulnerability, ability to ask for help.

Examples:

- Role play other ways to express anger.
- Make a collage of all the things that make me angry.
- Poster for room or unit entitled "what to do when you are mad."
- Write story "The Girl/Boy Who Got Mad."
- Make list of "100 things that make me mad."

- Do anger management work sheets.
- Make thermometer of how anger feels when it starts, levels of anger; use to specify current level.
- Role play working out of difficulties.
- Do work sheets on describing anger, causes.
- Draw picture of anger.
- Draw a picture that depicts events leading up to anger, how I look on outside, what is happening inside, and goes through whole sequence of events.
- Talk to others about times they felt afraid and what they did.
- Ask others, especially those admired, about times they have felt scared or confused or overwhelmed.
- Make poster about "how a guy/girl can be strong" that includes ways other than by violence.

If the child does not know how to make or keep friends:

Goal of tasks: Learn and practice effective friendship skills, experience positive peer interactions.

Characteristics of tasks: Practice skills with staff; be supported in positive play with peers.

Examples:

- Role plays, worksheets from book.
- Playing a game with a peer.
- Supported problem solving with peer.
- Reading book on friendship and giving report to group.
- Making poster of "what makes a good friend."

- Write story about the day a boy made a friend.
- Practice specific personal effectiveness skills.
- Play a cooperative game with a friend for a half hour.
- Choose a peer and work together on a project to beautify the unit.
- Interview three peers about likes and dislikes, present at meeting.
- Shadow a peer and get to know him or her.
- Role play with a staff problem solving strategies.

If the child is reacting to family problems:

Goal of tasks: Explore family issues and positive ways to change or endure them.

Characteristics of tasks: Opportunities for exploration and processing, referral back to therapist and family therapy.

Examples:

- Collage of "My Family Now and How I want it to be".
- Letter to family.
- List of good and bad things about my family.
- Pictures of family at different stages.
- List of "ways I can get along better with my family and who will help me."
- Invite family member to recreational activity.

If the child is overwhelmed by identifiable, external, stressful events and feeling hopeless:

Goal of tasks: Practice self-care, self-soothing, crisis management, how to get through difficult times, how to ask for and receive support from others; develop hope for the future.

Characteristics of tasks: Contain opportunities to learn and practice ways to take care of ones self; contain opportunities to connect with others and get support, a sense that the future may be better.

Examples:

- Make list of ways to distract oneself using all five senses.
- Make poster for room: Things to do when I get bad news or am worried.
- Explain to another child how to tolerate bad times.
- Make a soothing toy or blanket.
- Spend time with staff talking about how to get through bad times.
- Practice three self-soothing skills.
- Make and use a crisis kit.
- Spend time outside in nature.
- Engage in positive physical activity.
- Do something for others.
- Make a CD with soothing or uplifting music.
- Write a list of dreams, hopes, and goals.
- Write a list (make a collage) of ten things I have accomplished or learned in the last year.
- What would you say to a younger relative who was going through a bad time? Write or tell a story about it.

If the child's behavior results from a fear of being left by significant others, of being alone:

Goal of tasks: Develop ability to remember that the other person exists and cares about you even when he or she is not physically present.

Characteristics of tasks: include transitional objects and reminders of people the child cares about.

Examples:

- Write a letter to the person.
- Call their voice mail.
- Keep a journal that you will share with the person.
- Make a poster with names/pictures/sayings of people who have loved you.
- Write a story about someone who loved you in the past and what he/she would wish for you.
- Find music that reminds you of people you love.
- Plan a future activity with someone you care about.
- Make a collage of characteristics of people you have cared about that you would like to have.

Appendix F

Restorative Tasks for Making Amends

The first step in making amends is to figure out who was affected by your behavior. Who was hurt, inconvenienced, upset, insulted?

Then, consider what you can do to work it out with them and make their life better.

Working it out may include listening to their account of how they felt during the situation.

It may include your telling them steps you will take to avoid it happening again.

Tasks to make amends for damage done to an individual:

- Talk with them about how the experience felt for them.
- Write the story of the event from their point of view.
- Make a poster or card (drawing, collage) to explain what happened and how you were feeling before the event.
- Write the person a letter.
- Do a chore for them or with them.
- Replace something that was broken.
- Make them something: a decoration, food.
- Do an activity with them or play a game with them.
- Teach them something (like how to play a video game).

Tasks to make amends for damage done to individuals or unit community:

- Decorations
- Posters illustrating feelings and positive behaviors
- Posters or books illustrating steps to a task, i.e. getting ready for school

or unit chores

- Make food for unit
- Cleaning
- Weeding
- Setting out a treat for each child
- Doing a presentation on something in a community meeting, such as the dangers of smoking or why we should not pull fire alarms
- Lead an activity
- Teach something to younger children, or read to them
- Clean the van
- Repair something you broke. If you cannot repair it, do something nice for the people who do have to repair it (like bake cookies for the maintenance staff).

Appendix G

Outline for Case Presentation

1. Demographics
   Name, age, sex, race, unit, how long at placement
   Family composition
2. Question
   Focus of presentation
3. History
   Bio family
   Trauma history
   Placement history
   Important events
   Problem development
   Treatment history
4. Formulation: How do we understand this child?
   How are these behaviors adaptive?
   What self-capacities does he/she need to learn?
5. Current situation
   Family: mental health issues, substance use, medical issues, siblings/extended family?
6. Therapy and Visitation: How is it going?
7. Course of Treatment
   Diagnosis and medication
   Individual treatment
   Family treatment
   Behavior
8. Restate question- What do you want from group?

Appendix H

Complementary Therapies for Trauma-Informed Programs

Trauma-informed care is the foundation of the building that is a treatment program. It supports all treatment and pervades everything that the program does. From the moment that a client enters the building, an atmosphere of respect, collaboration, and empowerment characterizes every interaction. Every person the client meets is aware of the healing power of relationships, and attempts to offer the client an experience of a caring and trustworthy connection.

Many specific treatment modalities can then be implemented, built on this foundation. The following are some of the approaches that have been found to be helpful in congregate-care programs:

- Sensory Interventions
- Trauma-Focused Cognitive Behavioral Therapy
- Dialectical Behavioral Therapy
- Eye Movement Desensitization and Reprocessing
- Neurotherapy
- Yoga, Meditation and Mindfulness
- Animal Assisted Therapy

Sensory Interventions

The movement to eliminate the use of restraint and seclusion has been instrumental in bringing attention to the use of sensory interventions in helping people to calm down and stay regulated. Occupational therapists are taking a leadership role in the planning and implementation of sensory approaches across mental healthcare settings, including the use of sensory rooms, carts and kits. Sensory interventions can be used in many ways. An individual client can develop their own Crisis Kit, which contains items utilizing all five senses to help soothe the person. The kit could include essential oils, hard candy, CDs of soothing music, pictures of beautiful scenes, notes written by people who love this person, pictures of loved ones, soft fur or other textures, and anything else the individual finds helpful. The kit is often kept by staff and offered whenever the youth is having a hard time.

The development and use of sensory rooms, sensory carts, and sensory enhancements throughout the milieu is designed to offer sensory soothing options to everyone in an easily accessed way. Items in the room can include a rocking chair, weighted and plain blankets, music, fur, squeeze balls and other touchable items to play with, clay, different lighting fixtures, beanbag chairs, and many other options. Consultation with a skilled Occupational Therapist will bring expertise into the use of sensory interventions. Furthermore, an OT can often recommend specific sensory interventions for particular children or problems. For example, brushing the child's arms with a soft brush or applying lotion can be helpful. Children who bite can be given biting toys to channel their need for mouth stimulation. Vibrating pens and cushions can help fidgety children concentrate in school. (For more information and links to resources, see http://www.ot-innovations.com)

It is also helpful for clients to leave treatment settings with discharge packets to share with outpatient providers, family members, and caregivers. This packet should contain worksheets and information regarding the variety of techniques learned and practiced, and plans for incorporating these skills and ideas into daily schedules at home, school and/or work environments. This information sharing is an essential part of the discharge planning process.

Trauma-Focused Cognitive Behavioral Therapy

Trauma-Focused Cognitive Behavioral Therapy (TF-CBT; Cohen, Mannarino, & Deblinger, 2006) is a therapeutic intervention designed to be delivered in 12 therapy sessions with a child and, when possible, their parent. It can be integrated into residential or day treatment programs as one segment of the care.

TF-CBT's treatment model includes several core treatment components designed to be provided in a flexible manner to address the unique needs of each child and family. There is strong scientific evidence that this therapy works in treating trauma symptoms in children, adolescents, and their parents. This model was initially developed to address trauma associated with child sexual abuse and has more recently been adapted for use with children who have experienced a wide array of traumatic experiences, including multiple traumas. It is recognized as an evidence-based treatment by the National Child Traumatic Stress Network Empirically Supported Treatments, and Promising Practices.

Children and parents learn new skills to help process thoughts and feelings related to traumatic life events; to manage and resolve distressing thoughts, feelings, and behaviors related traumatic life events; and to enhance safety, growth, parenting skills, and family communication.

There is a free, excellent web-based training for TF-CBT that can be found at http://tfcbt.musc.edu/. Therapists generally augment this learning by attending live trainings regularly offered by the developers of the method, Judith Cohen, M.D. and Anthony Mannarino, Ph.D.

Dialectical Behavior Therapy

Dialectical behavior Therapy (DBT) is a complete treatment method that fits well with a trauma-informed approach (Linehan, 1993). The assumptions of DBT, such as "the client is doing the best they can," and the emphasis on the dialectic between validation and the push for change can greatly enhance the team's ability to provide excellent treatment. Furthermore, a key belief in trauma-informed care is that adults cannot simply insist that clients give up the behaviors/symptoms that have saved their lives. Instead, treaters need to teach the clients new ways of meeting their needs and managing their feelings. A DBT Skills Group and curriculum as implemented in congregate-care provide one of the most effective methods of facilitating positive change.

The skills taught in the DBT skills group are:

- Mindfulness
- Interpersonal Effectiveness
- Emotion Regulation
- Distress Tolerance
- Self-Management

The assumptions of DBT are:

- People are doing the best that they can.
- People want to improve.
- People must learn new behaviors both in therapy and in the context of their day-to-day life.
- People cannot fail in DBT.
- People may not have caused all of their problems, but they have to solve them anyway.
- People need to do better, try harder and be more motivated to change.
- The lives of people who are suicidal are unbearable as they are currently being lived.
- The most caring thing a therapist or treatment provider can do is help people change in ways that bring them closer to their own ultimate goals.
- Clarity, precision, and compassion are of the utmost importance.
- The treatment relationship is a real relationship between equals.

- Principles of behavior are universal, affecting clinicians no less than clients.
- Treatment providers need support.
- Treatment providers can fail.

These skills and assumptions fit perfectly with the beliefs that underpin trauma-informed care.

Eye Movement Desensitization and Reprocessing

More and more trauma treatment is focused on methods that involve the body. Since much of the damage through neglect, abuse, and trauma happened to clients before they had reached the verbal stage, change cannot be achieved entirely through words. One bodily method that has proved effective is Eye Movement Desensitization and Reprocessing.

Eye Movement Desensitization and Reprocessing (EMDR) is a psychotherapy treatment that was designed to alleviate the distress associated with traumatic memories. Originally created by Francine Shapiro, Ph.D., EMDR is a comprehensive, integrative psychotherapy approach, as Dr. Shapiro, (1998) explains on her website:

> EMDR psychotherapy is an information-processing therapy and uses an eight-phase approach to address the experiential contributors to a wide range of symptoms. It attends to the past experiences that have set the groundwork for symptoms, the current situations that trigger dysfunctional emotions, beliefs, and sensations, and the positive experiences needed to enhance future adaptive behaviors and mental health.
>
> One of the procedural elements is "dual stimulation," using bilateral eye movements, aural tones, or physical taps. During the reprocessing phases the client attends momentarily to past memories, present triggers, or anticipated future experiences

> while simultaneously focusing on a set of external stimuli. During that time, clients generally experience the emergence of insight, changes in memories, or new associations.

The clinician assists the client to focus on appropriate material before initiation of each subsequent set.

Neurotherapy

Another body-based treatment that is rapidly gaining both scientific evidence of effectiveness and increasing general awareness and acceptance is neurotherapy. Due to the rapid development over the last two decades of numerous brain-based technologies, healthcare professionals now have access to powerful tools that allow direct observation of the human brain's functioning. But unlike CAT, PET, SPECT scans or fMRIs, neurotherapy is both a powerful and cost-effective clinical tool for assessing and modifying human brain activity. In contrast to psychotropic medication, which impacts chemical activity throughout the human brain, evidence-based neurotherapy approaches can identify specific brain structures and determine whether their functioning exhibits atypical patterns of activity that have been associated with emotional, behavioral, or psychological disorders. Once specific areas or patterns of dysfunctional brain activity are identified, neurotherapy can effectively modify the atypical activity, creating positive and lasting results.

Neurotherapy (also referred to as 'neurofeedback' or 'EEG biofeedback') uses monitoring devices to provide moment-to-moment information to an individual on the state of their central nervous system and brain functioning. In a typical neurotherapy session, sensors are placed on the head that begin to read the electrical brainwave patterns of the individual. This information is then fed back to the trainee virtually instantaneously on a computer monitor. Whenever the trainee is able to generate the targeted brainwave frequency or pattern selected by the neurotherapy clinician, he receives a signal via the computer monitor. Due to the principles of learning, the trainee is able after repeated training sessions to change the specific brain patterns associated with their reported emotional and behavioral problem(s). There are no medications used, and the procedure is completely painless and non-invasive.

Effective evidence-based neurotherapy must be preceded by an objective assessment of brain activity and psychological status. In addition to a clinical interview and completion of standard paper-and-pencil assessments used to assist in identifying the individual's relative strengths and areas of concern, individuals participating in evidence-based neurotherapy treatment receive a quantitative electroencephalography (QEEG) assessment. The QEEG is a powerful tool for measuring the electrical activity within the brain and identifying whether the brain shows specific types of atypical activity as compared to a large database of same-age, well-functioning individuals. The results of the QEEG assessment are then used to inform the creation of a carefully tailored, individualized treatment plan. The treatment plan identifies the specific targets of treatment unique to that individual's brain. In addition, the QEEG-informed treatment plan will identify the appropriate neurotherapy approach necessary for assisting the individual to modify their atypical brainwave patterns so that problem symptoms are reduced and/or eliminated (Davis, 2010).

Yoga, Meditation and Mindfulness

There has recently been a groundswell of appreciation for the role that Yoga, meditation and mindfulness can play in healing from trauma. In their article on trauma-sensitive yoga, Emerson, Sharma, Chaudhry, and Turner (2009, pp. 12-13) state that: "An essential aspect of recovering from trauma is learning ways to calm down, or self-regulate. For thousands of years, Yoga has been offered as a practice that helps one calm the mind and body. More recently, research has shown that Yoga practices, including meditation, relaxation, and physical postures, can reduce autonomic sympathetic activation, muscle tension, and blood pressure, improve neuroendocrine and hormonal activity, decrease physical symptoms and emotional distress, and increase quality of life." For these reasons, Yoga is a promising treatment or adjunctive therapy for addressing the cognitive, emotional, and physiological symptoms associated with trauma, and PTSD specifically.

The clinical premise is that the experience of trauma affects the entire human organism – body, mind, and spirit – and that the whole organism must therefore be engaged in the healing process. Traditional trauma therapy is talk-based and focuses on the mind, the story, and tends to neglect the physical, visceral, and body-based dimension of trauma. Yoga, when skillfully employed, can uniquely address the physical needs of a trauma survivor, and provide a way for a trauma survivor to cultivate a friendly relationship to his or her body through gentle breath and movement practices."

Dr. Bessel van der Kolk, in a 2009 interview with *Integral Yoga Magazine*, states, "What most people do not realize is that trauma is not the story of something awful that happened in the past, but the residue of imprints left behind in people's sensory and hormonal systems. Traumatized people often are terrified of the sensations in their own bodies. Most trauma-sensitive people need some form of body-oriented psychotherapy or bodywork to regain a sense of safety in their bodies" (p. 12).

Mindfulness is the practice on focusing on the present, often through concentrating on the breath. Meditation is one vehicle towards mindfulness. However, because children and teenagers, especially those who have experienced trauma, find meditation difficult, many exercises have been developed to provide an experience of keeping the mind in the moment.

Animal-Assisted Therapy

Treaters in the trauma field are understanding the value of introducing animal therapy into the treatment package. As Cathy Malchiodi suggests in an article for The National Institute for Trauma and Loss in Children blog, "Increasing numbers of helping professionals are including animal-assisted therapy – sometimes called pet therapy – in their work with clients of all ages. In particular, this approach is being used with children who have been traumatized by abuse or neglect."

Animal-assisted therapy allows a child to participate in a relationship that does not rely on words. Children who have learned not to trust relationships with people may be able to enter into a relationship with an animal. In addition, interaction with an animal often involves the kind of rhythmic, repetitive, rewarding activity (stroking, petting, grooming) that has been associated with rebuilding the lower brain.

According to play therapist Rise VanFleet (blog post, 2011) animal-assisted play therapy is "the use of animals in the context of play therapy, in which appropriately trained therapists and animals engage with children and families primarily through systematic play interventions, with the goal of improving children's developmental and psychosocial health as well as the animal's well-being. Play and playfulness are essential ingredients of the interactions and the relationship." This form of intervention most often involves dogs, but other types of animals (cats, birds, rabbits, horses, and dolphins, among others) can be part of treatment, too.

Some of the benefits of animal-assisted therapy include:

- Reducing resistance and increasing attachment
- Enhancing empathy
- Teaching appropriate communication skills
- Building confidence
- Enhancing the ability to self-soothe
- Prevention of animal abuse (sometimes seen in children who have been abused or neglected)

Appendix I

Sample Individualized Crisis Prevention and Management Plan (ICPMP)

Client Section:

1. What makes me feel really scared or upset or angry or sad and could cause me to have a problem?

   Too much noise. Yelling. When a lot of people are talking it makes me upset. Being told "no." No structure or routine. I get scared when I feel lonely. I get scared when I call my mom and dad and they don't pick up the phone. Bedtime is hard for me.

2. What might I think or feel first when I am getting upset?

   I feel mad, sad, nervous, excited. My head feels hot and my ears might turn red. Clench my teeth. My heart beats fast and sometimes hurts.

3. What might I, or others notice or what might I think or feel when I am getting REALLY upset?

   I pace, yell, say mean things, stay alone in my room, refuse to follow directions, refuse to talk, repeat the same thing/question over-and-over again. Threaten and punch. I may "zone out" and clench my teeth.

4. What kind of things do I sometimes do or say when I am VERY upset?

   I swear and throw things. I kick, yell, pinch, and threaten to bite.

5. What is important to know about me when you are helping me when I am REALLY upset or sad or scared? (medical conditions, etc.)

   I don't like to hurt people but I sometimes do when I'm sad or angry or threatened. I might try to pinch you.

6. What are some things that help me calm down when I get upset?

   Individual attention, going away from situation, distraction, like talking about movies and telling jokes. I like to read and be read to. Asking if I need a hug. I like to be wrapped up in a blanket like a cocoon. I like my back rubbed, it calms me down.

7. What does NOT help when I am starting to get upset or angry or sad or scared?

   Confrontation. Yelling. A lot of talking. Being threatened with consequences. Being in groups. Too many people around me talking to me.

8. If staff has to restrain me or put me in a quiet room because I could be dangerous to myself or someone else, what helps me get through it?

   Hearing simple directions in a firm, calm, nurturing voice, staff saying how they understand my thoughts/feelings. Seeing staff through the window or at the door of the quiet room. Distractions help – talking about books, movies and jokes.

9. What else do I want you to know about me?

   I have trouble sleeping and like a back rub, bedtime story, being wrapped in my blanket.

Staff Section:

1. Known Crisis Management Risk Factors: (asthma or other physical health status/medical risk, disabilities or limitations, medications, size, boundaries, abuse history, dissociation, etc.):

   Bob has a difficult time during transitions and especially after a transition back to the unit from home. Bob also has a history of having difficulty around bedtime and needs extra support around this time. Bob had heart surgery about 1.5 years ago and has a pacemaker.

   Are there any prohibitions or modifications to isolations, seclusions, holds and restraints based on current medical and/or physical conditions? If so, what are they?

   The following are current recommendations from his Cardiologist:

   The left arm should be restricted above his head during any type of restraint.

   "If Bob is truly out of control, then his primary safety should be considered as he can potentially injure his pacemaker and the wire during his active period of being out of control."

   Everything possible should be done to protect his arms from hyperextension and from direct trauma to the pacemaker area. "If there is any concern that his pacemaker was injured or that there was a problem then he can be brought directly to the emergency room and a chest x-ray can be obtained to check the pacemaker wire and see if there is any obvious fracture."

2. Are there any prohibitions or modifications to isolations, seclusions, holds and restraints based on history of trauma and/or other psychological risk factors? If so, what are they? *See Above.*

Appendix J

Goals for Trauma-Informed Treatment Planning

Attachment

Develop Safety and Trust

Form reliable relationships

Accept help

Ask for help

Share self with adults

Bring problems to adults

Improve skills in Problem Resolution

Develop skills to work out difficulties

Increase ability to articulate needs

Increase assertive communication

Increase ability to resolve problems with adults

Increase ability to ask for things

Increase ability to say no

Increase negotiation skills

Increase ability to compromise

Develop skills of Attunement

Child can describe an event from another person's point of view

Child can accurately predict the emotions another may feel

Child can make attuned statements when others speak

Be able to experience joy and pleasure

Share fun activities

Increase age-appropriate friendships

Will initiate age-appropriate activities with others

Will initiate age-appropriate conversations with others

Decreased engagement of others through negative acting out

Will try new activities

Increase age-appropriate romantic relationships

Increase sharing self with others

Increase inviting others into activities

Maintain Appropriate Boundaries

Child maintains appropriate boundaries with others

Child responds respectfully to others' boundary preferences

Biological Hyper-Activation and Trauma Symptoms

Identification and Understanding of Own Trauma Symptoms

Better understand self and symptoms

Identification of triggers and patterns

Understanding and identifying flashbacks and dissociation

Develop and Use Coping Strategies

Develop own crisis plan

Crisis kits

Accept adult suggestions

Use grounding techniques

Use relaxation skills

Use sensory interventions when distressed

Develop and use other daily coping skills

Improve Ability to Take Effective Action

Participates in planning and shaping own life

Participates in shaping community

Takes active steps to resolve relationship problems

Takes active steps to repair damage done

Makes plan for future, and takes steps to implement

Improving Brain Function

Improve ability to calm self down

Improved bodily rhythms

Memory improvements

Feelings Management

Maintain Inner Connection to Others

Increased ability to retain connection

Willingness to use transitional objects, use symbolic representations of others to help calm oneself

Ability to spend time alone without feeling lonely

Willingness to use increasing numbers of adults as resources to calm down

Increased ability to face difficult situations alone

Speaks of drawing on others to manage stress when other is not there

Decreased sense of abandonment

Increase Self Worth

Develop and notice new achievements

Develop new skills

Child begins to notice own achievements

Explore sources of shame

Share more of self, especially vulnerable feelings

Child can make a mistake, identify it, and still stay regulated

Child takes steps to rectify own mistakes

Improve Skills of Feelings Management

Develop emotional vocabulary

Notice emotions in own body

Increased ability to notice emotions when they first begin

Increased range of emotions

Develop self-soothing strategies

Accept adult help with feelings management

Use Appropriate Methods of Expressing Emotions to Others

Demonstrates belief that having feelings is not dangerous

Able to think about feelings before acting on them

Ability to express feelings in words rather than act them out

Increased distress tolerance

Can experience difficult emotions without harming self or others

Symptoms and Crisis Management

Understand the Adaptive Nature of Symptoms

Have more understanding of function of behavior

Able to meet needs in new ways

Within Crisis Situation Use Skills

Accept adult help

Use of new coping skills

Decrease frequency/length/severity

After Crisis Use Crisis for Learning

Do chain analysis to explore, increase self-awareness

Understand patterns and triggers

Understanding impact on others

Making amends for difficulties caused to others

Family Treatment

Learn about Trauma and Parenting

Understand trauma, its effects and the healing process

Understanding parenting to heal trauma

Identification of resources

Exploring Self and How Their Own History Affects Them as Parents

Understand own history and relationship with child's

Own emotion management skills

Fears and worries

Support and stressors

Increase Skills of Attunement

Develop ability to attune to child

Increase attuned statements

Share self with child

Speak from heart

Playfulness

Acceptance

Curiosity

Empathy

Daily living activities

Modeling feelings management skills

Developing Improved Relationship between Child and Family

Fun Activities Together

Conflict resolution skills

Development of shared history

Identify commonalities

Actions to promote inner connection

Mutual compliments

Celebrations

Mutual help

Making amends

Explore past as needed and stay safe

Appendix K

Sample Handout: The Restorative Approach for Parents and Guardians

Welcome to ______________________________! We appreciate the opportunity to work with you and your child. We hope the following explanation of our approach will be helpful to you in understanding how we do things here.

We urge you to talk these ideas over with your therapist, and let them know any concerns that you have.

We believe that all healing takes place within relationships. We will do anything we can to create a strong relationship with your child and with you.

We understand that children and adults do things to try to meet their needs in the best way they know how at the time. Many of the children and families that we work with have experienced bad things in the past. These difficulties have changed them.

If people have been hurt by other people, they may stop trusting. They may not believe that relationships can be a source of help and can be counted on. Instead, they have come to see relationships as unreliable and painful. So, it is important that we try to show the children and families we treat that relationships can be trusted and that other people can help.

When bad things happen to people, it is easy to start seeing the world as a dangerous place. It feels important to always be alert and looking out for danger. This perspective makes it hard to relax, have fun and sleep. We hope to offer our children and families a safe place where they can learn to relax and learn ways to stay calm.

Many of the youth we work with have not learned the feelings-skills that we all need to get through the hard things in life. It is essential that we teach them these skills. Often, the children cannot remember that anyone loves them or is on their side. They have a hard time thinking about people who care when those people are not near them. So we hope to strengthen their relationships with people who care (especially you and your family) and teach them ways to keep those people with them in their hearts.

The children we treat have often come to believe that they are no good and that everything that has happened to them is their fault. We work with them in many ways to develop a strong and healthy sense of their skills and abilities.

A lot of the children in our programs do not know how to deal with their feelings. They cannot notice their feelings when they are just beginning, name them, or get through them without making things worse. We will ask you to join us in teaching the child how to understand and react to feelings, including teaching them some skills to calm down and get through bad times.

When something goes wrong for one of our youth, they do not trust that others can help them with it. They are already feeling hyped-up and anxious. They do not know what to do with all the feelings they are having. So they start to feel very bad, hopeless, and scared. They do something that makes them feel better in the moment, like yell, hit someone, hurt themselves or run away. They feel better at the time but then they have made things worse.

We have to help the child learn better ways to meet their needs, ways that do not hurt them and others.

When one of our children does something that hurts others, we try to figure out why they did it. What need were they trying to meet? Then we think about what they would have to know in order to handle this situation differently next time.

We give them a restorative task that offers them a chance to learn or practice a skill that will help them next time. So, if a boy gets mad very quickly and hurts others, we may ask him to make a drawing of what he was feeling just before the incident. Maybe he can make a poster of three ways he knows he is getting upset and three things he can do to help himself calm down.

Also, we believe that the children need to learn how to make up for damage that they cause. So, when a child hurts others we expect them to make amends, to do something good for the person or people they hurt. We will assign the child a restorative task to make life better for the people they hurt. So a girl who pulled a fire alarm might make cookies for all the units that had to leave the building at night. Or a child who hurt another child might do that child's chore the next day. We will help you use this approach within your family if you would like.

Sometimes it may seem that the learning and making amends tasks are not enough when the child does something hurtful. You may wonder if the child should also have a punishment or a restriction. We have seen that punishments do not help the child change very much. Instead, what helps them change is to learn skills so that they can meet their needs in a better way.

We look forward to being part of the healing journey for your child and you.

Appendix L

Sample Family Crisis Prevention and Management Plan

Child Section:

1. What makes me feel really scared or upset or angry or sad and could cause me to have a problem?

   Too much noise. Yelling. When a lot of people are talking it makes me upset. Being told "no." No structure or routine. I get scared when I feel lonely. I get scared when my mom is not home… Bedtime is hard for me.

2. What might I think or feel first when I am getting upset?

   I feel mad, sad, nervous, excited. My head feels hot and my ears might turn red. Clench my teeth. My heart beats fast and sometimes hurts.

3. What might I, or others notice or what might I think or feel when I am getting REALLY upset?

   I pace, yell, say mean things, won't come out of my room, refuse to follow directions, refuse to talk, repeat the same thing/question over-and-over again. Threaten and punch. I may "zone out" and clench my teeth.

4. What kind of things do I sometimes do or say when I am VERY upset?

   I swear and throw things. I kick, yell, pinch, and threaten to bite.

5. What is important to know about me when you are helping me when I am REALLY upset or sad or scared? (medical conditions, etc.)

   I don't like to hurt people but I sometimes do when I'm sad or angry or threatened. I might try to pinch you.

6. What are some things that help me calm down when I get upset?

   One-to-one time with my parents, getting away from the situation, distraction. Talking about movies and telling jokes. I like to read and be read to. Asking if I need a hug. I like to be wrapped up in a blanket like a cocoon. I like my back rubbed- it calms me down.

7. What does NOT help when I am starting to get upset or angry or sad or scared?

   Confrontation. Yelling. A lot of talking. Being told about punishments. Being in groups. Too many people around me talking to me.

8. What else do I want you to know about me?

   That I have trouble sleeping and like a back rub, bedtime story, being wrapped in my blanket.

Parent Section:

1. Known Risk Factors: (asthma or other physical health status/medical risk, disabilities or limitations, medications, size, boundaries, abuse history, dissociation, etc.)

   Martha has a difficult time during transitions such as coming home from school. Martha has asthma, which may be activated when she is stressed. Martha also has a history of having difficulty around bedtime and needs extra support around this time.

2. Are there any things parents should never do with Martha based on current medical and/or physical conditions? If so, what are they?

   Martha should always be given her inhaler when she asks for it or when parents notice any signs of distressed breathing.

Appendix M
Team Self-Evaluation:
Effective Services for Survivor Parents

Please rate your current practice – how much do you think your team does on this indicator, on a scale of 1-5, 1 being very little to 5 being this is a solid part of our treatment. Put N/A if this does not apply to your program.

Safety	
1. Parents feel welcome when they come to our program.	
2. Our program is flexible and adjusts to parents' needs in scheduling, service provision, etc.	
3. Our system is responsive to parents' concerns and complaints.	
Attachments	
4. Our program promotes relationships as the primary tool of healing.	
5. Our program maintains consistency of staff/client relationships as much as possible.	
6. Our staff is trained in how to promote healing relationships.	
7. We treat parents as collaborators and as experts in their own life.	
Biology	
8. Our staff is trained in the biological changes from trauma, how they affect parenting, and how they can heal.	
9. We offer psycho-education to our parents about trauma.	
10. We teach parents skills to manage their biological response.	
Feelings Management	
11. We develop our parents' capacity for inner connection.	
12. Our program understands the role of shame in the lives and parenting experiences of our clients.	
13. We help our parents experience success and develop self-esteem.	
14. We teach feelings-management.	
Parenting	
15. We actively help parents make the connection between their trauma experiences and their struggles in parenting.	

16. We know and teach parents the specific challenges to trauma survivors in parenting children of various ages, and offer strategies for success.	
17. We work from the assumption that symptoms and problems in parenting are adaptive, and that parents will change when they learn healthier ways to meet their needs.	
18. We teach parents ways to find help and to advocate for themselves and their children.	

Appendix N
Assessing Trauma-Informed Foster Homes

My Healing Home:
Indicators of Trauma-Informed Foster Care
Rate how much you currently do these things.

1	2	3	4	5
I very rarely do this behavior →				I always do this behavior

Foster Parents' Beliefs and Actions	**Current Practice**
1. I feel that "my child is doing the best he can" rather than believing he is acting intentionally (i.e., "he is acting this way because he wants to;" "he's not motivated;" "if he can choose to act up, he can choose not to").	
2. I explore the problem (i.e., "what's going on?" "what's wrong?") rather than immediately speaking to my child about consequences.	
3. I understand that my child is trying to meet her needs through her problem behavior. So I try to figure out what needs she is meeting and help her learn better ways to meet them.	
4. I actively listen to my child (i.e., listen carefully, restate the problem, empathize with feelings and needs).	
5. I avoid comments that could be shaming to my child (i.e. insist he do things that he can't do, isolate him, scold in front of others).	
6. I avoid power struggles with my child (i.e., arguing with child, proving child wrong).	
7. I refer to my child in descriptive ways rather than using negative labels (i.e., manipulative, bad, troublemaker, untrustworthy).	
8. I value flexibility in managing my child's behavior rather than strict compliance with rules.	
9. When my child is upset, I mainly work to help her calm down.	
10. I talk with my team about my strong positive and negative reactions to my child.	
11. I ask other people for help or allow people to help when I get stuck trying to manage my child's behavior.	
12. I work well with the other people in my child's life (treaters, bio family, school).	
13. I find ways to take care of myself and do the things I enjoy.	
14. I talk with my team about how providing foster care is affecting me over time.	

Appendix O

Guidelines for Trauma-Informed Behavior Management in the Home

What To Do
To Prevent Problems
Alliance comes before compliance.
Be reliable and honest. Be patient, as it will take a long time for the child to trust you.
Pay attention to helping the child feel safe in your home.
Help the child by using names for emotions and sharing your own ways of managing life's ups and downs.
Reassure the child that things are not as bad as they seem, while acknowledging the child's feelings.
Think about what problem the child is trying to solve, what advantages he/she gets out of his behavior.
Help him/her learn how to stay calm, model staying calm your self.
Help the child experience success, notice small progress.
Structure, rituals and schedules are extremely important.
Problems in the areas of bedtimes and hygiene should not be addressed through punishments or rewards. Support children through parent closeness and creative interventions.
During a Problem
Ask yourself: Is the child feeling safe?
As yourself: Is he over-stimulated?
Be aware of the intensity of shame, be careful not to shame the child, and understand the paralyzing effect of shame.
When a child is agitated, escalated or out of control, all parent efforts should be to help them calm down. Listen and understand, don't give advice.
Children who are having difficulty should be kept closer to parents.
Isolation to any room should not be used.
Behavioral difficulty should be handled through redirection and persuasion. Consequences should not be threatened or imposed except as a last resort.

After a Problem
Until the child has completed their restorative tasks, they should not participate in extra or just-for-fun activities. They should be part of all regular activities.
When the child has completed their restorative task and is back on track, they should return to all normal activity.
Parents, team, and child should process event and learn from it. How did it start? What contributed to problem? What needs was the child meeting? What helped? Ideas for next time?
Parents should talk about event with the child, share their own feelings about it, and listen to the child's.

Appendix P

Scenarios and Questions for Hiring Interviews

Scenario One:

A client returns from school, bursts into the house and swears loudly, throwing their backpack across the living room at the wall. There are other clients in the area but the backpack does not hit anyone directly. What are your initial thoughts, feelings and actions?

Scenario Two:

You are working second or third shift and the clients are in bed. As part of your nightly duties, you are completing room checks at the specified intervals. You walk into a double bedroom with two teenage same-sex clients and find they are engaging in sexual relations. What are your initial thoughts, feelings and actions?

Scenario Three:

You are working with another coworker who you think has shown poor boundaries with the clients. He or she is often tickling one client in particular and often goes into this client's room alone and shuts the door. You feel uncomfortable with their interactions when you observe them together. What are your initial thoughts, feelings and actions?

Scenario Four:

You are on the unit and Susie comes back from school, throws her book bag on the floor, goes to her room and slams the door. What would you do? What is the first thing you say to her?

Scenario Five:

You have just come on shift and a client is crying. She has a red mark on her face. You ask what's wrong and she states that another staff member hit her prior to you walking through the door. What would you do?

Scenario Six:

A client approaches you and asks to speak with you privately. You find a quiet space to talk with them and sit down. The client says, "I have something really important to tell you, but I need you to promise that you won't tell anyone." How do you react? Do you promise to keep a secret for the client?

Scenario Seven:

A client asks to speak with you and states that she is thinking about killing herself. She reports that she has a knife hidden in her bedroom and has no desire to go on living. What do you do?

Questions

What would you do if a youth friended you on Facebook or asked for your personal cell phone number?

What information do you think would be ok to share with our clients about yourself? What is never ok to share with clients?

What do you feel is too much to share about yourself with a client?

What does the phrase "it's not about me" mean to you?

What do all children need from adults?

What would your reaction to a child be if they asked you to adopt them?

What do appropriate physical or emotional boundaries look like to you?

What do you think might be the most difficult time of day for clients?

What can staff do to make clients feel safer or more comfortable around bedtime and/or shower?

Appendix Q

Trauma-Informed Care in Youth-Serving Settings:

Agency Self-Assessment

Directions: Please rate the items listed in the various categories. Please write comments about why you rated items in a particular way on the back of each page.

This list is meant to be comprehensive, recognizing that the process of implementing trauma-informed care generally takes multiple years. While implementation of these elements is the goal, the list represents an ideal to strive for.

	How much is this value embraced by your organization? **1=Not at all 2=Slightly 3=Moderately 4=Mostly 5=Very much**
Trauma-Informed Care Values The following values underlie all the elements of trauma-informed care listed below. These values underlie the relationships between staff and clients, staff and their peers, as well as supervisory staff and their supervisees. Inherent in these values is the belief that all aspects of the organization's functions should be shaped by consumer involvement and input.	
1. Safety – ensuring the children's physical and emotional safety.	1 2 3 4 5
2. Trustworthiness – creation of a feeling of trust and safety via clear and thoughtfully considered frame and boundaries governing all aspects of the organization's work.	1 2 3 4 5
3. Collaboration – inviting, whenever possible, the input of those served by the organization and staff of the organization; providing opportunities for decision-making and innovation.	1 2 3 4 5

4. Empowerment – sharing power with, and giving appropriate authority and decision-making power to, those served by the organization and staff of the organization; maximizing, when possible and as appropriate, choice and control for the organization's consumers and employees; recognizing and highlighting strengths; looking for opportunities to praise and reward positive behavior; viewing mistakes as learning opportunities.	1 2 3 4 5

	How much is this element present in your organization? **1=Not at all 2=Slightly 3=Moderately 4=Mostly 5=Very much**
A. Administrative Support for Program-Wide Trauma-Informed Services	
1. Organizational administrators support the integration of knowledge about violence and abuse into all program practices.	1 2 3 4 5
2. The organization has a "trauma-informed care initiative" (e.g., workgroup/task force, trauma specialist) endorsed by and authorized by chief administrator.	1 2 3 4 5
3. A competent person with administrative skills and organizational credibility is designated to lead this task force.	1 2 3 4 5
4. Administration supports the recommendations of the trauma task force and follows through on these plans.	1 2 3 4 5
5. Administration attends at least a portion of trauma training themselves (vs. sending designees in their places); they allocate some of their own time to trauma-focused work (e.g., meeting with trauma initiative representatives, keeping abreast of trauma initiatives in similar program areas).	1 2 3 4 5
6. The administration releases staff from their usual duties so they may attend trainings and deliver trauma services.	1 2 3 4 5
7. Necessary sources of funding for trauma training and education are found.	1 2 3 4 5
8. The administration is able to tolerate certain levels of organizational disruption in making the transition, including such things as staff confusion, conflict within treatment team, resistance to change, and property destruction by youth.	1 2 3 4 5
9. The administration values and rewards staff efforts to be flexible and to offer choices to the clients, even when the result is that the client is not immediately brought under control.	1 2 3 4 5

10. The administration develops a policy statement that refers to the importance of trauma and the need to acknowledge consumer experiences of trauma in service delivery.	1 2 3 4 5
11. The administration celebrates successes.	1 2 3 4 5
	How much is this element present in your organization? **1=Not at all 2=Slightly 3=Moderately 4=Mostly 5=Very much**
B. Organizational Structure	
1. Clinically-trained staff are in leadership positions of multi-disciplinary treatment teams and are integrated into the daily life of programs.	1 2 3 4 5
2. In congregate-care, organization has an organizational and supervisory structure where clinical and residential staff is integrated into treatment teams rather than belong to separate clinical and residential "silos."	1 2 3 4 5
3. Intake and discharge process are planful, recognizing the important meaning of relationship beginnings and endings for traumatized children.	1 2 3 4 5
4. Staff schedules are structured such that staff have time to meet, think about, and talk about the work rather than only doing the work.	1 2 3 4 5
5. Staff has regular clinically-oriented supervision, ideally individual supervision, where they can discuss their issues with clients, including their counter-transference and vicarious traumatization.	1 2 3 4 5
6. Forums (e.g., supervision, treatment team meetings, periodic retreats) are held regularly aimed at helping staff to acknowledge, address, and transform their vicarious traumatization.	1 2 3 4 5
7. Organization makes use of outside consultants who have expertise in trauma when necessary.	1 2 3 4 5
C. Trauma Screening and Assessment	
1. The program has a consistent way to identify individuals who have been exposed to trauma and to include trauma-related information in planning services with the client.	1 2 3 4 5
2. Trauma screening is relatively brief, not overly complicated, and avoids unnecessary detail that would increase likelihood of triggering traumatic memories.	1 2 3 4 5

The screening process avoids unnecessary repetition of the same questions at multiple points in the intake or assessment process, recognizing that it is often important to return to the questions in treatment after some appropriate time interval.	1 2 3 4 5
D. Milieu Treatment Practices and Behavior Management **(For congregate-care settings)**	
Staff and clinicians routinely think first about the meaning and function of behaviors before deciding how to intervene.	1 2 3 4 5
Staff displays an attitude of the child "doing the best that they can" rather than assuming intentionality.	1 2 3 4 5
Staff use active listening to explore the problem rather than immediately speaking to the child about consequences or solving the problem.	1 2 3 4 5
Staff refrains from power struggles with children.	1 2 3 4 5
Organization uses a relationship-based behavior management system (such as The Restorative Approach*) instead of "point and level" system. Phase system can be used.	1 2 3 4 5
During behavioral crises, staff recognize primary goal as helping children to calm down and get back in control of their behavior.	1 2 3 4 5
Staff is sensitive to the many ways their interactions with children can trigger shame.	1 2 3 4 5
Staff refers to children in descriptive ways and refrains from negative labels (e.g. "manipulative," "resistant," "borderline," etc.)	1 2 3 4 5
Staff values flexibility and individualized care in managing behavior rather than strict compliance with rules and treating all children equally.	1 2 3 4 5
Multidisciplinary team members function well as a team – manage conflict, care for each other, avoid splits such as therapist/child care worker splits.	1 2 3 4 5
Program has thoughtful physical touch policy that recognizes the critical importance of touch for healthy child development and is sensitive to issues of child abuse, allegations of abuse, and re-traumatization.	1 2 3 4 5
Staff is willing to talk with their peers and supervisors about their strong positive and negative reactions to clients and doing the work.	1 2 3 4 5
Staff feels free to ask their peers for help, or take over for a peer, when there is an impasse in managing a behavioral issue.	1 2 3 4 5

	How much is this element present in your organization? 1=Not at all 2=Slightly 3=Moderately 4=Mostly 5=Very much
E. Physical Environment and Layout of Agency Space, including waiting and reception area, is welcoming and inviting for clients and families.	1 2 3 4 5
Living or program space is nurturing (e.g., colors, plants, music) and affirming (e.g., display of child art/work, culturally competent).	1 2 3 4 5
Crisis or "calm down" rooms are safe and soothing places for children to get strong feelings under control.	1 2 3 4 5
F. Clinical Treatment Practices	
Utilization of crisis prevention plans (also called safety tools or personal safety plans) written in collaboration with child, family, and possibly previous providers.	1 2 3 4 5
Before addressing problem behavior, the team, led by the clinician, considers their understanding of the reasons for the behavior and uses this understanding to determine their interventions.	1 2 3 4 5
Treatment planning is built from the clinical formulation that considers the impact of trauma on the client's development and current symptoms/behaviors, and includes goals of developing emotion-regulation skills/self-capacities as well as healthy attachments.	1 2 3 4 5
Family therapy addresses family dynamics, builds parenting skills, and reinforces child's growth and changes.	1 2 3 4 5
Staff has an awareness of the role of trauma in the history of parents, and family treatment includes a trauma focus.	1 2 3 4 5
Discharge is careful, thoughtful, gradual, and includes referral to trauma-informed resources.	1 2 3 4 5
Program offers trauma-specific treatments such as: Trauma-Focused Cognitive Behavior Therapy (TF-CBT), Dialectical Behavior Therapy (DBT), Eye Movement Desensitization Reprocessing (EMDR), Trauma-Adaptive Recovery Group Education and Therapy (TARGET), etc.	1 2 3 4 5

Treatment utilizes sensory interventions to help children calm down and teach self-soothing.	1 2 3 4 5
Psycho-educational groups about trauma are offered to clients and families.	1 2 3 4 5
G. Restraint and Seclusion Reduction	
All levels of staff are aware of propensity for re-traumatization through restraint and seclusion with traumatized clients.	1 2 3 4 5
Restraints and seclusion used only when there is threat of imminent danger.	1 2 3 4 5
Staff training focuses on de-escalation techniques to avoid restraint and seclusion.	1 2 3 4 5
Staff values avoidance of trauma and re-traumatization due to restraint and seclusion over strict adherence to rules, property damage, and negotiation time.	1 2 3 4 5
Each child has an individual plan stating both medical and psychological risks in restraint, which includes specific guidelines for staff actions to avoid.	1 2 3 4 5
Organization monitors trends in restraint and seclusion. Increases in restraint/ seclusion trigger discussions aimed at understanding and addressing reasons or the increases.	1 2 3 4 5
H. Workforce Development	
Trauma training is required for staff at all levels and of all disciplines (see "Staff Trauma Training" below).	1 2 3 4 5
Staff that display mastery of trauma-informed practice are encouraged, celebrated, and promoted.	1 2 3 4 5
Organization promotes a culture of performance improvement, one that understands that mistakes will be made but learning will occur.	1 2 3 4 5
Trauma-informed values and concepts are integrated into staff orientation.	1 2 3 4 5
Hiring practices screen for staff whose values are consonant with a trauma-informed approach.	1 2 3 4 5
I. Staff Trauma Training	
All staff members receive foundational trauma training with a primary goal of sensitization to trauma-related dynamics and the avoidance of re-traumatization.	1 2 3 4 5
Staff members receive training in a trauma-informed understanding of unusual or difficult behaviors. Training stresses concept of symptoms as adaptations.	1 2 3 4 5
Staff trauma training also includes topics of: frame and boundaries; relationship building with traumatized children; how to use their responses to particular clients (countertransference); impact of, and how to address, secondary trauma such as vicarious traumatization (VT).	1 2 3 4 5

	How much is this element present in your organization? 1=Not at all 2=Slightly 3=Moderately 4=Mostly 5=Very much
J. Monitoring Trauma-Informed Initiatives	
Organization monitors the progress of trauma-informed care initiative in ongoing way.	1 2 3 4 5
Data related to implementation of a trauma-informed approach are collected, monitored, and used for quality improvement.	1 2 3 4 5
Organization develops a debriefing process to analyze incidents characterized by conflict, violence, and aggression to inform policy, procedures, and practices in order to avoid such incidents in the future.	1 2 3 4 5

Sources:

Evaluation created by Steven Brown, Psy.D., and Patricia Wilcox, LCSW, Traumatic Stress Institute (Brown, Baker & Wilcox, in press.)

Fallot, R.D., & Harris, M. (2006). *Trauma-informed services: A self-assessment and planning protocol, version 1.4.* Community Connections: Washington, D.C. (202-608-4796). (2006).

Lang, J.M., & Franks, R. (2008). *Connecticut TF-CBT Learning Collaborative Change Package.* Adapted from Markiewicz, Amaya-Jackson, L., Agosti, J., & Lang, J. (2007). TF-CBT Organizational Assessment. National Center for Child Traumatic Stress.

Massachusetts Department of Mental Health. (2008). *Resource guide: Creating positive cultures of care, second edition.* Boston, MA: Author.

National Association of State Mental Health Program Directors (NASMHPD) (2006). *Creating trauma-informed systems of care for human services settings: Curriculum.* Alexandria, VA: Author.

Saakvitne, K.W., Pearlman, L.A., Gamble, S., & Lev, B.T. (2000). *Risking connection: A training curriculum for working with survivors of childhood abuse.* Baltimore, Maryland: Sidran Press.

Appendix R
Theory of Change Exercise for Staff

What Helps People to Change?

Teaching Objectives:
Understand the many factors that promote change.
Appreciate the role of relationships in facilitating change.

Leader:
Our job is fundamentally to help children and families to change. Let's spend some time talking about what we think actually promotes change in people, ourselves included.

Exercise:
Ask participants to think of something they have done (or still do) that has negative consequences that they *have not* changed. Examples would be smoking, drinking, over-eating, not exercising, etc. Without asking them what the behavior is, ask, "What are some of the barriers to change?"

Ask participants to think of something they wanted to learn and tried to learn and were *unable* to master (such as tennis, knitting, anything that they tried but could not become good at). Ask for a couple of examples. What does that feel like? How would it affect them if some one offered to reward them for doing it? Or punish them for not doing it? What role does wanting to do it play? If they could ever imagine getting better at this skill, what would it take?

Ask participants to think of a time in their lives that they *did* successfully make a change – lose weight, quit smoking, etc. Ask for examples. What made it possible? What started their change effort? What factors made it possible to make the change at that time? What helped? Ask about the role of other people and relationships in making the change. What did you feel about having made this change?

How can you relate these insights to the clients making changes?

Leader:

Emphasize:

1. Rewards and consequences are not enough, they only increase/decrease motivation – also need skills and support.

2. What part of change is influenced by self-image, hope, feeling a different future is possible?

3. The role of relationships in supporting change.

Appendix S
Sample Behavior-Management Policy

At this agency we believe that incidents of behavioral dyscontrol – such as AWOLs, property destruction, or assaults – often arise from the child's attempts to cope with his or her intolerable feelings of despair, hopelessness, shame, and fear. The child does not at that time trust relationships with adults enough to ask for help and does not possess the feelings-management skills necessary to respond to setbacks in a less harmful way. In addition, the child often operates with a biological danger-alarm and survival system that has been skewed by trauma. The child engages in dangerous behaviors because they are adaptive and address the needs of the moment for the child by decreasing his or her intolerable emotions.

In order to help the children decrease such episodes, we must make sure that everything we do builds strong relationships that they can gradually come to trust. Within these relationships the child can develop a secure base, learn that he or she is worthwhile, and master emotion-management skills that will allow him or her to handle difficult situations without making them worse.

In general, there are not distinct, separate causes of AWOLs, property destruction, and assaults. All of these behaviors are outcomes of emotional dysregulation. Each child has developed his or her own multiple methods for reacting to emotional distress. The more a program is able to provide a caring, skillful, trustworthy treatment environment for a child, the less the child will need these behaviors.

The particular response to behavioral episodes reflects a restorative philosophy whereby the resident must complete tasks that help him or her a) learn skills that will decrease the need for such behavior in the future, and b) make amends through tasks such as community service to repair the relationship that he/she had damaged by his/her behavior.

Less severe behaviors are handled with redirection without the need to add additional consequences. If a child is refusing to complete a task (such as a chore), other activities and privileges (like watching TV) should stop until he or she completes it. Staff should encourage, support, and help him or her to complete it. As soon as the child completes the task, all privileges and community participation should resume.

When a child is upset, staff makes every effort to help him or her to calm down. Calming can be done with active listening, physical activity, distraction, calming techniques, use of crisis kits and sensory interventions, etc. Staff uses flexibility and patience to avoid escalation.

When a child behaves in a manner that hurts others, seriously disrupts the program, or significantly destroys property, he or she will receive a restorative response. This response can include two parts: a learning opportunity which allows the child to practice skills he or she needs to learn; and a "making amends" opportunity in which the child repairs damage to any relationships that have been hurt by his or her actions. The task is individualized to the child's abilities and maturity. The task should also reflect the child's treatment formulation. Possible tasks and approaches can be determined in advance by the treatment team. In general, it is a good idea for a child to make amends to the exact person he or she hurt. However, if that person is unavailable for several days, the child's return to programming cannot be held up. In that case the person hurt will assign a task the child can do with another staff.

If the child refuses to complete the activity, staff invites him to do it and is welcoming and offers help. He or she continues to participate in all therapeutic activities. However, he or she cannot engage in extra or purely play activities until the tasks are complete. The child is told that staff is willing to repair their relationship but until that is done they do not feel they can take him or her to fun events. As soon as the child has finished his or her restorative tasks to the satisfaction of staff, all restrictions are lifted.

Time-based consequences are not used at this agency. Children can be kept on the units if they are not safe (such as if they are on suicide precautions). Similarly, it is permissible to hold children back from off-campus activities for 24 to 48 hours after a serious incident (such as an assault) to assure that he or she is safe enough to be in the community. However, restrictions of specific time-lengths cannot be imposed. For example, a child cannot be grounded for seven days. A child can be kept on the unit until he or she completes his or her restorative tasks to the satisfaction of the staff. Other than that, when a child has processed the incident, done a learning exercise, and made amends to the best of his or her ability, he or she should return to full community participation.

Point cards are not used at this program. Level systems may be used when they are treatment-based, do not decrease, involve participation from the child and family (when appropriate), and are regularly reviewed. The increase in responsibility and freedom at higher levels should reflect the child's increasing ability to manage his or her own emotions and ask for help when needed.

The following are never restricted due to behavior: family contact, food, basic necessities, access to toilet, or physical movement. Children will never be humiliated, degraded, or made fun of. Our program does not use physical punishment. Restraints or seclusions are never used as punishments.

Appendix T

Sample Satisfaction Surveys, Family and Child

Family Survey of Trauma-Informed Practices

Unit:__________________________________

Please mark each of these items with your opinion of how well we do this at our program.

1.	Staff cares about why my child is doing something and is not just interested in making them stop it. ____ Not at all Somewhat A Lot
2.	Staff understands that my child and I are doing the best that we can. ____ Not at all Somewhat A Lot
3.	Staff listens to us. ____ Not at all Somewhat A Lot
4.	Staff avoids getting in arguments with my child to make him/her do things. ____ Not at all Somewhat A Lot
5.	The phase system is fair and makes sense. ____ Not at all Somewhat A Lot
6.	When my child or I are upset staff tries to help me calm down. ____ Not at all Somewhat A Lot

7.	Staff is careful not to embarrass me, especially in front of others. ______________________________________ Not at all Somewhat A Lot
8.	Staff does not use bad terms, such as lazy or manipulative, to describe my child. ______________________________________ Not at all Somewhat A Lot
9.	Staff is flexible and treats me and my child as individuals rather than just like every one else. ______________________________________ Not at all Somewhat A Lot
10.	Staff gets along well with each other. ______________________________________ Not at all Somewhat A Lot
11.	Staff gives my child hugs and other forms of touch if he/she wants them, but do not touch him/her in ways he or she doesn't like or that make my child or me uncomfortable. ______________________________________ Not at all Somewhat A Lot
12.	Staff helps each other out. ______________________________________ Not at all Somewhat A Lot
13.	When my child or I is upset staff tries to help me solve my problem rather than just talk about consequences. ______________________________________ Not at all Somewhat A Lot

14.	When one staff member starts getting upset with a kid, other staff come and help. ____________________ Not at all Somewhat A Lot
15.	My child has an individual crisis plan that says what helps him or her, and staff uses the ideas in it when he or she gets upset. ____________________ Not at all Somewhat A Lot
16.	Staff tries to understand my child and I. ____________________ Not at all Somewhat A Lot
17.	My child's living space is warm and comfortable and I feel he or she is safe there. ____________________ Not at all Somewhat A Lot
18.	The waiting area, receptionist, and staff make me feel welcome when I come to visit. ____________________ Not at all Somewhat A Lot
19.	My child's treatment is teaching them more about how to handle their emotions. ____________________ Not at all Somewhat A Lot
20.	My child's treatment is teaching them how to have better relationships with people. ____________________ Not at all Somewhat A Lot
21.	I have family meetings that are helping my family and I to get along better. ____________________ Not at all Somewhat A Lot

22.	My child is learning how to help him/herself calm down when he or she gets upset. ______________________________________ Not at all Somewhat A Lot
23.	I am learning about how our past affects my child and I now, and what to do about it. ______________________________________ Not at all Somewhat A Lot
24.	Staff tries hard to avoid restraints and only uses them when nothing else can keep my child physically safe or keep others physically safe from my child's actions. ______________________________________ Not at all Somewhat A Lot
25.	Staff tries many ways to help kids calm down before using restraint. ______________________________________ Not at all Somewhat A Lot
26.	My therapist understands my child and I and helps us to understand our selves. ______________________________________ Not at all Somewhat A Lot

Child Survey of Trauma-Informed Practices

Unit:____

Please mark each of these items with your opinion of how well we do this at our program.

1.	Staff cares about why I am doing something and are not just interested in making me stop it. ____________________________________ Not at all Somewhat A Lot
2.	Staff understands that I am doing the best that I can. ____________________________________ Not at all Somewhat A Lot
3.	Staff listens to me. ____________________________________ Not at all Somewhat A Lot
4.	Staff avoids getting in arguments with me to make me do things. ____________________________________ Not at all Somewhat A Lot
5.	The phase system is fair and makes sense. ____________________________________ Not at all Somewhat A Lot
6.	When I am upset staff tries to help me calm down. ____________________________________ Not at all Somewhat A Lot
7.	Staff is careful not to embarrass me, especially in front of others. ____________________________________ Not at all Somewhat A Lot

8.	Staff does not use bad terms to describe me such as lazy or manipulative. ____________________ Not at all Somewhat A Lot
9.	Staff is flexible and treats me as an individual rather than just like every one else. ____________________ Not at all Somewhat A Lot
10.	Staff gets along well with each other. ____________________ Not at all Somewhat A Lot
11.	Staff gives me hugs and other forms of touch if I want them, but do not touch me in ways I don't like or that make me uncomfortable. ____________________ Not at all Somewhat A Lot
12.	Staff helps each other out. ____________________ Not at all Somewhat A Lot
13.	When I am upset staff tries to help me solve my problem rather than just tell me about consequences. ____________________ Not at all Somewhat A Lot
14.	When one staff member starts getting upset with a kid, other staff come and help. ____________________ Not at all Somewhat A Lot

15.	I have an individual crisis plan that says what helps me, and staff uses the ideas in it when I get upset. ____________________ Not at all Somewhat A Lot
16.	Staff tries to understand me. ____________________ Not at all Somewhat A Lot
17.	My living space is warm and comfortable and I feel safe there. ____________________ Not at all Somewhat A Lot
18.	I have a nice space where I can calm down if I need to. ____________________ Not at all Somewhat A Lot
19.	My treatment is teaching me more about how to handle my emotions. ____________________ Not at all Somewhat A Lot
20.	My treatment is teaching me how to have better relationships with people. ____________________ Not at all Somewhat A Lot
21.	I have family meetings that are helping my family and I get along better. ____________________ Not at all Somewhat A Lot

22.	I am learning how to help myself calm down when I get upset. ____ Not at all Somewhat A Lot		
23.	I am learning about how my past experience affects me now and what to do about it. ____ Not at all Somewhat A Lot		
24.	Staff tries hard to avoid restraints and only uses them when nothing else can keep me physically safe or keep others physically safe from my actions. ____ Not at all Somewhat A Lot		
25.	Staff tries many ways to help kids calm down before using restraint. ____ Not at all Somewhat A Lot		
26.	My therapist understands me and helps me to understand myself. ____ Not at all Somewhat A Lot		

Appendix U

Indicators of Trauma-Informed Care:

Staff Behavior in the Milieu

Directions: Rate how often your staff currently displays the behavior in the milieu:

1	2	3	4	5
Staff very rarely displays this behavior in practice	Occasionally	Sometimes	Often	Staff always displays this behavior in practice

Staff Behavior In the Milieu	Current Practice
1. Staff displays an attitude of "the child is doing the best they can" **rather than** believing the child is acting out on purpose (e.g., "he is acting this way because he wants to;" "she's not motivated;" "if he can choose to act up, he can choose not to").	
2. Staff explores the problem (e.g., "what's going on? what's wrong?") **rather than** immediately talking to the child about consequences.	
3. Staff engages in active listening with children (i.e., listen carefully, restate the problem, empathize with feelings and needs).	
4. Staff avoids comments that could be shaming to children (e.g., insist child do things that stretches his/her ability too much; isolate child; scold in front of peers).	
5. Staff avoids power struggles with children (e.g., arguing with child, proving child wrong).	
6. Staff refers to children in descriptive ways **rather than** using negative labels (e.g., manipulative, borderline, troublemaker).	
7. Staff values flexibility in managing behavior **rather than** strict following of rules.	
8. When a child is upset, staff mainly works to help the child calm down.	

9. Staff tries to avoid restraint and seclusion of a child. They do **not** use restraint to get a child to follow the rules, stop property damage, and/or cut off a discussion with a child.	
10. Staff talks with their peers and supervisors about their strong positive and negative reactions to clients and doing this kind of work.	
11. Staff asks peers for help, or allow peers to help, when they get stuck trying to manage a child's behavior.	
12. Treatment team members work well as a team (i.e., manage conflict, care for each other, avoid splits such as between therapists and direct care workers).	

Appendix V

Trauma-Informed Care Belief Measure

Date 1/24/18

Choose the number that best describes your belief about the statement.

1	2	3	4	5
Strongly Disagree	Disagree	Not sure	Agree	Strongly agree

4	1.	The clients I work with could behave better if they really wanted to.
5	2.	My relationship with clients is my most important tool to change the behavior of clients.
4	3.	Often the clients are manipulative and try to trick staff just to get what they want with no concern for others.
5	4.	The clients I work with are generally doing the best they can at any particular time.
5	5.	Having intense feelings in response to clients is an inevitable part of working in mental health.
1	6.	It is better not to form close relationships with clients because I will not know them that long.
2	7.	Even though the clients have had bad breaks, the best way for them to learn is to experience the "real world" consequences of their mistakes.
5	8.	When I feel myself "taking my work home," it's best to bring it up with my supervisor.
5	9.	I am most effective as a treater when I focus on strengths of the client, even if they are not readily apparent.
5	10.	When managing a crisis, flexibility is more important than strict compliance with rules.
5	11.	Having strong feelings of anger at a client or sadness for a client is a sure sign that I am letting the work affect me too much.
1	12.	Controlling clients' negative behavior is one of the most important features of an effective treatment approach.

1	13.	The most effective way to de-escalate a crisis is to remind clients about the consequences of their actions.
2	14.	The best way to deal with feeling burnt out in your job is to not dwell on it and it will pass.
4	15.	When a client is angry with me, I should start by asking them to express their anger respectfully.
5	16.	Restraints should only be done as a last resort, when there is imminent danger of the client hurting themself or someone else.
1	17.	The most powerful tool I have as a treater to influence clients' behavior is the rewards and punishments I set up in response to behavior.
1	18.	Even when I feel especially burnt out in my job, it doesn't affect my work with clients.
1	19.	I should not tell anyone if I have strong feelings about the work because they will think I am not cut out for this job.

Difficult to complete - creating boundaries @ internship site now

References

Allen, J. (2001). *Traumatic relationships and serious mental disorders.* New York: Wiley and Sons.

Achenbach, T.M. (1992). *Manual for the child behavior checklist/2-3 and 1992 profile.* Burlington, VT: University of Vermont Department of Psychiatry.

Achenbach, T.M. (1991). *Manual for the child behavior checklist/4-18 and 1991 profile.* Burlington, VT: University of Vermont Department of Psychiatry.

American Psychiatric Association (2000). Diagnostic and Statistical Manual of Mental Disorders (4th ed., text rev.). Washington DC: Author.

Bloom, S. L. (2006). *Organizational stress as a barrier to trauma-sensitive change and system transformation.* White Paper for the National Technical Assistance Center for State Mental Health Planning. (NTAC). National Association of State Mental Health Program Directors.

Bloom, S. L., & Farragher, B. (2010). *Destroying sanctuary: The crisis in human service delivery systems.* New York: Oxford University Press.

Brenner, J. D., Randall, P., Scott, T.M., Bronen, R.A., Seibyl, J.P., & Southwick, S.M., et al. (1995). MRI-based measurement of hippocampal volume in patients with combat-related posttraumatic stress disorder. *American Journal of Psychiatry, 152,* 973-981.

Briere, J., & Scott, C. (2006). *Principles of trauma therapy: A guide to symptoms, evaluation, and treatment.* Thousand Oaks, CA: Sage.

Briere, J., Elliott, D.M., Harris, K., & Cotman, A. (1995). Trauma symptom inventory: psychometrics and association with childhood and adult trauma in clinical samples. *Journal of Interpersonal Violence, 10,* 387-401.

Brom, D., Pat-Horenczyk, R., & Ford, J. (2009). *Treating traumatized children: Risk, resilience and recovery.* New York: Routledge.

Brown, S. (2001). *Streetwise to sexwise: Sexuality education for high-risk youth.* (2nd Ed.). Morristown, NJ: Planned Parenthood of Greater Northern New Jersey.

Brown, S. (2010). *Embedding attention to vicarious traumatization.* Newsletter. Traumatic Stress Institute. Retrieved from: www.traumaticstressinstitute.org.

Brown, S.M., Baker, C.N., & Wilcox, P. (In press). Risking connection trauma training: A pathway toward trauma-informed care in child congregate-care settings. *Psychological Trauma: Theory, Research, Practice, and Policy.*

Center for Disease Control. (2008). ACE Study. http://www.cdc.gov/ace/index.htm

Clark, D.B., Lesnick, L., & Hegedus, A.M. (December 1997). Traumas and other adverse life events in adolescents with alcohol abuse and dependence. *Journal of the American Academy of Child & Adolescent Psychology, 36*(12), 1744-1751.

Cohen, J.A., Mannarino, A.P., & Deblinger, E. (2006). *Treating trauma and traumatic grief in children and adolescents.* New York: Guilford.

Cohn, J., Campbell, S., & Ross, S. (1991). Infant response in the still-face paradigm at 6 months predicts avoidant and secure attachment at 12 months. *Development and Psychopathology, 3,* 367-376.

Cornell University Residential Child Care Project. (2012). Information available from http://rccp.cornell.edu/tcimainpage.html

Costello, E.J., Erkanli, A., Fairbank, J.A., & Angold, A. (2002). The prevalence of potentially traumatic events in childhood and adolescence. *Journal of Traumatic Stress, 15*(2), 99-112.

Crisis Prevention Institute. (2011). *Instructor manual for the Nonviolent Crisis Intervention® training program.* Milwaukee, WI: Author.

Davis, R., Psy.D., Personal communication. (2010).

Diamond, A., & Lee, K. (2011). Interventions shown to aid executive function development in children 4 to 12 years old. *Science, 333,* 959-963.

Emerson, D., Sharma, R., Chaudhry, C., & Turner, J. (2009). Trauma-sensitive yoga: Principles, practice, and research. *International Journal of Yoga Therapy, 19.* Brookline, MA: Justice Resource Center.

Felitti, V., Anda, R., Nordenberg, D., Williamson, D., Spitz, A., Edwards, V., Koss, M., & Marks, J. (May, 1998). Relationship of childhood abuse and household dysfunction to many of the leading causes of death in adults: The adverse childhood experiences (ACE) study. *American Journal of Preventive Medicine*, 14(4), 245-258.

Harris, M. (1998). *Trauma recovery & empowerment: A clinician's guide to working with women in groups.* Free Press.

Harris, M., & Fallot, R. (Eds.) (Spring, 2001). Using trauma theory to design service systems. *New Directions for Mental Health Services, 89.* San Francisco: Jossey-Bass.

Herman, J. (1997). *Trauma and recovery: The aftermath of violence—from domestic abuse to political terror.* New York: Basic Books.

Holden, M.J. (2009). Children and residential experiences: Creating the conditions for change. Washington, D.C.: Child Welfare League of America. *Child & Family Press, 2.*

Hopper, E., Bassuk, E., & Olivet, J. (2009). Shelter from the storm: Trauma-informed care in homelessness services settings. *The Open Health Services and Policy Journal, 2,*133.

Hughes, D. (1998). *Building the bonds of attachment: Awakening love in deeply troubled children.* Lanham, MD: Jason Aronson.

Hughes D. (2007). *Attachment-focused family therapy.* New York: W.W. Norton.

Hughes, D. (March, 2009). *Attachment-focused parenting: Effective strategies to care for children.* New York: Norton Professional Books.

Kim, J.J., & Diamond, D. (2002). The stressed hippocampus, synaptic plasticity and lost memories. *Nature Reviews Neuroscience 3,* 453-462.

Kotter, J. (1996). *Leading change.* Cambridge, MA: Harvard Business Press.

Lebel, J., Stromberg, N., Duckworth, K., Kerzner, J., Goldstein, R., Weeks, M., et al. (2004). Child and adolescent inpatient restraint reduction: A state initiative to promote strength-based care. *Journal of the American Academy of Child & Adolescent Psychiatry, 43,* 37-45.

Levine, P.A., & Kline, M. (2007). *Trauma through a child's eyes: Awakening the ordinary miracle of healing.* Berkeley, CA: North Atlantic Books.

Linehan, M. (1993). *Cognitive behavioral treatment of borderline personality disorder.* New York: Guilford Press.

Malchiodi, C. (April 26, 2011). *Animal-assisted therapy and children: Calling in the furry therapist.*http://tlcinstitute.wordpress.com/2011/04/26/animal-assisted-therapy-and-children-calling-in-the-furry-therapist. Retrieved February, 2012.

Markiewicz, J., Ebert, L., Ling, D., Amaya-Jackson, L., & Kisiel, C. (2006). *Learning collaborative toolkit.* Los Angeles, CA, and Durham, NC: National Center for Child Traumatic Stress.

McCann, I. L., & Pearlman, L. A. (1990a). *Psychological trauma & the adult survivor: Theory, therapy, and transformation.* New York: Brunner/Mazel.

McCann, I. L., & Pearlman, L. A. (1990b). Vicarious traumatization: A framework for understanding psychological effects of working with victims. *Journal of Traumatic Stress 3*(1), 131-149.

McEwen, B.S. (1999). Stress and hippocampal plasticity. *Annu. Rev. Neurosci. 22,* 105-122.

Mohr, W., Olson, J., Martin, A., Pumariega, A., & Branca, N. (2009). Beyond point and level systems: Moving toward child centered programming. *American Journal of Orthopsychiatry, 79*(1), 8-18.

Morrissey, J.P., Ellis, A.R., Gatz, M., Amaro, H., Reed, B.G., Savage, A., Finkelstein, N., Mazelis, R., Brown, V., Jackson, E.W., & Banks, S. (2005). Outcomes for women with co-occurring disorders and trauma: Program and person-level effects. *Journal of Substance Abuse Treatment, 28*(2),121-133. (Department of Health Policy and Administration, School of Public Health, University of North Carolina at Chapel Hill).

Mueser, K.T., Goodman, L.B., Trumbetta, S.L., Rosenberg, S.D., Osher, F.C., Vidaver, R., Auciello, P., & Foy, D.W. (June, 1998). Trauma and posttraumatic stress disorder in severe mental illness. *Journal of Consulting and Clinical Psychology, 66*(3), 493-499.

Naar-King, S., & Suarez, M. (2011). *Motivational interviewing with adolescents and young adults.* New York: Guilford Press.

Najavits, L. (2001). *Seeking safety: a treatment manual for PTSD and substance abuse.* New York: Guilford Press.

National Association of State Mental Health Program Directors. http://www.nasmhpd.org

National Child Traumatic Stress Network. www.nctsn.org

Noether, C.D., Brown, V., Finkelstein, N., Russell, L.A., VanDeMark, N.R., Morris, L.S., et al., (2007). Promoting resiliency in children of mothers with co-occurring disorders and histories of trauma: Impact of a skills-based intervention program on child outcomes. *Journal of Community Psychology, 35*(7), 823-843.

Nunno, M. A., Holden, M. J., & Leidy, B. (2003). Evaluating and monitoring the impact of a crisis intervention system on a residential child care facility. *Children and Youth Services Review, 24*(4), 295-315.

Nunno, M., Day, D., & Bullard, L. (Eds.). (2008) *For our own safety: Examining the safety of high-risk interventions for children and young people* (pp. 201–215). Washington, DC: Child Welfare League of America.

Ogles, B., Melendez, G., Davis, D., & Lunnen, K. (2000). *The ohio youth problem, functioning, and satisfaction scales technical manual.* Ohio University.

Panksepp, J. (1998). *Affective neuroscience: the foundations of human and animal emotions.* New York: Oxford University Press.

Parent Resources for Information, Development, and Education (PRIDE). (2008). CWLA Press.

Pearlman, L. (2009). Living and working self-reflectively to address vicarious trauma. In C. Courtois and J. Ford (Eds.), *Treating complex traumatic stress disorder: An evidence-based guide.* 202-221. New York: Guilford Press.

Pearlman, L., & Saakvitne, K. (1995). *Trauma and the therapist: Countertransference and vicarious traumatization in psychotherapy with incest survivors.* New York: W.W. Norton & Company.

Pearlman, L. A. (1998). Trauma and the self: A theoretical and clinical perspective. *Journal of Emotional Abuse, 1,* 7-25.

Pearlman, L. A. (2001). The treatment of persons with complex PTSD and other trauma-related disruptions of the self. In J.P. Wilson, M.J. Friedman, & J.D. Lindy, (Eds.). *Treating Psychological Trauma & PTSD* (pp. 205-236). New York: Guilford.

Perry, B.D. (1999). *Stress, trauma, and post traumatic stress disorder in children.* Houston, TX: Child Trauma Academy Interdisciplinary Education Series.

Perry, B., & Szalavitz, M. (2007). *The boy who was raised as a dog: And other stories from a child psychiatrist's notebook.* New York: Basic Books.

Project Adventure. Resources for activity-based learning. Available from 719 Cabot Street Beverly, MA, 01915. (978) 524-4500. www.pa.org

Project Joy. www.projectjoy.com

Pryor, K. (2002). *Don't shoot the dog!: The new art of teaching and training.* Ringpress Books. 3rd edition. (November, 2006).

Saakvitne, K., Pearlman, L., Gamble, S., & Lev, B. (2000). *Risking connection: A training curriculum for working with survivors of childhood abuse.* Lutherville, MD: Sidran.

Substance Abuse and Mental Health Services (SAMHSA). (2006). *Road map to seclusion and restraint free mental health services* [CD or download]. Washington, DC: Author.

Shapiro, F. (1998). *EMDR: The breakthrough "eye movement" therapy for overcoming anxiety, stress, and trauma.* New York: Basic Books.

Stamm, B. H. (2002). Measuring compassion satisfaction as well as fatigue: Developmental history of the compassion satisfaction and fatigue test. In Charles R. Figley (Ed.), *Treating Compassion Fatigue* (pp. 107-119). New York: Brunner-Routledge.

Tronick, EZ. (2005). Why is connection with others so critical? The formation of dyadic states of consciousness: coherence governed selection and the co-creation of meaning out of messy meaning making. In J. Nadel & D. Muir (Eds). *Emotional Development.* 293-315. New York: Oxford University Press.

Traumatic Stress Institute of Klingberg Family Center. (2009). *Milieu indicators.* Unpublished manuscript.

van der Kolk, B. A., & Pynoos, R. S. (2009). Proposal to include a developmental trauma disorder diagnosis for children and adolescents in *DSM-V.* Official submission from the National Child Traumatic Stress Network Developmental Trauma Disorder Taskforce to the American Psychiatric Association.

van der Kolk, B. (Summer, 2009). Yoga and post-traumatic stress disorder: An interview. *Integral Yoga Magazine*, 12-13.

VanFleet, R. (1998). *Affective neuroscience: The foundations of human and animal emotions.* New York: Oxford University Press.

The NEARI Press
New England Adolescent
Research Institute
70 North Summer Street
Holyoke, MA 01040
Phone 888.632.7412
www.nearipress.org

Ancient Ethics for Today's Healers
by Geral Blanchard.
NEARI Press. Paperback, 224 pages.
ISBN 978-1-929657-74-2

Ancient Ways: Indigenous Healing Innovations for the 21st Century
by Geral Blanchard.
NEARI Press. Paperback, 256 pages.
ISBN 978-1-929657-53-7

Assessing Youth Who Have Sexually Abused: A Primer
by David S. Prescott.
NEARI Press. Paperback, 98 pages.
ISBN 978-1-929657-27-8

Awakening Motivation for Difficult Changes
by David S. Prescott and Robin Wilson.
NEARI Press. Paperback, 96 pages.
ISBN 978-1-929657-62-9

Beyond Workbooks: Improving Clinical Outcomes with Adolescents who have Sexually Abused
by David S. Prescott.
NEARI Press. Paperback, 32 pages.
ISBN 978-1-929657-61-2

Brain Detective: A Practical Tool for Helping Misunderstood Children and Teens
by Penny Cuninggim
and Shannon Chabot.
NEARI Press. Paperback, 56 pages.
ISBN 978-1-929657-63-6

Contemporary Practice with Young People Who Sexually Abuse: Evidence-based Developments
by Martin Calder (Editor).
NEARI Press. Hardcover, 368 pages.
ISBN 978-1-929657-55-1

Current Applications: Strategies for Working with Sexually Aggressive Youth and Youth with Sexual Behavior Problems
by David S. Prescott
and Robert E. Longo, (Editors).
NEARI Press. Hardcover, 368 pages.
ISBN 978-1-929657-43-8

Current Perspectives: Working with Sexually Aggressive Youth and Youth with Sexual Behavior Problems
by Robert E. Longo
and David S. Prescott (Editors).
NEARI Press. Hardcover, 720 pages.
ISBN 978-1-929657-26-1

Current Perspectives & Applications in Neurobiology: Working with Young Persons who are Victims and Perpetrators of Sexual Abuse
by Robert E. Longo,
David S. Prescott, John Bergman,
and Kevin Creeden (Editors).
NEARI Press. Hardcover, 360 pages.
ISBN 978-1-929657-67-40

Enhancing Empathy
by Robert E. Longo
with Hogen Laren Bays
and Steven Sawyer.
NEARI Press. Paperback, 80 pages.
ISBN 978-1-929657-04-9

Enhancing Motivation in Treatment: A Case Study and Professional Development Planning Method
by David S. Prescott.
NEARI Press. Paperback, 38 pages.
ISBN 978-1-929657-68-1

Evicting the Perpetrator: A Male Survivor's Guide to Recovery from Childhood Sexual Abuse
By Ken Singer.
NEARI Press. Paperback, 268 pages.
ISBN 978-1-929657-46-9

Evolving Residential Work with Children and Families
by James R. Harris, Jr.
NEARI Press. Paperback, 160 pages.
ISBN 978-1-929657-36-0

For Now: Words of the Girl Who Fought Back
By Anna Nettie Hanson.
NEARI Press. Paperback, 96 pages.
ISBN 978-1-929657-59-9

Growing Beyond: A Workbook for Teenage Girls
by Susan L. Robinson.
NEARI Press. Paperback, 216 pages.
ISBN 978-1-929657-17-9

Growing Beyond Treatment Manual: A Guide for Professionals Working with Teenage Girls with Sexually Abusive Behavior
by Susan L. Robinson.
NEARI Press. Paperback, 42 pages.
ISBN 978-1-929657-15-5

Illegal Images: Critical Issues and Strategies for Addressing Child Pornography Use
By David L. Delmonico
and Elizabeth J. Griffin.
NEARI Press. Paperback, 88 pages.
ISBN 978-1-929657-72-8

The Impact of Pornography on Children, Youth, and Culture
By Cordelia Anderson.
NEARI Press. Paperback, 32 pages.
ISBN 978-1-929657-51-3

Intellectual Disability and Problems in Sexual Behaviour: Assessment, Treatment, and Promotion of Healthy Sexuality
by Robin Wilson and Michele Burns.
NEARI Press. Paperback, 208 pages.
ISBN 978-1-929657-58-2

An Introduction to Autism Spectrum Disorders, Sexual Behaviors, & Therapeutic Intervention
by Gerry D. Blasingame.
NEARI Press. Paperback, 157 pages.
ISBN 978-1-929657-50-6

Lessons from the Lion's Den: Therapeutic Management of Children in Psychiatric Hospitals and Treatment Centers
by Nancy S. Cotton.
NEARI Press. Paperback, 316 pages.
ISBN 978-1-929657-24-7

Men & Anger: Understanding and Managing Your Anger
by Murray Cullen.
and Robert E. Longo.
NEARI Press. Paperback, 125 pages.
ISBN 978-1-929657-12-4

The Mindfulness Toolkit: For Counselors, Teachers, Coaches and Clinicians of Youth
by Jack Apsche
and Jerry L. Jennings.
NEARI Press. Paperback, 96 pages.
ISBN 978-1-929657-69-8

The Mindfulness Toolkit: Youth Companion
by Jerry L. Jennings
and Jack Apsche.
NEARI Press. Paperback, 80 pages.
ISBN 978-1-929657-70-4

Moving Beyond: Relapse Prevention Student Manual
by Thomas F. Leversee.
NEARI Press. Paperback, 52 pages.
ISBN 978-1-929657-18-6

The NEARI Way: A Unique Intervention Model for Working with Students with Emotional and Behavioral Self-Regulation Issues
by Penny Cuninggim
NEARI Press. Paperback
ISBN 978-1-929657-03-2

New Hope For Youth: Experiential Exercises for Children & Adolescents
by Robert E. Longo
and Deborah P. Longo.
NEARI Press. Paperback, 142 pages.
ISBN 978-1-929657-20-9

Passport to Independence: A Good Lives Workbook
by Peel Behavioural Services
with Robin J. Wilson
NEARI Press. Paperback, 292 pages.
ISBN 78-1-929657-02-5

Paths To Wellness
by Robert E. Longo.
NEARI Press. Paperback, 144 pages.
ISBN 978-1-929657-13-1

Paths To Wellness en Español!
by Robert E. Longo.
NEARI Press. Paperback, 144 pages.
ISBN 978-1-929657-31-5

Pornography and its Place in the Assessment and Treatment of Adolescents who have Sexually Abused
By David S. Prescott and
Siegi A. Schuler.
NEARI Press. Paperback, 36 pages.
ISBN 978-1-929657-52-0

The Prevention of Sexual Violence: A Practitioner's Sourcebook
by Keith L. Kaufman (Editor).
NEARI Press. Hardcover, 536 pages.
ISBN 978-1-929657-45-2

Promoting Healthy Childhood Development Today
by James R. Harris, Jr.
NEARI Press. Paperback, 92 pages.
ISBN 978-1-929657-30-8

RESPECT: A Professional Manual
by Tom Keating.
NEARI Press. Paperback, 216 pages.
ISBN 978-1929657-47-1

RESPECT: Student Workbook
by Tom Keating.
NEARI Press. Paperback, 136 pages.
ISBN 978-1-929657-48-3

Responsibility And Self-Management: A Client Workbook of Skills to Learn
by Jack Apsche and Jerry L. Jennings.
NEARI Press. Paperback, 224 pages.
ISBN 978-1-929657-29-2

Responsibility And Self-Management: A Clinician's Manual and Guide for Case Conceptualization
by Jack Apsche and Jerry L. Jennings.
NEARI Press. Paperback, 118 pages.
ISBN 978-1-929657-28-5

The Safe Workbook for Youth: New Choices for a Healthy Lifestyle
by John McCarthy and
Kathy MacDonald.
NEARI Press. Paperback, 210 pages.
ISBN 978-1-929657-14-8

Smoothies For The Brain: Brain-Based Strategies To Defuse Behavior Problems in the Classroom
by Penny Cuninggim
and Shannon Chabot.
NEARI Press. Paperback, 48 pages.
ISBN 978-1-929657-35-3

Stages of Accomplishment
by Phil Rich. NEARI Press.
Clinician's Manual
Paperback, 96 pages.
ISBN 978-1-929657-41-4

Introduction to Treatment, Stage 1
Paperback, 72 pages.
ISBN 978-1-929657-37-7

Understanding Yourself, Stage 2
Paperback, 96 pages.
ISBN 978-1-929657-38-4

Understanding Dysfunctional Behavior, Stage 3
Paperback, 120 pages.
ISBN 978-1-929657-39-1

Hitting the Target: Making Change Permanent, Stage 4
Paperback, 168 pages.
ISBN 978-1-929657-40-7

The Thursday Group
by PeggyEllen Kleinleder
and Kimber Everson.
NEARI Press. Paperback, 280 pages.
ISBN 978-1-929657-44-5

Trauma Informed Treatment: The Restorative Approach
by Patricia Wilcox.
NEARI Press. Paperback, 368 pages.
ISBN 978-1-929657-64-3

Try and Make Me! Power Struggles: A Book of Strategies for Adults Who Live and Work with Angry Kids
by Penny Cuninggim.
NEARI Press. Paperback, 112 pages.
ISBN 978-1-929657-23-0

Using Conscience as a Guide: Enhancing Sex Offender Treatment in the Moral Domain
by Niki Delson.
NEARI Press. Paperback, 104 pages.
ISBN 978-1-929657-22-3

Using Conscience as a Guide: Student Manual
by Niki Delson.
NEARI Press. Paperback, 52 pages.
ISBN 978-1-929657-19-3

Very Different Voices: Perspectives and Case Studies in Treating Sexual Aggression
by David S. Prescott and Robin J. Wilson
NEARI Press. Paperback, 242 pages.
ISBN 978-1-929657-79-7

Who Am I and Why Am I In Treatment?
by Robert E. Longo with
Hogen Laren Bays
and Steven Sawyer.
NEARI Press. Paperback, 96 pages.
ISBN 978-1-929657-01-8

Why Did I Do It Again? and How Can I Stop?
by Robert E. Longo with
Hogen Laren Bays
and Steven Sawyer.
NEARI Press. Paperback, 176 pages.
ISBN 978-1-929657-11-7

Youth with Sexual Behavior Problems: A Practical Guide for Therapists Working with Youth and Their Families
by Rene McCreary
NEARI Press. Paperback
ISBN 978-1-929657-06-3

For prices and shipping information,
or to order, please call: **888.632.7412**
Find us online at: **www.nearipress.org**